CW01019814

vacant city

NAi PUBLISHERS

vacant city

BRUSSELS' MONT DES ARTS RECONSIDERED

N   A   I

ROTTERDAM / 18/06/2009

TABLE OF CONTENTS

7   Introduction

I. FRAGMENTED PANORAMA

16   The Westbury Tower
      BRUNO DE MEULDER

18   The Telex building
      RONNY DE MEYER

21   The Sabena Air Terminus
      MAURIZIO COHEN

22   The Shell building
      JO BRAEKEN

25   The Gare Centrale
      ERIC DE KUYPER

26   The Galerie Ravenstein
      DIETER DE CLERCQ

29   The Palais des Beaux-Arts
      KARINA VAN HERCK

30   The Old England
      VIRGINIE JORTAY

33   The Bibliothèque Royale
      DAVID VANDERBURGH

34   The Palais de la Dynastie
      KOEN VAN SYNGHEL

II. IN THE SHADOW OF THE PALACE

40   The metamorphoses of an area between two fires
      BRUNO DE MEULDER, with NANCY MEIJSMANS, KARINA VAN HERCK, ILKE VERHOEVEN

58   Modernity versus identity: Leopold II and Charles Buls
      KARINA VAN HERCK AND BRUNO DE MEULDER

72   A Belgian labyrinth: Victor Horta and the Mont des Arts
      BRUNO DE MEULDER AND KARINA VAN HERCK

84   The Carrefour de l'Europe
      BRUNO DE MEULDER

100   The "invisible" Museum of Modern Art: the peak of modesty?
      JOHAN LAGAE

III. ARCHITECTURAL ARCHIVES DISCLOSED
107

IV. THE STATE OF THE ARTS

190 The Mont des Arts as terrain vague?
DIETER DE CLERCQ

216 Counter-arrangement
TOM AVERMAETE

228 City without excitement
KRISTIAAN BORRET

234 How public are the temples of culture on the Mont des Arts?
KOEN VAN SYNGHEL

246 Art and culture on the Mont des Arts: a descent and an ascent
KOEN BRAMS AND DIRK PÜLTAU

V. MUSEUM AND CITY: ELEMENTS OF REFLECTION

267 The Mont des Arts as a ruin in the revanchist city
ERIK SWYNGEDOUW

282 The Mont des Arts: between museum and city
KARINA VAN HERCK AND HILDE HEYNEN

292 The Mont des Arts, Brussels 2000 and the Fondation Roi Baudouin
MARIE-LAURE ROGGEMANS

VI. LABORATORY FOR THE CITY OF TOMORROW

298 The Mont des Arts: one nation under ground
MAX.1 & CRIMSON

306 De-masking the Mont des Arts
DESIGN + URBANISM

314 Sleight of hand, signal or manipulation?
HILTON JUDIN

322 Old knowledge, nothing new
BART VERSCHAFFEL

328 Agent provocateur
ATELIER SERAJI

336 Cet obscur objet du désir
JOÃO LUÍS CARRILHO DA GRAÇA

344 A proposal for a significant and dynamic cultural collage
CATHÉRINE DAVID

352 The Mont des Arts as theoretical spectacle
ISABELLE GRAW

360 Brussels as it might have been
RIKEN YAMAMOTO & FIELD SHOP

368 Food for thought. Ideas for the Mont des Arts
PAUL VERMEULEN

INTRODUCTION

February 1st, 1998. Discussion with Guido Minne about Brussels, architecture, and Brussels 2000, European City of Culture, apparently three disparate subjects caught within their own absurdities. There is everything and more probably nothing to be achieved. Can something be done? One of the proposed avenues, which leads to the *Vacant City* project, is the idea of organising *Denkoefeningen* (Think-ins). A list of representative sites among the plethora of impossible candidates found all over Brussels was established with the idea of organising an international design project; a designerly research which can enrich the "imagining" of the city and its architecture and which would mentally fill the physical and symbolic emptiness of these spots with refreshing designs capable of reopening the flagging debate on the city and its architecture in Brussels. A cool outsider's look as a diagnosis, but also as a catalyst for release, as a first move towards renewal. The list of suitable sites is almost endless: the canal zone, the Heysel, the Gare de l'Ouest or the future TGV station in Schaerbeek, etc.

A little later the Mont des Arts somehow crept onto the bottom of the list at an unguarded moment, and straight away the theme "museum of the 21st century" is coupled to this site. Of all the possible sites around Brussels on which to organise an architectural *Think-in*, the impossible Mont des Arts seems the least likely. For is it not simply one of history's lost opportunities to which there seems nothing to be added, the battle field of a burnt out, long abandoned war, a site that is both symbolically and materially overfilled and immovable, with no freedom at all to change anything? Does anybody still care about the Mont des Arts? Is there any significance to the endless stream of historical projects and plans relating to it? Should we not rather choose one of the other sites at the top of our list, as Erik Swyngedouw contends in the following pages, whose urgent need can be instantly recognised, sites clearly manifesting an urban dynamism where a design study can be given free rein? Closer examination shows the Mont des Arts to be one of the sites most ravaged by modernisation in the whole of Brussels. After quite some time the site chosen for the first *Think-in* turns out to be the diamond-shaped area between the Place Royale, the Marché aux Herbes, the Place de la Justice and the Marché au

Bois, the whole dominated by the Mont des Arts (see pp. 382-383). At first this seems a forced and somewhat unfortunate choice, in view of the previous history of the site, but it is nevertheless a sound one. As will be argued by Dieter De Clercq, it is both materially and semantically a "Belgian space," a *terrain vague*. Indeed, the apparently paradoxical conditions of emptiness and accumulation can be found on the Mont des Arts. A designerly research on this site can go deeper than the usual obligatory and risk-free exercise in redeveloping e.g. a post-industrial site, and can thus become an innovative experiment – not that there are any guarantees in the conduct of experiments.

The *Vacant City* project, the result of co-operation between Brussels 2000, OSA (Onderzoeksgroep Stedelijkheid en Architectuur of the K.U.Leuven) and the Fondation Roi Baudouin, avoided clinging to a single guiding principle and opted instead for a multi-facetted exploration of the Mont des Arts. This is reflected in the table of contents of this book which contains the provisional results of the project. *Fragmented panorama* endeavours to expand the reader's familiar expectations by bringing to the fore a capricious series of buildings as the site's *eye-catchers*.

The second part, *In the shadow of the palace*, examines both the site's shaky position and its latent power by plunging into its history: the area's morphological structure and the pile of architectural, urban and infrastructural projects designed for this site over the past 250 years. They are further documented by Maureen Heyns in part three, *Architectural archives disclosed*. This documentation is, throughout the book, complemented by other historical documents, such as photographs, news paper reports and other texts (e.g. Sophie De Schaepdrijver). Thus, not only projects are documented but also debates and discourses.

In *The state of the arts* the area is analysed from a present-day perspective, the starting point of the analysis being public space, urbanity, and the role of cultural institutions within the city. These themes are examined as such (like the concept of urbanity in Kristiaan Borret's contribution), as well as their mutual interaction. Koen Van Synghel, for example, links the discourse on urbanity and public space to the cultural institutions present on the site by considering to what degree these institutions contribute to creating a public space capable of supporting a "museum district." Koen Brams and Dirk Pültau also examine the impact of the institutions on the public domain from the point of view of the discursive construction of "the public." Tom Avermaete for his part examines the public space on the Mont des Arts in the light of present-day urban practices. Erik Swyngedouw's *Manifesto For Benign neglect* opens part five, *Museum and city: elements of reflection*. The contribution by Karina Van Herck and Hilde Heynen in this section expands the concept of the Mont des Arts as a 19th and 20th century enlightenment project into a broader reflection on the museum and the city.

All this leads up to the sixth and crucial part, the *Laboratory for the city of tomorrow*. This takes a plunge into the site's future and generates material for a discussion on possible innovative scenarios for development. Two instruments are used to this end: on the one hand, the urban and architectural design and on the other the theoretical programme, the discursive scenario. This international laboratory for the city of tomorrow is populated by architects, urban designers, philosophers, curators and art critics – the architects Atelier Seraji (France), João Luís Carrilho da Graça (Portugal), Design + Urbanism (USA), Max. 1 & Crimson (the Netherlands), Riken Yamamoto & Fieldshop (Japan & Switzerland) and the "programmers" Cathérine David (France), Isabelle Graw (Germany), Hilton Judin (South Africa) and Bart Verschaffel (Belgium). In the capital of blissful nonchalance and dismal rigidity, this international company of thinkers and designers operates, with a clarity born of distance, towards creating spatially or programmaticaly inspired elements for a vision of the future development of the Mont des Arts as an urban site.

The capacity for transformation of the architectural heritage embodied in the Mont des Arts – spatially fragmented and a heterogeneous pattern-card of architecture – is tested. Its cultural significance is examined, as well as the meaning of consumption and production of culture, of museum clusters and cultural institutions in the broad sense of the word, for the city of tomorrow. Design and programme, the dual unity of architecture, are thus employed as research instruments, as the means of developing generative metaphors. In other words, architectural design is called upon for its capacity to visualise spatial strategies in an inspiring manner. Individuals from the cultural world, active at the junction between cultural production and criticism are called upon for their ability to come up with programmatical development strategies. It will be evident that the latter, where the programme is, so to speak, farmed out beyond the bounds of the discipline of architecture, is no straightforward step. Utopian projection is after all an integral part of architectural discipline. Sysiphus-like, architecture is constantly constructing an ideal world that is undermined by reality again and again. To shift the cultural field in order to think in terms of realistic urban development presumes the acceptance of analogous reasoning. This projection of architectural strategies into the world of culture proved to be a somewhat bold but none the less interesting experiment. None of the above implies that the diverse architectural projects and development scenarios contained in this book should be regarded as utopian projects. On the contrary, they provide concrete fuel for the debate on the Mont des Arts of tomorrow, the city of tomorrow, of the yuppie museum shopper and ragged tramp, the plodding commuter and somewhat irritable inhabitant, the authorities and developers. They now have the floor. Paul Vermeulen closes the laboratory's open house with an interpretative appraisal of the data and ideas, some contradictory, some compatible, found in all of the above, and by sifting through it and throwing light on it, invites further discussion.

As we were saying, this debate was the object of the exercise. This book is not the last word on the Mont des Arts: it is merely the opening sentence of a discussion that we hope will be as rich and intriguing as the city and the site concerned. The *Vacant City* project is only one manner of speaking. Besides words, there are deeds. The project does in fact not stand alone. As Marie-Laure Roggemans' contribution shows, delicate and praiseworthy attempts are being made by the Fondation Roi Baudouin, with angelic patience all its own, to initiate renewal on the site itself. All sorts of short-term projects, from the renovation of the Jardin de l'Albertine, to building up collaboration between the institutions, are being launched and steered through a maze of junctions. Parallel to the development of elements for a long-term vision for the Mont des Arts – as reported here – a short-term development as active as it is intensive is taking place. The ultimate ambition of the *Vacant City* project is to fuse the short-term development fostered on a daily basis by the Fondation Roi Baudouin with the long-term vision that Brussels 2000 has contributed to the *Vacant City* project into a communicative public event. This book and the accompanying exhibitions of the historical projects and the proposals of the architects and "programmers" are the instruments for achieving this; discussion the method.

During the three years that the *Vacant City* project on the Mont des Arts evolved, many people's help was sought. The work of the architects, planners and authors involved in this extensive operation was made possible by a great deal of goodwill, numerous suggestions, stimulation and support, and especially by much thankless and exhausting work behind the scenes. Apart from all the institutions and authorities which helped us, we particularly wish to express our thanks here to: Guido Minne, Programme Co-ordinator, Brussels 2000 and Marie-Laure Roggemans, a director of the Fondation Roi Baudouin seconded as Programme Co-ordinator to Brussels 2000. Special thanks are also due to: Els Baetens, Karl Beelen, Jeroen Beerten, Geert Bekaert, Sébastien Carpentier, Bieke Cattoor, Veronique Charlier, Tine Daems, Lieven De Cauter, Chris Dercon, Alexander D'Hooghe, Oswald Devisch, Patricia De Peuter, Hilde Heynen, Maureen Heyns, André Loeckx, Tom Louwette, Nancy Meijsmans, An Petre, Michael Ryckewaert, Christine Sommeillier, Raf Suttels, Thierry Timmermans, Willem Van Bockstal, Veerle Van Hassel, Els Van Meerbeek, Bert van Meggelen, Ilke Verhoeven, Joris Vlasselaers and the students in Cultural Studies, Sofie Wouters, and last but not least Véronique Patteeuw, whose constant and indefatigable energy kept everything moving in the right direction every day.

September 1st, 2000. The preparation stage of the experiment is complete, the text for this introduction drafted, translated, edited. Soon the book will go to print, the exhibits will be set up, the invitations to the presentations and discussions despatched. All Guido has to do now is to tot up the expenses, perhaps look out for the next *Think-in*, draw up shortlists, initiate discussions, line up the institutions, and make a sound choice. Any volunteers?

Bruno De Meulder

FRAGMENTED PANORAMA

#01.

THE WESTBURY TOWER
Bruno De Meulder

Narrow-minded provincial town and some-what decadent capital city: as a small out-post between major centres of power like Paris, London and Berlin, Brussels has a contradictory identity. After all, its central location gave this insignificant city a neu-trality that could be turned into cash. International conference centre, capital of Europe, Nato headquarters and so on, descended on Brussels and were the motor behind its on-going modernisation. As a overflow area for the surrounding cultures, Brussels grew – in spite of itself – to become a free haven, a place where you can escape from the dominant codes and flaunt every authority with impunity. Plans that drag on and nonchalance are tra-ditional habits here.

The friction resulting from the combination of a provincial mentality with the func-tion of an international crossroads produced a dramatic conflict of scale that marked the city in an exceptionally brutal way and – fostered by the proverbial nonchalance – led to an improbable spatial chaos. The incompatible meeting of contradictory conditions (on-going modernisation versus nonchalance and liberty) yields a constellation in which daz-zling architecture can arise amid chaos and rubble. Apparent flukes. Architecture as lucky shot, *poésie instantanée*.

The Westbury Tower (1961), better known as the Lotto Tower, is a success of this kind, one of a series of unsurpassed masterpieces of metropolitan high-rise buildings in Brussels that includes the Martini Tower and the Lotimo slab. Almost indiscriminately they were and are cursed by the right-thinking man in the street as atypical, while in fact more than any-thing else they determine the paradoxical quality of Brussels. Practically every one of these towers emerged "spontaneously" from the armpits of busy intersections, points of conver-gence of traffic flow. They settled themselves in the few hectic points of provincial Brussels that have a metropolitan character.

The Lotto Tower by architect Goffaux is the prime example: with the boulevards above, the north-south rail link to the rear, and the large-scale east-west link designed by Henri Maquet bypassing its curved socle side, it marks the end of the Rue des Colonies where it branches into the Rue de la Loi and the motorway to Liège. It looks like localised conges-tion, a fast piece of the metropolis springing up like a mushroom.

So it stands just beyond the edge of the Îlot Sacré, a tower from the swinging sixties, a packaged piece of speculation. At first glance the tower looks out of place and strange, but a second look provokes a compassionate smile at this flippant architecture that is unable or unwilling to age. The alternation of concave and convex sides for the socle and tower elic-its unruly excitement. It is as if the tower could be catapulted into the sky at any moment for a date with the future. Eighteen floors of offices. The promoter removed six of them

before construction as a concession to the urban planners and the mayor's concerns about the skyline. When an international hotel chain showed an interest, part of the tower was quickly converted into a hotel while building was still going on. Behind the aluminium curtain façade emerged a mixed programme of hotel rooms, offices, a restaurant, shops, a bank and a car park. Modernism in Brussels had never been doctrinaire, but hybrid. The finances, the programme, the architecture – all by hook or by crook. Feasibility. Yield.

Which brings us to the final characteristic of the unsurpassed towers in Brussels. Despite the moaning about monofunctionality and formless monotony that dominates right-minded criticisms of modernisation (christened bruxellisation in a moment of self-pity), remarkably enough, the hallmark of this architecture is its hybridity. Martini or Westbury, they remain successful pieces of mischief, cheerful experiments that earned a pretty penny.

#02.

THE TELEX BUILDING
Ronny De Meyer

The Telex building does not seem to belong here, to the Carrefour de l'Europe. With its huge canopy and façade of louvres it shows absence and rejection. The side facing the Lower Town, with the stylised louvres on the front façade, is predominantly closed and static. The vertical window openings in the side façades are abruptly cut off by a lift shaft and a huge concrete slab. The side facing uptown is dominated by a transparent façade, but that is closed off by the base of the former Westbury Hotel. Just like the Gare Centrale, a funnel to an invisible, because underground, railway network, the Telex building forms a gateway into or out of Brussels. In view of the telex equipment it used to contain, you could call the Telex building a virtual port or gate.

The Telex building may appear to be just another "floating" modernist building which could have been built anywhere. However, it is not just literally "anchored." Its concrete skeleton accurately traces the underground tunnel of the north-south railway link. Every floor is rather like a tunnel, with a clear span of 20 m. Apparently the original programme for telex equipment could have been located anywhere. However, this location was chosen because it offered a junction of telex cables and the proximity of the Gare Centrale – and thus a connection for the commuting personnel.

In the age of the fax and the internet, the number of telex subscribers has fallen dramatically. This has reduced the remaining operational equipment to an anachronism, a museum piece. These days, almost all floors of the buildings are used for the call centre from which Belgacom offers its services. If you visit the Telex building now, you will notice an unusual atmosphere. Inside, every reference to a definite location or situation disappears. The louvres on the front façade block any view. The view on both sides is interrupted

by the lift shaft and concrete slab. The people working in this digital temple inhabit an open plan office dominated by wall-to-wall carpet, connected through headsets to potential customers, fighting deadlines with their eyes focused on the data on the computer displays. This flight simulator lacks any experience of space or the city, time is all there is: one is nowhere anymore, except on the way to somewhere.

This apparent virtuality is interrupted on the roof where the city and architecture reclaim reality: the majestically laid out roof terrace offers a splendid view of Brussels. In the centre of the terrace there are a number of modernist cabins with thin concrete roof shells, on tall slender steel columns: not board rooms but small sleeping cells. Both the telex and the call centre operate around the clock. At this privileged place in – or rather above – Brussels you can lock yourself into a cell with opaque glazing, without any reference to the city, except the sound of church bells nearby. Should Belgacom ever leave the building then a use should be found which ties in with how, in 1979 in a discussion with Albert Bontridder, architect Léon Stynen described his Telex building built in 1959: "In petrified silence this building suggests something of the accuracy of an electronic device, something of the mystery of the Gothic church nearby."

#03.

THE SABENA AIR TERMINUS
Maurizio Cohen

Built in the modernist surge that Brussels was experiencing in the 1950s, this building is an example of the intention to provide the country with new infrastructures meant to create a capital oriented towards progress and the future. The terminus is the work of Maxime Brunfaut, built between 1952 and 1954. The objective was to link the city centre with the new airport 12 kilometres away, to link the different modes of transport: cars, planes and trains. Although air travel at the time was pure luxury for most citizens, the aim was to display the power and capacity as well as, of course, the presence of the national airline company next to the Gare Centrale.

It was a complex programme. A link had to be created with the Gare Centrale at track level. In order to allow the smooth operation of the numerous activities, a large number of circulatory and linking elements punctuate the building and characterise it without necessarily being put to the fore. The "L" shape simplifies the reading of the volumes and clarifies the usage of the spaces. The curved volumes enrich the architecture's vocabulary by expressing the interior volumetrics. A bus station linking the city centre to the airport by motorway was planned on the Rue de la Putterie, opposite the Gare Centrale.

The building is notable for its lack of monumentality and by a pragmatic and functional layout that bring to mind the plans of the Dutch architect Dudok. All superimposition is erased in favour of a clear relationship with the urban environment. The internal spaces initially gave panoramic views of the old city, with its spaces and monuments (at the time of its construction, the terminus faced the unbuilt esplanade of the Boulevard de l'Impératrice).

The programme's complexity forced Brunfaut to refrain from accentuating any particular element, but rather to create an urban entity that acts as a condenser of energies and activities, favouring a functional solution for the interaction between different infrastructures and activities. At the time of its construction, it was hailed as a free work of architecture that affirmed its own status as a station and place for the transfer, of reception and exchange of travellers. It is notable that it does not fit into the conventional street alignment, but is laid out according to its pragmatic rather than representational exigencies. The contrast with Victor Horta's Gare Centrale, which was conceived as an "island building" (*îlot-bâtiment*) seeking to define a line of urban continuity, is all the more underlined by the clarity of the forms, which show indifference to this concern. The terminus is a self-contained building or a "building island" (*bâtiment-îlot*), a condenser of urban flux and a support to the movement of travellers and citizens. The spirit of modernity is even more evident in the refusal to make any concession to the urban scene of ordered urbanism, a legacy of the 19th century that was ill suited to the new needs.

#04.

THE SHELL BUILDING
Jo Braeken

"The measure of this time is a gigantic and precise measure. Why should the gigantic, or what was still known by the name yesterday, not have its elegance and beauty?" The editorial of the architectural journal *Bâtir* took an optimistic view of the future in 1934. A whole issue was devoted to what was considered as the new standard in modern office construction. And this was only the start. The first tower block in Brussels was soon to rise on one of the most strategic sites in the Upper Town as a beacon of the city of the future, the new financial, commercial and cultural heart of the capital.

The Shell building (1931-1934) is the last in a series of commercial office complexes that were erected in the capitals of Europe in the 1930s by the oil giant Shell. As monuments of the new era, they embodied the growing power and demands of the multinational corporations and the world of commerce. Shell commissioned the architect Alexis Dumont to design an imposing building in a stark formal idiom – "the strength of the new industrial forms" – and as the bow of an ocean liner, surmounted by the corporate logo. The building is characterised by its stacked volumes and flowing lines. The interior organisation of the complex, equipped with air conditioning, a battery of lifts, a shopping arcade and underground car park, meet the most forward-looking standards of efficiency and comfort.

But even progress has its limits. The square 90-metre-tall tower block that was to rise from the core of the complex was already the third high-rise project planned for this site, including Victor Horta's only escapade in this field. It sparked off a grim skyscraper debate in Brussels architectural circles, but was firmly rejected by the authorities as a "cyclopean mass of stone" which, for vulgar publicity purposes, would take its place in full view of the royal palace between the towers of the city hall and the cathedral, the symbols of the city's past. A Shell building with the symbolic value of the Antwerp Tower building could have made the skyscraper debate in Brussels take a very different turn. Without its tower, you can hardly call the Shell building a building at all. That it is why it is one of the least known monuments in Brussels, a socle without a statue. Many a passer-by walks past without noticing it. Unjustifiably so.

#05.

THE GARE CENTRALE
Eric de Kuyper

What a strange building this is. Strange because it is so easily overlooked. As a traveller, you could use it every day without noticing its obstinacy. You move along with the flow of passengers, underground. Or you surface, walking in the opposite direction. And gradually, or suddenly, you discover its originality. As happens with many things in Brussels.

It all has to do with access, the entrances and exits, of which there are quite a few, each with its own character. From the obvious and clearly present, to the secret and hidden. The wide, spacious, gentle stairs leading down and into the corridors to the platforms are the most obvious. In effect these stairs transfer you in stages from the large and open, through the narrow to…your own space, the intimacy of your place in the train compartment. The opposite journey, from down below, upwards, is not simply a reversal of the route. Moving from the narrow to the broad and spacious, you reach a plateau, the station hall, from which you can slide through the exits into the city. Here, Brussels lies at your feet. Unfortunately, this view is now somewhat restricted by the hotel on the Carrefour de l'Europe. The stairs which coordinate all this are remarkable in their serenity. Other stations, in Milan or Antwerp for example, also have majestic staircases. They are beautiful and showy, while the stairs in the Gare Centrale stand out by the nature of their discretion.

There are two, even three other entrances, but they are usually used as exits. The largest and most widely used takes you straight from the underground hall into the street, without passing through the large waiting and ticket hall. The second is most imposing and playful, but unfortunately hidden. It was reserved for those in the know. It is an immense circular hall that takes you with a broad sweep close to the Grand'Place, via stairs or a bridge. Unfortunately, that is the way it used to be, because I do not know if this bizarre part of the Gare Centrale even exists nowadays. Then there is another corridor somewhere, rather like a stage door, which I have rarely if ever passed through, I do not even know which part of the district it leads to.

The secret of the Gare Centrale comes from the tension between high and low, between the different spaces that are stacked loosely. It is not surprising that stairs have such an important role to play. When you realise that you can reach another building through the Galerie Ravenstein, the Palais des Beaux-Arts, with a similar playful arrangement of levels, above ground and underground, it becomes clear that there is a rich cohesion. The station as mirror image of the palace? From the platform you can walk through a veritable labyrinth into the Salle Henry Le Boeuf or the Rue Royale! And the other way round. Amazing. The Gare Centrale becomes something like a key to the whole district. Maybe even to Brussels itself, a city of "ups" and "downs." A city with a strong suggestion of sliding up and down.

Alexis and Philippe Dumont wanted their design for the Galerie Ravenstein, built between 1954-1958, to create a lively commercial centre on the Mont des Arts. A hybrid programme of offices, shops, cafés and restaurants was to breathe new life into this part of the city that was almost totally dominated by cultural and administrative institutions at the time. The proximity of the Gare Centrale and the national airport – passengers used to check-in at the Sabena Terminus – raised the already high expectations: "The commercial arcade will form a pleasant and extremely useful transition area (…) and will restore this old district of Brussels to its former splendour and liveliness after having unfortunately been subjected to half a century of demolition."[1]

Unlike the free-standing modernist buildings nearby, such as the Sabena Terminus and the Telex building, the Galerie Ravenstein fits better into the existing urban logic. It links the Gare Centrale with the Palais des Beaux-Arts, thereby partly restoring the connection between the Upper and the Lower Town. However, the arcade does not just have a connecting function; it also accentuates the contrast between the two parts of the city. The architecture of this urban passage is modern, but it also refers to the spatial organisation of the 19th century arcade. The paintings on the ceiling, the overhead lighting, the rotunda and the architectural details are still reminiscent of the prestigious character of the arcade

---

1. "Nouvelle Galerie à Bruxelles," in *Habitat et habitations* vol. 14 (September 1954, nos. 9-10, pp. 123-125, p. 123). The designers planned that the complex would house not only a cinema but also 81 shops, 12.000 sq m of offices, and 248 underground parking lots.

at the time of the World's Fair in 1958. Stylish boutiques and a link to a design centre beneath the adjacent Generali building lent the Galerie Ravenstein a certain *élan* at first. However, like its illustrious 19th century predecessors, after a few years of relative success the arcade entered a period of rapid decline.

Today the commercial apparatus in the arcade is completely geared to the traffic of commuters and passers-by. An underground passageway integrates the Galerie Ravenstein with apparent ease into the logic of the system of corridors of the Gare Centrale and the metro. In doing so, it assumes virtually all the features of the average station environs, from dingy cafés and snack bars to beggars, tramps and breakdancers. Although the Galerie Ravenstein – like the 19th century arcades in which Walter Benjamin saw the portents of a budding modern experience and a new urban public life – is potentially a very hybrid public space, it is degenerating more and more into an inhospitable corridor. It is one of the few buildings on the Mont des Arts that still combines different functions and different publics. Despite its urban potential, however, for the time being the Galerie Ravenstein is unlikely to shake off its baleful lethargy.

#07.

THE PALAIS DES BEAUX-ARTS
Karina Van Herck

The completion of the Palais des Beaux-Arts (PBA) in 1928 fulfilled the long-cherished dream of enriching Brussels with an impressive exhibition hall for the fine arts and music. As a cultural centre *avant-la-lettre*, it was to incarnate the cultural resurrection of the nation after the First World War and to transform Brussels into an international arts centre, a "Geneva of the Arts."

At first sight, the PBA does not look like an impressive palace, nor like Horta's masterpiece. The rather squat, grey building that seems hardly able to hold up its monumental façade articulations provokes bewilderment rather than admiration. But appearances are deceptive. Indoors, a layered and labyrinthine space opens up, which ingeniously reveals a complex programme. Wedged into the hillside, the PBA is a seemingly small building. Despite what the façade suggests, the interior gives full vent to the palatial aspirations that are subdued on the outside. A mass of stairways, steps, ramps and foyers provides access to no less than two exhibition routes, a theatre, a film hall, halls for musical recitals, shops, a restaurant, conference rooms, and the biggest concert hall in Belgium. With five entrances on different levels, with a complex spatial organisation combining organic methods of composition with a classical system of axes and with an amazing number of associations and organisations of all kinds that are active in it, it is not easy to get a clear picture of the PBA straight away. It remains an elusive building in which you discover different areas, different entrances or routes each time.

The PBA is an urban building, and not just in a metaphorical sense. Horta designed it as part of a trajectory extending from the Place des Palais and the Rue Royale to the Gare Centrale, and even as far as the Grand'Place, the historical heart of the city. Located in a bend between Galerie Ravenstein and Rue Baron Horta, the PBA remains today the topmost step in the steep climb to the Upper Town, or the first in the flowing movement down to the Lower Town.

The PBA is Horta's masterly answer to an extremely complex architectural assignment. A very ambitious programme had to be realised on a small site defined by strict limitations and conditions. Out of a whole series of apparently incompatible demands, this work of architecture develops a figure and a strenght entirely of its own. At the same time it fits seamlessly. The Palais des Beaux-Arts is a hybrid palace, a unique synthesis of the large and the small scale, of timeless classicism and contemporary modernism, of urban planning and architecture. As a radical urban building and as one of the first buildings in the world to house concert halls, exhibition areas, shops and a restaurant under one roof, it can be considered as the essence of Horta's vision for the entire Mont des Arts.

#08.

THE OLD ENGLAND
Virginie Jortay

From one century to the next, ideas take hold, a little bit like: "Oh, it's New Year, I'll give up smoking..." So, from one century to the next, let's start afresh and, after all, why not raze everything? Really, this Montagne de la Cour, it was... steep, it was... arduous, but, especially, these houses, so dirty and so close to where it shouldn't be dirty... "Let's eliminate, eliminate, eliminate," proclaimed the King; "Preserve, preserve, preserve," dared the locals; but no, no – the decree says so and so it will be. The King wants his museums, the bourgeoisie its neighbourhoods, after all, steel earns big money. Have you seen what Eiffel has done in Paris? Let's innovate the Grand Magasin, the Old England and its brilliant architect get supplied from the Clabecq steelworks. Leafy capitals, prismatic mouldings, channeled shafts, this is an all white world that makes its way to the terrace where five o'clock tea flows. "– What have you bought today? – Me this. – How nice! – What's happening down below?" A black world comes home at night. Workers go to get washed, the big ship is about to sink and the century to turn. "I want my museums," screams the King, feeling the approach of Death. "How many hands have you cut off?" replies a voice he does not recognise. "That has nothing to do with my museums," refutes the King.

The King is dead, there are still no museums, but the waltz goes on at the Old England. The world is squaring up for a fight, the negroes die, the miners spit, but the waltz goes on at the Old England. And time passes, time passes. The fashion is a bit less English, other

shops are selling white, but the world is still imperial and that is why there will be fighting. King, another small war and you will have your museums! Let's go for it: atomic bomb, reconstruction and, finally, construction: the … Mont des Arts! Another time, another style, the big store is outdated, laws of the market, to relocate, are you scared of burning too? The building is sold and will remain empty for 30 years.

Abandoned, neglected, the gables, domes and turrets rot away, the signs of the old order rot away, it's enough to make one take up smoking again. Is it going to be left to crumble? Patience, patience, even the King had to wait! From one century to the next, what a brilliant idea to turn it into a museum!

#09.

THE BIBLIOTHÈQUE ROYALE
David Vanderburgh

The challenge, of course, is in the section. How otherwise to understand such a dichotomy between the serene façade and the crazed interior of the Bibliothèque Royale? Or the negation of any lateral connection to the Jardin de l'Albertine? The Bibliothèque Royale stares helplessly across at its sister Palais des Congrès – the latter, at least, giving directly onto the esplanade. A thousand questions go unanswered. An "armchair" (or perhaps "throne," given its royal patronage) created by the excavated space places library and convention centre as the "armrests," and leaves the level change entirely up to the "backrest," in manifest opposition to the steady rise of the staircase and cascading gardens it replaces.

Outside, *mine de rien* (unobtrusively), the Albertine façade gives only the barest hint of what is happening in the tortuous entrails of this complex edifice. Inside, for the visitor, the pleasantly disorientating visit of a sort of battle field awaits, where the building has fought to accommodate its various constraints: above all, the relentless upward march of the site and the conservation in extremis of the Chapelle de Nassau. But also the uncompromising boundaries on both long sides, esplanade and street, lead to a dodging and weaving in section, repeated by every visitor looking for one department or another. Among its 67.000 square metres of countless double and half floors that will not or can not line up, one must go up in order to go downstairs, and down in order to go up.

The Bibliothèque Royale plays an odd game of hide-and-seek with classical frontality. The entry sets the "0" level well above the Esplanade, roughly the same as the Chapelle de Nassau, as if the Bibliothèque Royale already belonged to the aristocratic heights. But the portico, with its row of blade-like columns, rests on a shear plinth that neither asks of, nor gives to, the countersunk Albertine void. Its bureaucratic stripped classicism is the architectural language of 20th century power. Stripped to bare armatures, the last trace of sensuality hangs on by the skin of its creamy stone-faced teeth (and the Chapelle de Nassau is caught in them like traces of its last meal), facing a vast flatness whose only motive is to show that its makers *could*. If making flatness is a fundamental act of occupation, this particular one speaks above all to the memory of all the earth moved to make it possible.

#10.

THE PALAIS DE LA DYNASTIE
Koen Van Synghel

The tautly rhythmical façades, the forceful detailing, the echo of classical roman buildings. Is this fascist architecture? The buildings of Houyoux and Ghobert on the Mont des Arts certainly owe a debt to the architectural vocabulary of the 1930s, which in an unprecedented, villainous manner coagulated the power of nation states into solid structures. However, in contrast to the regimes of Mussolini and Salazar, Belgium seems to be a model democracy choosing the Mont des Arts as an architectural shrine for a monarchical state. The Palais de la Dynastie can easily be seen as symbolising an overconfidently nationalist Belgian architecture enhanced by the war. Hollow rhetoric, because despite the solid stone, the "false" façade hides a dubious building programme. While today the Palais de la Dynastie does indeed form part of the Palais des Congrès, it was never designed as a conference centre.

The monumental entrance building on the Boulevard de l'Impératrice, with its high bronze gateway and barely visible stately approach road for royal visits, conceals a majestic but macabre hall. Macabre because the cool white marble of the hall keeps alive the memory of Leopold II's plans to use the blood money extracted from the Congo, safely put away in the royal foundation and so protected from "recuperation" by the Belgian state, to build, among other projects, a mausoleum and a palace to the glory of the dynasty. But in the 1950s, when work started on building the Palais de la Dynastie, the royal question was raging round the person of Leopold III so that the palace rapidly gained another, less explosive function. That is how it happened that the present architecture is more evocative of the chilly spirit of the Belgian dynasty than a hospitable setting for conference participants.

This is also how it happens that the Palais de la Dynastie recalls the architecture of Claude Nicolas Ledoux, and in particular *La Saline Royale* in Arc et Senans. Ledoux built this pre-industrial complex according to absolutist principles: socially stratified and in honour of Louis XV. However, when the French Revolution raged over the recently-built Saline, and Ledoux landed up in a revolutionary prison, he did manage to give a radical reorientation to the ideological basis of his project by proposing it as an ideal, even republican, city for the *citoyen*. It is open to question whether today a similar – second – transformation is possible for the Palais de la Dynastie, originally a half-hearted expression of a monarchical state. For otherwise, what is the significance of opening up the Palais de la Dynastie as an

urban hallway, a crossroads for the streams of commuters and indifferent citizens, Belgian and foreign, people of all sorts, passing by on their way from the Lower to the Upper Town, from the underground car park to the station and back? The Palais de la Dynastie, with its monumental hall, its imposed conference hall and grotesque carillon, is the product of an unintentional act of façadism. Who knows, perhaps these buildings would be better off if they were completely "filleted," so allowing them to present themselves as large urban hallways. The Palais de la Dynastie lacks transparency, particularly in the vertical sense. By hollowing out the architecture, literally, the building would not only gain in symbolism but would even be able to function as "illuminating" and mediating space for users of the underground car park – and thus for the temporary exhibition space that it regularly becomes.

It is difficult today to regard the architecture of Houyoux and Ghobert neutrally, let alone describe it that way. This architecture cries out for new life, something that would require surrealist intervention at the very least. Or is the SOS for *Mehr Licht*? Light to warm the heart of the architecture?

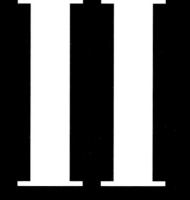

II

IN THE SHADOW OF THE PALACE

... D'Jardin des grands Arbalestiers. pag. IX 10 dien le Hal La Maryth Sayp.
9r La Jardin des Archers.   210. D'Hôtel du Gils vander Noodt.
98 Le Jardin des Couleuvriniers.   211. Bastion de la Comne Hepaire.
200 L'Hôpital de S. Jacques.   212. L'Hôtel-dieu de la S. Trinité.
202 La Chap. de S. Corneille.
203 L'Hôp. de S. Laurent.
204 La Chapelle de S. Michel.
205 La Chap. de S. Christophle.
206 La Chap. de Salazar.   De Tur aut où il y a des Points
207 L'Hôtel-dieu des Boulangers.   la été Bombardé en 1695.
208 L'Hôtel-dieu de S. Elizabeth.

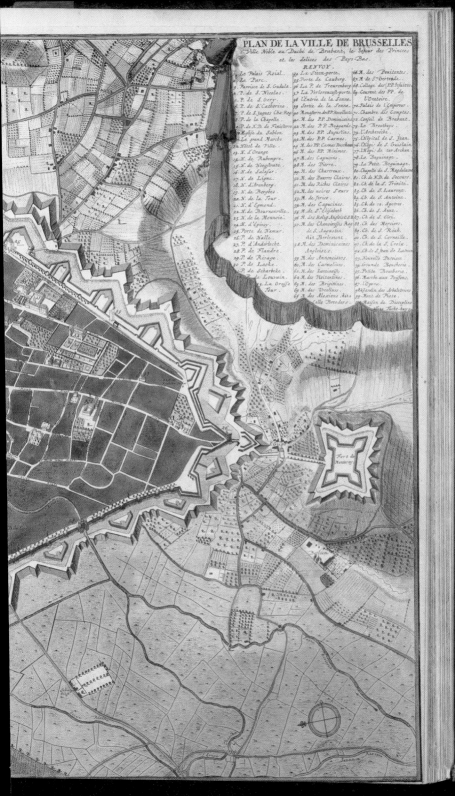

THE METAMORPHOSES
OF AN AREA BETWEEN TWO FIRES

Bruno De Meulder, in co-operation with
Nancy Meijsmans, Karina Van Herck, Ilke Verhoeven

A mediaeval urban structure

Brussels was originally no more than a strategic bridge over the marshy valley of the Senne, where the north-south passage of the river crossed the east-west route between England and Germany. The junction rapidly became a transit point and grew into a town. Emanating from the encampment on the Île St. Géry a simple pattern developed, somewhat modified by the twists and turns of the meanders in the Senne. Around the 10th century, the citadel was moved to the hill known today as the Coudenberg. The new site of the citadel, which with the passage of time would develop into the Ducal Palace, had a significant impact on the town's structure and generated a bipolarity (up town/down town, ducal authority/free town, nobility/trade) that, in spite of the countless transformations and shifts that have occurred, still exists in Brussels today: a harsh friction between the city of the inhabitants or the citizens and the wielding of power that comes from elsewhere, of "identity" versus "the other."

The building of the first ramparts in the 11th century and of the later second ramparts, encapsulates the bipolarity of Brussels in a nutshell and turns it into a two-in-one city. The connections between the gates of the first and second walls graft a radial pattern onto the design of the Brussels town centre. A highly specific urban structure results from the long preservation of the first wall and its gates: a town centre – destined to crystallise into the Îlot *Sacré* – surrounded by a crown consisting of very tightly knit enclaves accessible only through a limited number of openings, the gates in the first wall – e.g. the Marolles (the working class district stretching from the Rue aux Laines to the Rue Haute) or the Quartier Notre-Dame aux Neiges. Such enclaves are in a way archetypal for Brussels, which even today resembles a conglomeration of villages, a loose patchwork of independent nuclei. It is often described as a collection of baronies.[1] The Upper Town turns out to be a very special enclave indeed in this series. The separate jurisdiction of the Upper Town – the seat of power –

previous page:
City map (Eugène-Henri Fricx, 1711)

clearly promotes this. The Warande was laid out on this site, a kind of domesticated hunting ground with the Ducal Palace in the corner. Thus the more complex spatial configuration resulting from the grid, the radial pattern, town walls and gates does not detract from the bipolarity mentioned above.

The east-west axis – the trade route that passes through the Rue de Flandre, Rue de la Madeleine, Montagne de la Cour and Rue de Namur – cuts right through the town and knits together a whole series of important points (Porte de Flandre, the port, Grand'Place, Hôtel de Nassau, Place des Bailles, Porte de Namur). The Place des Bailles, the square in front of the Ducal Palace, is a point of some importance, a hinge between the very different worlds of the town and the palace, which largely faces the Warande. Lying on the route into or out of the town, the Place des Bailles is a resting place where one can stop to honour or pay one's respects to the duke. It is a sort of lobby to the palace, to the Upper Town. It is also a borderline space with a life of its own. Traders set up temporary constructions. It becomes a place of bargaining and barter. Thus the ephemeral nestles in the margin of the permanent, the everlasting, squeezed between the Ducal Palace and the town. Historical prints show the construction of the gallows, and customs and rituals such as *Joyeuses Entrées* and varied types of official celebrations. Thus the Place des Bailles, which we can regard as the historical starting point of the Mont des Arts, has from of old been an accumulation of contradictions and confirmations. It is a scene both of the theatre of daily life and that of grand occasions. It is a town in a nutshell.

A town on the hill

In the interstitial space between the Upper and Lower Towns, an intermediate zone develops on the hill of the Coudenberg. Due to a recess in the first town wall it should belong to the Lower Town, but in fact it protrudes from it. This zone belongs to neither, but rather exists thanks to the tension between the push and pull exerted between the two poles – the ducal domain on the one hand and the district of free citizenry on the other. Morphologically the zone is less than pure: its form fades into a radial pattern and the flat valley bottom becomes a steep hill. The big change in level is accounted for in two ways: on the one hand there are tightly-knit parallel

1. P. Abercrombie, *Bruxelles. Etude de développement et de tracé urbain* (Brussels: Emulation, s.d.).

streets with steps perpendicular up the hill (these include the so-called Jewish steps) and on the other hand there are large building complexes which absorb the difference in level internally (such as the Hôtel de Nassau). This divergent morphological construction contributes to the difference of the intermediate zone, though this is derived primarily from what it contains. The district indeed seems to attract those elements that neither fit in with the upper crust nobility and dukes of the Upper Town nor with the industrious Lower Town of free citizens and craftsmen. It seems to be the place for those things the town needs, but is not quite willing to accept. On the hillside in the shadow of power is the site of the Jewish ghetto: neither excluded nor included, but placed in between. Following the expulsion of the Jews, this intermediate zone becomes literally and figuratively "the Montagne de la Cour," the district at the foot of the ducal residences, where numerous dignitaries and functionaries set up house and build hotels or palaces: Ravenstein, Granvelle, Nassau, Thurn, etc. They too live in the shadow of the palace, like the Jews between acceptance and exclusion. In a region where changes in regime follow one another in rapid succession, they were never entirely sure of finding favour at court. Thus the Montagne de la Cour remains a distinct district, separate from both the Upper and Lower Towns. The pious reign of the archdukes was also a period when many large monasteries were established (including Carmelites, Jesuits, Annunciates, Minimes). The hotels and monasteries permeate the texture of the town here in a coarse-grained pattern.

The Montagne de la Cour, site of "otherness," becomes increasingly swallowed up in a sea of normality with each new stride of urbanisation. The entire east-west axis becomes a continuous ribbon of trade with the Rue de la Madeleine as the fashionable segment. Successive building waves break open the bilateral relation between the Îlot Sacré and the crown of enclaves around it, via cross-connections such as the Rue de l'Infante Isabelle (1625) which connects the palace and the Cathédrale St. Michel. The town centre acquires a polycentric wholeness, the street pattern becomes ever more hybrid. Nevertheless the morphological distinctions remain. There remains a world of difference between the Upper and Lower Towns that is resolved within a specific interstitial space. There remains a very marked difference too between the Îlot Sacré, still surrounded by the first wall, and the enclaves between the first and second walls. Between the Montagne de la Cour and the Sablon, originally the horse market and by now being taken over by the nobility on the Montagne de la Cour, there are still no direct connections: the old rampart here is still a strong line of separation, a fundamental boundary.

The Place Royale

A few archaeological remains are all that are left of the Ducal Palace since the devastating fire of 1731, covered over by the neo-classical district that emerged from 1775: the new Parc and the Place Royale.[2] Their construction marks the beginning of modern urban development and forms the first episode in a breathtaking saga of destruction and renewal that is so typical of Brussels in general and of the Montagne de la Cour district in particular. In transforming the ducal domain into a part of the city, a *quartier urbain*, (later the Quartier Royal), the map of progress, of enlightenment, was drawn. The strongly classical framework ensures a rigorous distinction from the medieval Lower Town. Paradoxically enough the transformation from domain to an urban district results in no annexation or homogenisation, but on the contrary in an accentuation of the difference. The Upper Town becomes a separate entity in the city with its own geometry, its own architecture, its own class and also its own public. The hunting reserve becomes a park, (with the formal figure of the goose-foot) while laid out on top of the Ducal Palace and the Place des Bailles, the equally severe Place Royale cuts an introverted, classical architectural figure. The relation with the Lower Town is primarily visual. From the Upper Town there is a view over the urban landscape with the tower of the town hall – in a direct line from the Place Royale – proudly rising above it.

The character of the Parc determines what is built around it, interspersed with a number of *impasses* (dead-ends) giving no access to the Lower Town but permitting panoramas of it. The physical connection with the Lower Town runs, as of yore, via the Rue de la Madeleine, of which the part on the hill is now called Montagne de la Cour. The Place Royale assumes the function of the Place des Bailles. It becomes the hinge between the Lower and Upper Towns,

2. Complete review in: A. Smolar-Meynart and A. Vanrie, *Le Quartier Royal* (Brussels: CFC, 1998).

PLATES PP. 113-115

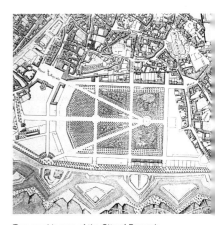

Topographic map of the City of Brussels (Louis-André Dupuis, 1777)

Place Royale, circa 1905

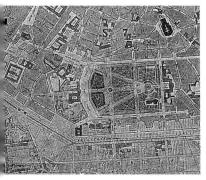

City map (Philippe Vandermaelen, circa 1838)

between the world of classicism and that of the Flemish renaissance. The Place Royale, in which distinguished businesses such as Old England, the Café d'Europe and several insurance companies are located, retains a specific significance in the old trade circuit. It is always busy. Horses and carriages arrive and depart – followed a century later, when the Place has already gained dynastic significance, by the tram. National ceremonial processions, the taking of oaths, independence celebrations, royal weddings and funerals cannot prevent progress from taking possession of the spot too. The Place Royale is no longer simply a place criss-crossed by daily life and major events, it is just as much the spot where the stealthy inroads of modernity present a bulwark against the royal household's regressive recuperation. Silent tracks, trams and still later: the car.

Nevertheless the early 19th century saw the construction of the ring boulevard on the dismantled ramparts, with main roads such as the Rue du Trône, Rue de la Loi and Rue Belliard leading off it to shape the urban expansion to the east. These roads also penetrate inside the Pentagone (the inner city), but because of the big difference in height with the Lower Town they never reach beyond the Rue Royale and its successive extensions (the Rue de la Régence which breaks open the Place Royale and connects with the Sablon and later with the Palais de Justice). The Rue Royale and the Rue de la Régence serve here as the boundary of the Upper Town. As a connection between two royal residences the Rue Royale also develops into a representative main road. Everything along the route simply belongs to the Upper Town and furthermore is situated on a trajectory of national importance. Thus the eastern urban expansion fuses with the Upper Town – whose geometrical logic it takes over – but not with the Lower Town. This development fundamentally alters the significance of the Rue de la Madeleine, the Montagne de la Cour and its continuation, the Rue de Namur, which in the Upper Town is as it were enclosed by the newer and faster access routes to either side (Rue du Trône and Avenue Louise). The old road is reduced de facto to a local relief route. This reduction in traffic simultaneously permits the development referred to earlier of the Rue de la Madeleine and the Rue de Namur into an exclusive commercial sector extending from the Lower Town to Ixelles, with the Place Royale as the link between distinct segments.

As a stopping place in the overall east-west movement through the city the Place Royale has also largely lost significance. These days the traffic bustles much more between north and south. The Place Royale seems to incarnate the essence of the city's development. A whole series of modifications to the infrastructure which go together with the 19th century transformation of Brussels into a major industrial city, such as the deviation of the railway to the west, the cutting of the canal, the central boulevards and the (plans for) a north-south rail connection, brought about a brutal distortion of the city's mediaeval structure. The city is pushed willy-nilly into a north-south corset. In terms of the whole Brussels agglomeration, the Rue Royale and the Rue de la Régence also become a north-south axis and a dividing line. Godefroi de Bouillon's statue, placed in the middle of the Place Royale, does anything but contribute to the static repose of the square, on the contrary it fails in this purpose entirely. Standing as it does amidst the rush of cars and passing trams, it serves more to delineate a traffic island whose faltering function is to disentangle without too much turbulence the eastbound traffic from the unequal north-south flow.

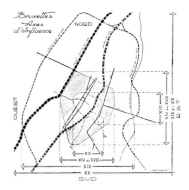

From place to junction

In the 19th century and the beginning of the 20th century the connection between the Upper and Lower Towns became progressively more difficult due to the major increase in the flow of goods and people together with the development of motorised transport. The limited steps taken early in the 19th century, to link the Upper and Lower Towns proved to be inadequate and Leopold II sought a more radical approach. The bustling district of the Montagne de la Cour became the focus of a far-reaching programme of reconstruction, modernisation and modifications of the infrastructure.

The construction of the Maquet Curve was indeed a decisive step. The differences in height were reconciled in the first phase by a sweeping double curve which increases the effective distance between the Upper and Lower Towns. A first curve, completed in 1897, which begins on the very steep Montagne de la Cour and later rejoins it (the later Rue Coudenberg) only cuts through the Quartier St. Roch. But for the second, much wider, curve, which connects the Montagne de la Cour at the top with the Marché aux Herbes at the

PLATE P. 120 (5)

PLATE P. 119

3. In one of the early versions of the repeatedly amended Maquet project it was still the intention to keep the viaduct partly visible and make it a pivotal point and urban terrace, an intermediate stopping point between the Lower Town and the Place Royale, in order to maintain the contiguous texture of the Lower Town.

4. M. Smets, *Charles Buls. Les principes de l'art urbain*, (Liège: P. Mardaga, 1995), pp. 117 et al.

5. T. Demey, *Bruxelles. Chronique d'une capitale en chantier*, T 1, (Brussels: Legrain, 1990), p. 250.

6. H. Teirlinck, *Brussel 1900*, (Antwerpen: Elsevier-Manteau), p. 49.

PLATES PP. 133, 136-137

bottom, a far larger piece of the mediaeval urban fabric was destroyed. The characteristic texture of the neighbourhoods on the slope with their numerous, close-knit little streets and dead-end alleyways was almost entirely swept away, while a great many problems arose in connecting the new flowing arc to the existing finely-woven street pattern. For the existing levels do not correspond with those of the new route. Part of the Rue Ravenstein, as the newly created Maquet Curve later became known, indeed rests partly on a viaduct.[3] Not only the formal, but also the functional unity of the Montagne de la Cour area is grievously damaged by these east-west connections. The construction of the Coudenberg and the semi-circular open space at its southern extremity spelled the end for the busy Montagne de la Cour which with its upmarket shops had been the "heart" of the Quartier St. Roch. As the then mayor, Charles Buls, remarked, the damage wrought upon the infrastructure was not only a goal in itself, but also a means of preparing the way for the creation of the museum complex that Leopold II was planning – and which to reduce the fire risk needed to be completely free of any surrounding buildings.[4] The Montagne de la Cour was to become a Mont des Arts.

The construction of the east-west route can be interpreted with certainty as an imperial gesture of Leopold II, as a Haussmann-style "annexation" of the Montagne de la Cour area into the Upper Town. By breaking out of the introverted urban architecture of the neo-classical Upper Town, the distinction between the Montagne de la Cour and the latter was erased and the Montagne de la Cour became a kind of offshoot of the Upper Town. The project met with little resistance from the city council, whose elders expressed scant concern as to the impact of the proposed upheaval, appearing to take for granted the amalgamation of the Upper Town with the Montagne de la Cour. The cleaning up of the picturesque but obscure Quartier St. Roch evidently had priority. Certainly the old Jewish ghetto, with its "worthless buildings" and "horrid little streets" where "sun and light never penetrate"[5] had a bad reputation, but strangely enough this was never elaborated upon. Herman Teirlinck also wrote edifyingly, though somewhat vaguely, about the area "somewhat lower than the just acceptable part of the Montagne de la Cour,"[6] so that we may assume that in the shadow of the high class shops in the Rue

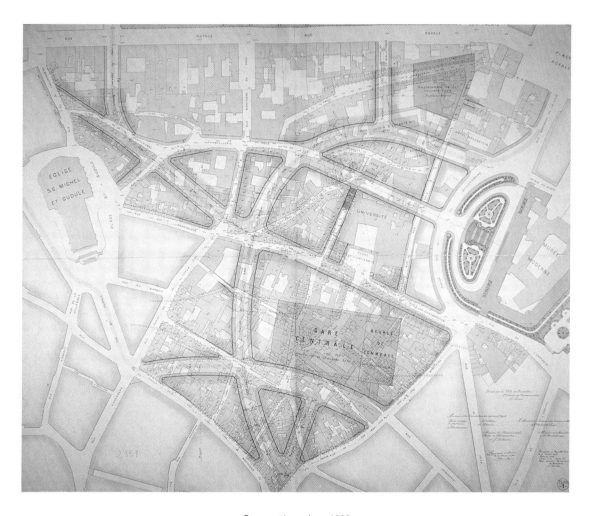

Convention plan, 1903

Montagne de la Cour less honourable services were available that were taboo for good right-thinking burghers.

Financially the project only became feasible when Leopold II, using his influence and his immense colonial fortune, effectively appropriated the Montagne de la Cour,[7] while arranging for the construction of the wide Maquet Curve to be combined with the building of a central station in the city centre. At a stroke, the Maquet Curve was joined via the Rue des Colonies with the Rue de la Loi. All these public works were "definitively" set down in a convention between the Belgian state and the city of Brussels in 1903: the construction of a commercial exchange and a central station (already specifying the route for the north south rail connection), the isolation of the Cathédrale St. Michel from surrounding buildings, and the cleaning up of the Putterie, the Montagne de la Cour and the area around the Cathédrale St. Michel. In this way a major part of the costs could be channelled off from the city to the state and the national railway company. The ambition to confer upon Brussels the statute of *Grande Ville*, shared by the city elders and Leopold II alike, nevertheless proved to be beyond their abilities – particularly those of the city treasury. Thus the city came to be largely handed over to the state, all vociferous declarations regarding the city's autonomy notwithstanding. The demolition of the Quartier St. Roch and the construction of the Rue Coudenberg in 1897 effectively gave the starting signal for the Montagne de la Cour and the districts of Isabelle, St. Roch, Terarken and the Putterie to be razed to the ground. A series of symbols of modernity were planned in their place: railway station, stock exchange, national museum and "modern" boulevards, adapted to the electric tram, motor traffic and suitable for "contemporary" buildings, in this case offices for the national capital. As drawn up, the intermediate area is effectively added to the Upper Town. The bulge in the Lower Town is to be transposed into an extension of the Upper Town. The state is to run the show. That at least is the gist of the convention.

The 1903 convention set down a coherent, but no less megalomaniac for all that, all-embracing plan for the complete transformation of the intermediate area between the Upper and Lower Towns. Its unexpectedly far-reaching ramifications, plus two world wars, projects that were never started, and the government's periodic indecision over the continuation of the north-south rail link, all helped to open the door to a whole series of disagreements between city and state and, more importantly, allowed all sorts of adaptations, amputations and additions to creep in. The coherent convention project was never completed in detail and those parts that were realised differ through and through from the original plan. The master plan was effectively thrown to the winds virtually from the outset. By way of poetic licence for example, a double expansion of the Maquet Curve was permitted so as to enable more connecting roads to penetrate into the Lower Town. The arc became ever wider, but cut ever deeper into the old town.

With the passage of time, individual parts of the plan increasingly stand on their own. The north-south rail link, which finally received the go-ahead and was built in this segment largely between the late 1930s and early 1950s, is the most striking example. Its route was drawn along the lower edge of the hill between the Lower and Upper Towns. On top of the railway line (which is more or less at the original ground level here) an oversized roadway was built, intended to serve as an artery for a series of additional, all equally oversized crossroads, with the Gare Centrale as the central pivot. This virtually makes the underbelly of the Mont des Arts into one big turntable, a set of oversized infrastructural elements ramblingly hitched together. The Carrefour de l'Europe (European Crossroads) was the name given to an odd fragment of this network, as if all Brussels, all Belgium and places beyond must find their way here and change direction. A gigantic traffic intersection. Brussels, the historic bridge over the Senne, erases itself in an attempt to become a pivotal point towards the future that does not exist, a crossroads that leads nowhere. This process of self-effacement and of becoming a traffic intersection stems from the paradox of scale found in Brussels. The small provincial town evidently aspires to a place on the world map by opening itself to international currents. This appears to be peculiar to Brussels and finds one of its most symbolic expressions at the foot of the Mont des Arts.

The Mont des Arts and its surroundings come off badly from the numerous infrastructural interventions. The numerous swathes cut through the original intermediate zone on the hill destroy its coherence. Now it is primarily an artificially raised thoroughfare

7. J. Stengers, *Combien le Congo a-t-il coûté à la Belgique?* (Brussels, 1957).

Aerial view of the Carrefour de l'Europe, 1935

dedicated to movement and the passage of everything that is "other." Trains, trams, buses, cars, the metro. The buildings are secondary and are a negative of the traffic infrastructure: a collection of hastily knocked-together fragments, often in the form of solitary buildings (Gare Centrale, Westbury Tower, Telex building, Sabena Air Terminus), torn loose from their urban context and with little mutual connection apart from that single common datum: the illusion of expanse, the bath in a sea of asphalt. The original, characteristic intermediate zone between Upper and Lower Town has been erased to make way for a new one. The irregular character acquired by this intermediate zone and the dominance of the traffic infrastructure nevertheless still distinguishes it from the reasonably intact Upper Town and the coherent *Îlot Sacré*. It still belongs neither to the one nor to the other. It remains an "other" place and a place for the "other."

The infrastructural interventions also made the area ripe for the realisation of extensive building projects. Leopold II's plan for systematically transforming the Montagne de la Cour into a Mont des Arts is executed step by step, and the 19th century already sees the building of the Musées Royaux des Beaux-Arts, followed one by one in the 20th century by the Palais des Beaux-Arts, Bibliothèque Royale, Archives Générales du Royaume, Palais des Congrès, Palais de la Dynastie, etc. In short, numerous cultural institutions of national importance were placed here. The Montagne de la Cour became the Mont des Arts that we know today: a slightly breathless, not quite homogenous cluster. At first sight, the Mont des Arts seems completed: a cascade of buildings is tumbling down the hill from the Rue Royale to the Boulevard de l'Impératrice. The plinth at the Rue de Ruysbroeck is matched by the plinth of the library on the Jardin de l'Albertine. The overall effect is hardly taut, but certainly "full." Everything still to be added has to be dug out and put underground, an option that Roger Bastin indeed chose for the latest addition – the Musée de l'Art Moderne. It seems like an anticlimax: the completion of the Mont des Arts is a pit. But as Johan Lagae's contribution makes clear, there was absolutely no need for it to be thus. For in spite of the apparent completion of the Mont des Arts, there still exists a margin for a critical examination, by means of architectural design, of the original set-up of the site.

Aerial view of the Mont des Arts, 1970

Fragments of an in-between zone

From the 1950s onwards, the wholesale demolition caused by the
creation of the north-south route and the limited depth between
the Rue Royale and the morphological fault line of the railway line
put the whole area from the Jardin Botanique to the Rue de
Ruysbroeck under ever-increasing pressure. It has been literally
marked by the brutal distortion of Brussels' historical east-west
axis into a north-south one. The entire district was completely
transformed and has disintegrated today into a number of connected fragments, each of which with its own particular shape
occupies the hill between Upper and Lower Towns: the Cité Administrative du Royaume that reaches from the inner ring road to the
Place du Congrès, a cluster of office blocks encircling and trying to
dominate the Cathédrale St. Michel (the Banque Nationale, the
offices of the Crédit Communal, the Ministry of the Flemish
Community, the Telex building); a battery of offices around the
Marché au Bois (Westbury Tower, Shell building, Fortis Bank, ...).
Also the amorphous bundle of hotels at the Carrefour de l'Europe,
the Gare Centrale, the Sabena Air Terminus, and the Telex building
in a sense form a similar cluster. The conventional Mont des Arts
(the agglomeration of the Musées Royaux, Bibliothèque Royale,
Archives Générales du Royaume, and the underground Palais des
Congrès) forms the last chunk in this series of fragments and as a
coherent building complex, bridges the gap between the Upper
and Lower Towns. The entire interstitial area on the hill between
Upper and Lower Towns comes to an end with the Mont des Arts.
Here there is a distinct morphological boundary. The Sablon and its
surroundings bridge the gap between Upper and Lower Towns with
traditional urban fabric: building blocks with a finely interwoven
border that creates the leeway to integrate large scale projects. The
boundary between the Sablon and the Mont des Arts is still marked
by the first town wall. This fundamental fault line in the morphol-
ogy of the Brussels inner city is underlined by the break in scale
that the Musée de l'Art Ancien imposes on the Rue de Ruysbroeck.
On account of the gradient, the museum is placed on a heavily
elaborate plinth and this emphasises the idea of the town wall, of
the boundary.

Map of the City of Brussels, 1995

PLATES P. 258-259

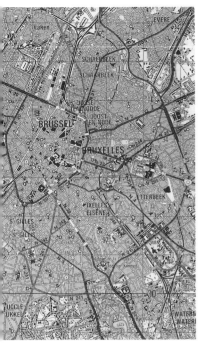

Topographic map of the City of Brussels, 1986

Dispersed centrality

As a segment in the east-west route and essential threshold between the Upper and Lower Towns, the Montagne de la Cour enjoyed a natural centrality and public presence for centuries. Everything and everybody passed this way. Since the 19th century the centre of gravity of the swelling metropolis nevertheless moved eastwards. Successive waves of urban development spread to valley after valley: the Maelbeek, the Woluwe. In its wake various important institutions set up house, such as the European Union and Nato, spreading ever further from the city centre. The city's centre of gravity not only shifted eastwards but in a sense also evaporated. The development of the new territorial networks, such as the motorway system, pose a challenge to the compact 19th century city. Important present day motors of urban activity, such as the Heysel with its annual trade fairs, are orientated primarily towards the motorway ring road network. Formerly peripheral elements such as the airport are becoming centres of development, junctions in the network.

All this puts the Mont des Arts in a difficult position. An important part of its centrality has been lost. The shift in the city's power and influence centres and the genesis of the new network-oriented urbanity draws people away from the spot. The motors of urban activity that attract or generate people in significant numbers are nowhere near here. The place is no longer a magnet in the city. All you can find here, so to speak, are dusty old books and droll national art, relics of a distant past, whilst in Diegem people are buying CDs and in Waterloo expensive works of art are being traded, in Vilvoorde or in the American theatre at the Heysel television shows are being produced and in Zaventem the business parks are spreading like carpets over the countryside. Only the Gare Centrale, which daily spews out 60.000 commuters and sucks them back in again, offers any competition.

Particularities and margins

The phenomenal investments in infrastructure, the conversion from place to junction, appear to have been wasted effort. The infrastructure here appears more than ever oversized. Perhaps the best way to regard this gigantic and partly useless infrastructure today is as a margin to manoeuvre. Since an intermediate level exists for the entire length of the north-south link between the railway lines and the boulevards placed on top of them, it is not only possible to operate on the profile, but equally on the cross-section. The infrastructure – or structure if you prefer – can be partly dismantled, partly recuperated as a carelessly built and oversized raw construction. Working on the cross-section sometimes unexpectedly reveals useable space. Superfluous infrastructure can be dismantled in other places so as to reinstate historical connections. To simply ignore these possibilities, as Sarfati's current proposal for the reconstruction of the Boulevard de l'Impératrice does, strikes us in this sense as a missed opportunity to use public space to work towards a redefinition of the area. This argument with regard to the north-south link applies equally to the Rue Ravenstein or the Rue de la Régence which consist in whole or in part of viaducts.

The Mont des Arts functions today as an island within the urban context, because of its large-scale traffic infrastructure and its narrowly defined main theme. Nevertheless it remains one of the essential connections between the east and west of Brussels and hence much traffic flows through the district. The Mont des Arts is both a bridge and an island. This duality creates an interesting tension and invites confrontation: between low and high culture, between free flows and fencing off, between dynamic and static, or perhaps more precisely: between the temporary or ephemeral and the permanent.

A major part of what has been built on the Mont des Arts has as it were been pushed into the hill, and this gives rise to a rich gradation between the above-ground and underground spaces. Many of the spaces have an ambiguous nature. From below they are above ground, from above they are below ground. Streets cross at different levels. It turns out that a viaduct, such as that of the Rue Ravenstein, houses a surprisingly decorative curved space of majestic dimensions. Above, below, inside, outside, in the hill, on the slope, apparently above, in fact below and reversed, original and artificial levels, situations such as these, all contribute to a rich spatial gradation, from vertical co-ordination to a dense interweaving. Various interventions by city planners and architects on the Mont des Arts made intensive use of this confusion of levels. The Palais des Beaux-Arts, for example, has no real level of reference, situated as it is on the Rue Ravenstein, Rue des Sols, Rue Royale, Rue Baron Horta, Rue

Terarken and Rue Villa Hermosa. Horta planned entrances to the Palais des Beaux-Arts on different levels in each of these streets, and exploited this complex feature in masterly fashion. Other interventions, such as the constructions below ground of the Palais des Congrès and the Musée de l'Art Moderne which ended up in a pit, are less subtle. At other points, such as the Hôtel Hoogstraten, (the former Cour des Comptes) we find an astonishing mixture of constructions dating from the middle ages to 20th century. The Musées Royaux des Beaux-Arts (1875-1881, architect Alphonse Balat) also shows an imaginative approach to the slope with its massive plinth.

The underground spaces brought into being throughout the complex past of the Mont des Arts today form a sort of hollow base that forges the site into a single entity, thereby undermining all the foregoing analyses. The area may only apparently be fragmented, for it in fact possesses an exceptionally strong spatial support, albeit an invisible one. That its potential remains largely underemployed is beyond dispute. Its latent strength today is at most acknowledged by marginal and temporary use of underground spaces such as the superb rotunda of the Gare Centrale for rave parties and suchlike; in the chance resonance of a polyphonic piece in the archaeological maze under the Hôtel Lalaing; in the occasional experimental performance in the viaduct of the Rue Ravenstein; in the raucous disco noise reverberating though the Galerie Ravenstein, an ambiguous space half above, half below ground. The below ground can only deploy its potential in competition with the above ground, a thoroughly unswinging place to be today, exuding an air of deathly, dusty sacredness. It seems paradoxical, the ground level here houses that which is dead: sacred works of art that are stored and buried. The library – described by Borges as the impenetrable world of knowledge inhabited only by strange old men, all skin and bone, who have lost all awareness of life in the real world outside – is just as dead. The same applies to the Archives Générales du Royaume. Only in the untrammelled imagination of Schuiten do the archives reveal a dizzying tension. The upper side of the Mont des Arts is, rather, a necropolis, as indeed Charles Buls once foresightedly described it. As rock-solid as it may look above ground, so temporal and feeble however are the sparks of vitality that are waiting below ground to one day set the Mont des Arts ablaze.

VACANT SPACES

 vacant in the near future

potentially vacant

vacant

partially vacant

CONNECTING SPACES

storage PBA, groundfloor Galerie Ravenstein and Shell building, Jardin de l'Albertine, groundfloor Palais des Congrès, patio Bibliothèque Royale

car parks (Shell building, Galerie Ravenstein, Albertine) and patio Bibliothèque Royale

entrances and hall Gare Centrale

underground spaces Gare Centrale (Rotunda)

possible connections

STRUCTURING GRID / LABYRINTH

underground car parks

intermediate level between railway and boulevard

elevated streets

(sculptural) architectural elements

FEEDERS AND PEDESTRIAN PASSAGEWAYS

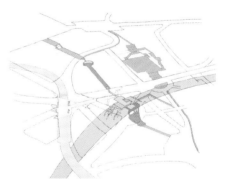

subway, subway corridor and railway as feeders

Upper Town and Lower Town as commuter and tourist destinations

pedestrian passageways (above ground and under ground)

connections between main passageways

JOURNAL DE BRUXELLES ILLUSTRÉ

G. ONKELINX del.

Rédaction & Administration :

4, Impasse de la Fidélité BRUXELLES

DEUX ASPECTS PITTORESQUES DE BRUXELLES-DÉMOLITIONS

1. Le Marché-au-Bois. — 2. Comment on se rend de la Grande Harmonie à Sainte-Gudule

Bruxelles-Démolitions

Les gravures que nous publions en premières pages sont réellement bien curieuses.

Il en est une notamment qui donne une impression frappante d'Alpes ou de Pyrénées. Et pourtant toutes deux ont bien été prises à Bruxelles en Brabant.

Il est vrai qu'elles y ont été prises en l'an de grâce 1911 et c'est, on le sait, pour la topographie bruxelloise, un temps fertile en miracles

Nos gravures donnent une vue en contrebas du pont en bois de la rue provisoire qui doit permettre, dès le 1er janvier, de raccorder la ligne de trams électriques du boulevard Anspach à celle de la rue Royale.

Des paliers du pont sont déjà plantés dans du béton. Le pont aura quatre-vingt-dix mètres de long, et son tablier douze mètres de largeur. Ce n'est que du provisoire, il est vrai, et du provisoire qui aura coûté cher. Mais la Ville de Bruxelles est tenue, sous peine d'avoir à payer une indemnité de plusieurs millions, par contrat avec la Société des Tramways Bruxellois, à rendre possible la jonction des lignes.

Comme elle n'a pas fait à temps les travaux définitifs qui lui incombaient, elle est obligée d'effectuer aujourd'hui un travail provisoire qui coûtera un demi-million.

Mais les contribuables sont là, n'est-ce pas, pour payer !...

vent
chemi
d'une
songer

— C
combi
cher
les je
grand

Les
form
coule
dans
l'irré
lette,
bleus,
toujo
ble à
plus s
penser

Que
Elle a
faire
sourit
mens
passé
l'emp
une h

Plu
émoti
que je
le sai
elle a
son v

MODERNITY VERSUS IDENTITY
LEOPOLD II AND CHARLES BULS

Karina Van Herck and Bruno De Meulder

Leopold II, the construction of the new

Brussels derives its identity as the capital of a country originating at the intersection of different cultures, as an artificially-created buffer between antagonistic states, having in fact arisen out of "nothing." Its existing town centre was removed, a development prompted by Leopold II, who drew upon his colonial fortune for this purpose. The Montagne de la Cour and its surrounding neighbourhoods (St. Roch, Terarken, Isabelle, and Putterie), in short, the whole area between the Lower and Upper Town, were completely cleared for the benefit of the infrastructural "violence" from the improved east-west connections (large and small "Maquet Curves") and from the north-south rail connection. What for centuries had been of prime importance in the city and had also nestled itself in the heart of the collective memory was consequently erased: the Putterie disappeared for the benefit of a railway station (Gare Centrale) and a stock exchange (the Bourse), while the Montagne de la Cour area with its picturesque narrow streets and numerous historic buildings, which was an essential part of the identity of Brussels as *Vieille Ville*, was also swept from the cityscape. The town centre was thus thoroughly evacuated to be refilled with new projects, which were meant to give shape to the aspirations of Brussels as a modern capital. To execute this, Leopold II fostered, from its inception, a megalomaniac project: a Mont des Arts.

PLATES PP. 133, 136-137 The first plans for the Mont des Arts date back to 1882 (by architect Alphonse Balat, succeeded in 1895 by his student, Henri Maquet). They include the expansion of the Musées Royaux des Beaux-Arts and the Bibliothèque Royale, and the establishment of a Palais de l'Industrie and the Archives Générales du Royaume. This colossal building complex was conceived as the symbol of the cultural status of Belgium. In complexity and size it competed with Poelaert's Palais de Justice, the largest building of its kind in the world at that time. As an urban element embedded in an axial system, it needed to form an "architectural trilogy" together with the Palais de Justice and the town hall to represent the traditional powers of the city. The enormous scale and the uniformity of the façade that encapsulates the existing and new buildings make the museum complex into a proud building that dominates its surroundings. A gigantic base, where the natural difference in levels of the site is counterbalanced, allows it to tower above the lower part of the city, as an "Acropolis" or "Valhalla," erected to the "honour and glory of the fatherland."[1] By distancing it from its context – the area between the Rue Coudenberg and the complex was turned into a public garden for the sake of fire security – a respectful distance was established between the museum and the surrounding city.

The gigantic scale and the neo-classical arrangement of the complex make the Mont des Arts an "expansion" of the Quartier Royal. The traditional urbanism is completely pushed back to the Lower Town, the *Vieille Ville*, which as an endearing witness from a distant, popular past is assigned a function as tourist attraction. The visual relationships between both parts of the city reinforce these shifts. From the Lower Town, the Upper Town can be perceived as a fortress or bastion of power placed above a massive base. From the Upper Town, panoramic views of the Lower Town unfold through linear views and broader perspectives. Two antagonistic worlds are presented: the medieval city with its *couleur locale* which, apparently protected from every modernity, is frozen as an *Îlot Sacré*, versus the modern city, with its imposing royal museum complex like a protruding bastion, forced into the foreground. Each has its own style and characteristics: a neo-classicism that makes universal claims, the representation of a civilisation in which Belgium wants to participate, and the organic and picturesque city as a representation of the local, earlier – medieval – culture. This paradoxical dual identity of Brussels, international capital and provincial town, manifests itself fully in the enormous difference in scale that arises between the large-scale museum complex and the texture of the historical fabric.

With its museums, archives and libraries that collect the knowledge and culture of the country, the Mont des Arts of Leopold II gives shape to the memory of the nation. The "Flemish Primitives," Rubens, Van Dijck, and everything else important that was produced in the Southern Netherlands (Belgium) are brought together to lay claim to a contribution to civilisation. This is displayed in the

1. See M. Smets, *Charles Buls. Les principes de l'art urbain* (Liège: P. Mardaga, 1995), p. 118.

Montagne des Aveugles (C.E.V.B., 1911)

treasure house of the nation, literally displayed on the altar of the fatherland. On the Mont des Arts, in other words, a national history is constructed, the unity of the Belgian people is presented and re-presented. At least, that was the intention of Leopold II. Due to its extravagant cost, the plans for the museum were voted down in 1908 by the parliament. All the same, the expropriation and clearing of the neighbourhood steadily went its own way and after the Second World War, against better judgement, the Mont des Arts achieved its imperfect completion. The ultimate construction of the Mont des Arts between 1951 and 1984 really appears to be a posthumous Pyrrhic victory of the meanwhile hopelessly outdated urbanistic views of Leopold II.

Charles Buls and Guillaume Des Marez, the construction of the historical city

Rue de la Madeleine (C.E.V.B., 1914)

Before the completion of the Mont des Arts, Brussels had, willingly or unwillingly, learned to live for years with a vacuum in the heart of the city. Although spared from destruction during the First World War, the centre of Brussels looked nevertheless like a ruined city. Where the ruined regions were immediately rebuilt, in Brussels the surplus of indefinable open space remained for years.[2] It produced a very alienating effect that undoubtedly confirmed the "deficiency" of the demolished patrimony and encouraged a certain mythologising of the earlier neighbourhoods. Suddenly Putterie and Terarken, neighbourhoods over which until then nothing had been recorded, proved a valuable microcosm of Belgian history.[3] The deficiency that perhaps would have failed to appear in the case of immediate reconstruction undoubtedly contributed to an "alternative urban project" taking shape in Brussels, an urban project that paraded itself as "rational urbanism" and which takes as an offshoot respect for the existing city and more specifically for the urban fabric. Since the mid-1920s this attitude has been public property and set down as the canon of urbanism. The seed of this thinking was, however, already sown at the end of the 19th century by Charles Buls – then mayor of Brussels – who was one of the very few who objected to Leopold II's Mont des Arts project and resigned as a result of this conflict. The sweeping away of all the existing buildings on the Montagne de la Cour was for Charles Buls a direct assault on the individuality of the city, which for him by definition was historic, and an infringement on its urban autonomy. With the help of the city archivist, Des Marez, he gave shape to an urban project that departed from history and tradition, and that ideologically was to a large extent determined by its resistance to the modern project of Leopold II.

Buls was in disagreement with Leopold II from the very outset about the way in which communication between the Upper and Lower Towns should be achieved on the Montagne de la Cour. For Leopold II, who promoted the Maquet project, the new road (the small Maquet Curve or the Rue Coudenberg) would begin high up on the Montagne de la Cour and go straight across the St. Roch neighbourhood. For Buls, who in 1893 proposed an alternative project for the east-west connection, a shorter curve on the lower part of the site, where the slope was at its steepest, would have sufficed. In principle, Buls kept the possibility of constructing a second east-west connection – the large Maquet Curve – open, strongly speculating that delay would lead to its cancellation. Buls remained convinced by the *Projet d'ensemble pour l'amélioration de la voirie et la transformation de divers quartiers de la ville de Bruxelles* (1883), from the then city engineer Charles Van Mierlo, which is based on a distribution of traffic flow between east and west via an assortment of connections between the most important destinations in the inner city and the different approach roads from the agglomeration. In this way the connection between east and west could be interwoven in the existing urban structure without large scale interventions, as the previous layout by Buls for the Rue Coudenberg actually illustrates. Whereas Maquet translates the problem of the east-west connection into an abstract layout – determined by a purely technical study based on the smallest degree of inclination – that imposed on the existing fabric, Buls generates, following Van Mierlo, a solution for the stated problem starting from the structure of the urban fabric. The layout for the "alternative project" begins with the layout of the existing streets, takes into account the relief and avoids the demolition of historically important buildings, for which not only monuments but houses are also considered. The intervention into the fabric is minimal while the task – the realisation of an east-west connection and the accompanying redevelopment of the St. Roch neighbourhood – is still

2. This has to do with the long-term expropriation procedures, the indecisiveness of the Belgian government after the first world war about not placing the north-south railroad connection, and the disputes between the city of Brussels and the state about the reconstruction.

3. "The older people from Brussels don't miss anything as much as the Isabelle and Terarken neighbourhood. It hasn't been long since it disappeared. They're still upset. Its history was like a microcosm of the history of Belgium." A. Guislain, *Bruxelles Atmosphère 10-32* (Brussels-Paris: L'Eglantine, 1932), p. 217-218.

PLATES P. 120

carried out. The benefits of this pragmatic approach are countless, according to Buls: "One maintains the local and national character of the city, one does not destroy memories of the past except where modern life strictly requires it, one obtains picturesque effects, one manages the communal finances, and one interjects fewer disruptions into the habits and interests of the population."[4]

Buls' project exemplifies a clear conviction that the city is a living and moving organism which, in each stage of its existence, is capable of growing and producing something new. In the organically evolving city, each change follows the preceding one, the future lies contained within the present. For Buls modernisation should graft itself onto what already exists and further develop the already present potential. With his "alternative project" Buls in fact labels Maquet's project as "improper." Maquet's abstract intervention not only ignores the generative capacity of the fabric, but also destroys it. Whereas "living" material is dynamic, extends itself over the past and the future, a modern intervention that is imposed from the outside only relates to the present and "stands cold" in its context. According to Buls this has far-reaching consequences for the inhabitants. Disturbing the collective and continual evolution of the inhabitants and their city will eventually lead to alienation or, as Herman Teirlinck (then city clerk) with regard to this area dramatically expressed, "will prevent loving children from recognising their mother."[5] Teirlinck mirrors the familiar historical surroundings with the heart of the family – the mother figure – in which source and individuality merge, identity is established, and then considers each important intervention in this urban fabric as an incurable wound (Buls was referring to fatal wounds[6]), as a loss "of its own nature," a "conceding to the degradation of what was its historical integrity."[7] In one stroke Teirlinck associates the urban fabric that is subject to history with the idea of the wounded organism, with identity (via the mother figure), with cultural individuality (through historical integrity) and with community (the father's house and the mother), and by this stands in agreement with Buls who situates the locus of the collective memory (that which a society defines as culturally central or its "own") in the historical city. As part of everyday experience, the streets, houses and squares of the old city form an active and permanent stimulus for the remembering of a collective past: "The stones speak to the spirit; ... they reconnect the present to the past and cause a venerable and original accent to resonate and cut the uniformity and banality of modern life."[8] The built environment becomes an artefact upon which the collective history of an urban community can be read.

Buls' opposition to the destruction of the Montagne de la Cour was the catalyst for a global urban project: the reconstruction of *La Vieille Ville*, the small-scale city, for which Buls' pamphlet *Esthétique des Villes* (1893) quickly became one of the fundamental reference texts. For Buls the Montagne de la Cour is, just like the Grand'Place, one of the symbolic sites in the city that comprises an essential part of Brussels' identity as *Vieille Ville*. In *L'Origine et Développement de la Ville de Bruxelles* (1927), by the then city archivist Des Marez, the history of Brussels and of the Montagne de la Cour flow seamlessly into one another. What was at stake for Buls and Des Marez was therefore the old city itself. One could seriously wonder whether Des Marez would not have made an equally poignant story of any other, until that time blank, historical neighbourhood that was demolished.

When in 1903, with the Convention between the Belgian state and the city of Brussels definitively sealing the fate of the Isabelle and Terarken neighbourhoods, Buls and his allies – all representatives of the bourgeois elite – the *Comité d'Etudes du Vieux-Bruxelles* (C.E.V.B.), directed their attention to systematically documenting the monuments, houses and sites that were characteristic of Brussels. The Isabelle and Terarken neighbourhoods were meticulously studied, photographed and archived (this never took place at the St. Roch neighbourhood, which did not have a very good reputation). The reproduction of the most characteristic elements of these neighbourhoods should preserve the memory of this symbolic area. The whole undertaking can be interpreted as simultaneously both a search for and construction of what is "typically Brussels." It is often the lavishly decorated Flemish bourgeois houses from the 15th, 16th and 17th centuries with their pitched roofs, the twisting streets and alleys laid out in close association with the topography, and the picturesque views, which are selected as valuable; are given a central place in the collective memory and thus are immediately defined as the building blocks of Brussels' identity. The house, with its many common everyday qualities and aspects that contribute to local

4. Ch. Buls, *Esthétique des Villes* (Brussels: Bruylant, 1894), p. 15.

5. H. Teirlinck, *Brussel 1900* (Antwerp-Amsterdam: Elsevier-Manteau, 1981), p. 16.

6. Thus writes Buls about the lower part of Rue de Montagne de la Cour: "one can say that this long sinuous road, where we believe we have rediscovered the traces of generations who have wandered through them for centuries, is a vital artery of our old city and one of the traits of its beauty. We would not be able to distort it without delivering a fatal wound." Ch. Buls, o.c., p. 40.

7. H. Teirlinck, o.c., p. 16.

8. Ch. Buls, o.c., p.23.

Rue de l'Impératrice (C.E.V.B., circa 1909)

colour, is assumed by the *Comité d'Etudes du Vieux-Bruxelles* to be preserved as the bearer of the urban structure. La *Vieille Ville* is the city of
the house and its connection to texture, the city of bourgeois culture.
Neither monuments or churches but rather the residential fabric,
which is recognised as the framework for all sorts of uses and customs, is prominent as bearer of a collective lifestyle that will determine the specificity of place. Teirlinck with his poetic jargon did not
mourn the demolition of churches, but lamented the many madon-
nas (images, statues, etc.) no longer being carried in processions.[9]

Housing was claimed by the members of the *Comité d'Etudes du
Vieux-Bruxelles* as an immediate reflection of a splendid bourgeois
culture. In his historiography of the districts Isabelle and Terarken,
Des Marez tells how housing heroically withstood the successive
waves of foreign rule. Whereas public buildings and churches were
built in Italian renaissance, baroque and French neo-classical styles,
houses were continually built according to local traditions. The
house can thus be considered as the "true" witness of the past and
as an "authentic" expression of what is local. (Local is here actually
equated with Flemish and with national, which for a nation such as
Belgium is especially problematical.) For Des Marez most of the
blame could be assigned to the importation of the French styles in
the 18th century, from which housing was not spared. What he
especially regretted was the fact that "... deprived of their antique
ornaments, all modelled after a cold and desperately uniform type,
our houses lost their own individuality."[10] Upon further consideration it was possibly the typical values that were cherished by the
bourgeois elite around the turn of the century – the articulation of
individualism as an expression of free citizenship – that Buls and
Des Marez selectively read in history and retain as building blocks
for their *Vieille Ville*.

In the reconstruction project of Buls and Des Marez not only the
buildings, but also the generative structure of the city – the "pattern"
that is considered as unchanging and original – serves as the bearer
of meanings and memories that nourish civil consciousness and wel-
fare. Des Marez takes an especially hard stab at French neo-classicism,
because the physiognomy of the historical fabric is thoroughly disrupted by the construction of such monumental boulevards and
monolithic buildings. The centuries-old, topography-determined

Marché aux Herbes (C.E.V.B., 1911)

urban structure is recognised as "typical Brussels," whereas what does not result from it is seen as a mutation or a strange implant. The large Maquet Curve can in this way be interpreted as a blundering offshoot of the neo-classical boulevards, by which the Putterie and Terarken are permanently estranged from the origin of the place or the *Genius Loci*. The *Comité d'Etudes du Vieux-Bruxelles* concentrates especially on ensembles. Streets, an arrangement of houses, the cluster, and the neighbourhood become a preservation issue, with the objective of marking the origin or the "individuality" of the place.

Conservation, however, also means fixation. Where Van Mierlo's alternative project for the east-west connection, and also Buls' alternative project initially, still depart from the idea of a continually evolving city, the city is fixated in the reconstruction project based on a certain perception of the past. What is preserved is the often painterly testimony of a rich Flemish past, its heroic and illustrious "golden age." The Flemish renaissance becomes the national style – Buls proposes, for example, to erect "the acropolis of our national art" on the site of the Palais de Nassau in the style of the Flemish renaissance.[11] The cityscape in its totality is fixated via the protection of panoramic views. In this way the glorious past is collected and stored, and made available for appropriation by later generations.

The modern, "destructive" and ruthless urban project of Maquet and Leopold II and the historicising vision of Buls and Des Marez represent two contrasting modes of urban planning. Neither of these modes, however, gained the upper hand on the Mont des Arts. In this obviously unresolved conflict that arises from the dual identity of Brussels lies the explanation for the impasse from which Brussels in general and the Mont des Arts in particular suffer so much. The simultaneous will to achieve a *tabula rasa* and incremental renewal, set against the desire for preservation – and even a "museumisation" – of the existing city leads in practice to an insidious decision-making process and immobilisation.

9. H. Teirlinck, o.c., p. 16.

10. G. Des Marez, *L'Origine et le développement de la ville de Bruxelles. Le quartier Isabelle et Terarken* (Brussels: Van Oest, 1927), p. 149.

11. This proposal was published in April 1894 in *L'Emulation*. o.c., A. Brauman, M. Culot, M. Demanet e.a., *100 ans de debat sur la ville. La formation de la ville moderne a travers les comptes rendus du conseil communal de Bruxelles 1840-1940* (Brussels: A.A.M., 1984), p. 180.

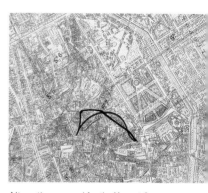

Alternative proposal for the Maquet Curve (Van Mierlo, 1887)

QUE SERA LE MONT DES ARTS?

REVUE DES PRINCIPAUX PROJETS

UNE REVUE DES PROJETS.

Voici plusieurs années que ministres et députés, architectes et esthètes cherchent une chose qui semble plus difficile à trouver que la pierre philosophale : la meilleure solution à donner au problème du Mont des Arts à Bruxelles.

Nos lecteurs connaissent les éléments de ce problème. Ils savent aussi qu'en dernière analyse, M. le Ministre des travaux publics s'était rallié, en ce qui concerne l'aménagement des terrains de l'ancienne Montagne de la Cour, et une nouvelle appropriation des terrains de la rue de l'Empereur, à un projet conçu par l'architecte français Vacherot. La Chambre a exprimé le désir que rien de définitif ne soit entrepris pour

Gouvernement et du Parlement.

Le moment est donc opportun de passer en revue les principaux projets qui sollicitent cette approbation.

LE PROJET MARQUET

Des deux photographies que nous publions l'une représente la façade principale. L'angle supérieur de cette façade se dresse au coin de la petite rue du Musée, l'angle in-

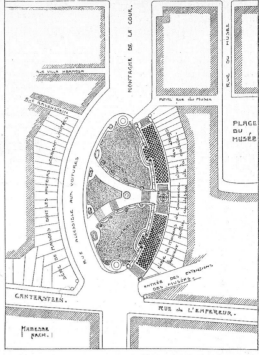

PROJET PAUL HAMESSE

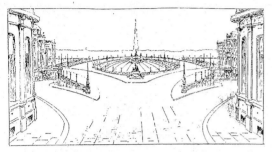

PROJET HERMANUS. — Vue perspective de l'Esplanade prise de la Place Royale vers la tour de l'Hôtel-de-Ville dans l'axe exact.

l'instant. On ne fera donc rien d'ici l'an prochain, si ce n'est niveler le terrain compris entre la rue Caudenberg et l'ancienne Montagne de la Cour et y jeter un tapis de fleurs. La question du Mont des Arts elle-même demeure réservée jusqu'à ce qu'un projet définitif ait reçu l'approbation du

férieur au coin de la rue de l'Empereur où les bâtiments auront une élévation de quarante mètres. La tour, amenée là, pour les besoins de la perspective, aura une hauteur de 80 mètres.

L'autre photo représente la façade postérieure du côté de la rue de Ruysbroeck. Le

raccordement avec une des façades latérales du Musée Ancien prolongera cette partie du palais des Beaux-Arts jusqu'à la rue de la Régence.

LE PROJET VACHEROT.

Le projet de M. Vacherot, architecte parisien, projet que M. le Ministre des travaux publics avait adopté, comporte l'établissement sur le terre-plein actuel de la Montagne de la Cour d'un square horizontal se terminant, face à la rue de la Madeleine, par une sorte de petit temple grec semi-circulaire et à colonnades. Du haut de ce square l'on découvre tout le panorama de Bruxelles. Sur l'emplacement du côté gauche de la rue de l'Empereur (en descendant vers la place de la Justice) s'élèvent en pente douce des jardins directement raccordés au square de la Montagne de la Cour. Au centre de ces jardins, vers le milieu de la rue de l'Empereur, s'érige une fontaine monumentale. L'ensemble du pro-

PROJET HERMANUS. — Vue perspective vers la Place Royale.

La Façade Principale.

PROJET MAQUET.

La reproduction de ce projet a déjà paru, en plus grandes dimensions, dans notre numéro du 1er mars 1908.

jet Vacherot forme les assises fleuries et arborées sur lesquelles l'on pourrait édifier plus tard le palais du Mont des Arts dont les dimensions et le caractère seraient à discuter ultérieurement.

cès, de plain-pied, sur le toit de cette immense rotonde laquelle pourrait être aménagée en promenade avec bancs, candélabres, etc. Au centre de cette rotonde et de tous ces magasins, il y aurait place pour

Une colonnade monumentale limiterait la galerie-promenade; entre les cintres viendraient s'encadrer les perspectives vers la ville et les échappées vers les jardins étagés.

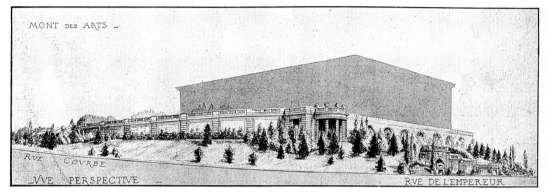

PROJET VACHEROT

LE PROJET HERMANUS.

M. Hermanus s'est inspiré du désir fréquemment exprimé par les mandataires de la capitale de voir conserver au quartier de la Montagne de la Cour son ancien caractère commercial. M. Hermanus trace une seconde rue courbe face à celle qui existe déjà et sur l'emplacement situé au milieu de ces deux boucles, il édifie en rotonde une série de magasins qui seraient assez élevés du côté de la rue de la Madeleine et iraient en se rapetissant vers la place royale. En arrivant de la place Royale on aurait ac-

une salle de fêtes, dans laquelle l'on pénétrerait par la rue de l'Empereur.

PROJET DE M. HAMESSE.

De la montagne de la Cour, M. Hamesse fait un passage couvert, bordé d'un côté de magasins de luxe et de l'autre d'une colonnade. En face, serait un large square. La galerie, de cinq à six mètres de largeur, est réservée aux promeneurs; ceux-ci pourraient examiner à loisir les vitrines des maisons de commerce, dont les étages, construits en saillie, constitueraient le plafond de ce passage et prendraient jour et air vers les squares.

Des balcons arrondis établis le long de la promenade ménageraient des points de vue vers le square et la cité.

Et pour corriger la pente trop forte de cette galerie, il y est prévu une succession de terrains reliés de distance en distance par quelques marches. On se trouverait ainsi, au bas du passage, de niveau avec la rue de la Madeleine.

D'autre part, de l'espace compris entre les palissades actuelles, le projet fait un square elliptique, sorte de musée de sculpture en plein air, rempli de statues, de fontaines et de fleurs, et traversé de chemins reliant la galerie couverte à la rue Coudenberg.

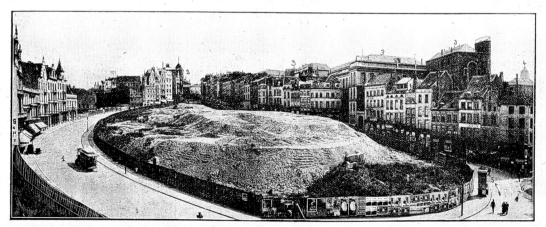

ETAT ACTUEL. — 1. Rue Courbe. — 2. La Place Royale et l'église St-Jacques. — 3. Les Musées. — 4. Le Palais de Justice. 5. Montagne de la Cour. — 6. Rue de l'Empereur.

Square du Mont des Arts (Vacherot), 1910-1955

AROUND THREE O'CLOCK, dressed in my best, I used to go for a stroll on the Montagne de la Cour.

In those days, the Montagne de la Cour was the place where, in the winter, women of all classes would go at the same time, between three and five, to do their shopping, take a stroll and check each other out. Men were less present.

Women were at home there. All the dress, hat, fine lingerie, fur jewelry and luxury shoe shops were concentrated on this steep old street. One would walk down it, and via the Rue de la Madeleine, go as far as the Passage and then go back up. Having tea was unheard of: rather, one might have a piece of cake at Brias', on the Cantersteen, although not necessarily...especially in my case, as I didn't have enough money. Twenty-five years ago, in Brussels, if you hadn't been for a stroll on the Montagne-de-la-Cour, you had never been out.

I was happy as Larry as young, pretty and well dressed, I strolled in this elegant milieu, because the Montagne-de-la-Cour was an intimate place where people recognised each other without knowing each other.

"See that short woman with wavy hair: she must be foreign," said the ladies as they looked me over. People tend to lower their voices in Belgium.

"Ah! Here's that lady with the beautiful furs," I would think. And we would carry on going up and down, tirelessly, until five o'clock at the latest.

From *Keetje* by Neel Doff, 1918.

C'EST UN MANTEAU *"Lamalux"* SIGNÉ : *Destroopers*

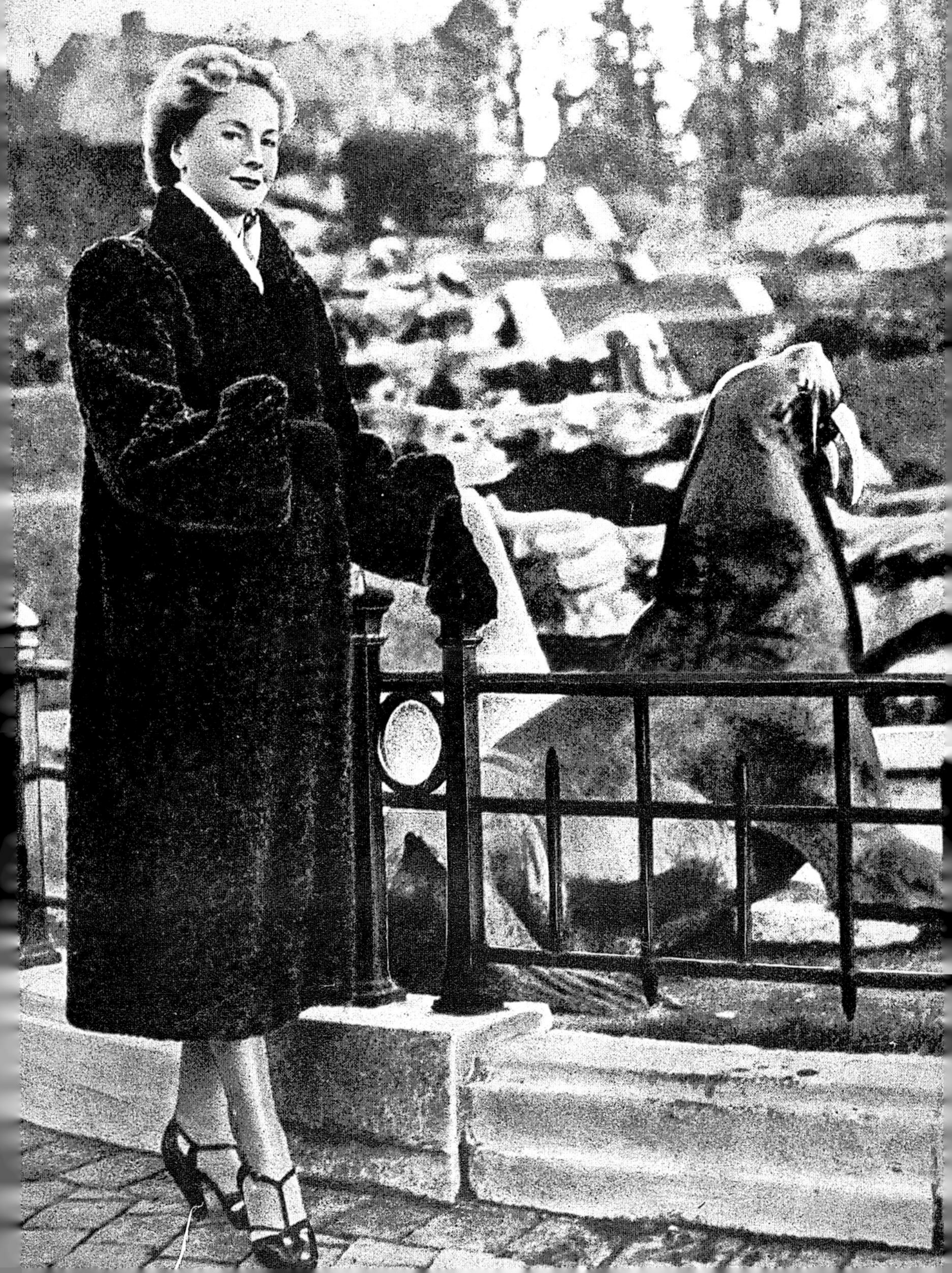

A BELGIAN LABYRINTH

VICTOR HORTA AND THE MONT DES ARTS

Bruno De Meulder and Karina Van Herck

Horta's work is without question the 20th century's most valuable architectural contribution to the Mont des Arts, largely because dogmatic or instrumental opinions on architecture were foreign to him. He did not adopt a doctrine, nor was he tempted by discourse – whether that of Charles Buls or Leopold II – because his primary concern was to make architecture. Not surprisingly, his architecture (which he spoke of as Art) displayed a purely architectonic way of dealing with programmes, structure, circulation and urbanism. Although Horta worked extensively on and around the Mont des Arts, and indeed carried out a thorough study of the neighbouring Quartier Royal,[1] he never designed a master plan for it. None of which detracts from the fact that Horta's plans for the Gare Centrale, the Municipal Development Project, the Palais des Beaux-Arts and the museum complex on the Mont des Arts itself, fit together like pieces of a jigsaw puzzle. Although these projects were developed independently, it is tempting to combine them into a comprehensive plan, Horta's Mont des Arts.

PLATES PP. 113-115

PLATES PP. 144-155

At first sight, these projects do not seem to express a very definite opinion on urban design. The Gare Centrale, the Municipal Development Project and the Palais des Beaux-Arts followed one another in splendid sequence, but in fact did nothing more than fill in, painstakingly and uncritically, the building blocks provided by the routes taken by the notorious Maquet Curve and the north-south railway link. Building lines, ridge heights and sight lines were all respected. When the city council decided to put two diagonal lanes through the building block originally reserved for the Gare Centrale, as a way of achieving four different building blocks, and so created for private sale three pieces of building land next door to the station, Horta was not one bit concerned. He retreated to the extremely narrow triangular site and worked the station into it. The more impossible the task, the more ingenious the solution developed within the prescribed outlines and the greater the contrast between the exploded spaciousness inside and the neutrality outside. From the outside it remained a neatly defined building block. Horta does not seem to have questioned the urbanistic layout – an unmannerly habit common to most architects – but rather to have subscribed to it. For Horta, restrictions were no impediment to architecture; indeed he seemed rather to find them stimulating, practically unavoidable challenges, obstacles catalysing the achievement of architecture.

This seemingly unassuming fundamental attitude did not in any way prevent Victor Horta from providing a network of shortcuts, bridges and passages – openings left in the grid of structures which created a pattern of courtyards and enclosed spaces – through the sequence of independent buildings which he planned for the Mont des Arts. The result was that the various elements fused together to form a single whole: a gigantic labyrinth, with breathtaking spatial effects and striking spatial sequences, forming an intermediate zone between the Upper Town and the Lower Town and giving itself the ambiguous character of both compound and element. Not that this zone conflicted in any way with the Upper or the Lower Town: the projects were smoothly integrated into both. From the Upper Town, the Quartier Royal he esteemed so extraordinarily highly, he consciously borrowed the measuring system based on the axis which ran between the Place Royale and the town hall and so embodied the city's fundamental bipolarity.

1. V. Horta, "Le Quartier Royal," in V. Horta, Questions d'architecture et d'urbanisme. Textes choisies, T11 (Brussels: Académie Royale de Belgique, 1996), pp. 111-137.

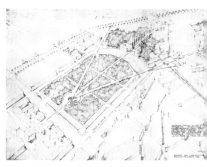

Study of the Quartier Royal (Victor Horta, 1938)

Horta followed the same logic in both the Palais des Beaux-Arts and the Municipal Development Project, painstakingly assigning proportions in accordance with this same triangulation system, so confirming the primacy of the Quartier Royal. Visual axes leading to the town hall and panoramic views of the Lower Town were respected. His intervention was therefore primarily an addition to the Upper Town. From the Lower Town, Horta's projects borrowed its programmatic complexity and vitality. The Gare Centrale, the Municipal Development Project and the Palais des Beaux-Arts were allocated a multiplicity of functions, all mixed up together. The Municipal Development Project, for example, combined housing, offices, and shops. The Gare Centrale included the normal functions of a station but also shops, a post office, a buffet, offices, and a short cut through the building for the local buses. The Palais des Beaux-Arts contained shops, offices, exhibition and concert halls, auditoriums, etc. The profusion and variety of programme elements seem to have acted as a catalyst for Horta's virtuoso skills as a designer. The complexity of the interwoven programme achieved in the Lower Town incrementally was reproduced by Horta in a single *tour de force* of design.

To achieve this Horta also borrowed elements of the rich morphological vocabulary of the Lower Town: courtyards from former places of worship, monasteries and noble mansions, passages (such as the Galerie St. Hubert) and the variegated pattern they created in the fabric, that nevertheless remains enclosed by the form of the building block. These elements were translated in the systematics of the architectonic composition. The programme was in fact of secondary importance. The variety of measures and proportions, and the wealth of morphological and typological vocabulary permitted programme variations which, as in a city that grew naturally, allowed for continuous evolution. Horta found it no more difficult to design a school on the site between the Gare Centrale and the Palais des Beaux-Arts than to design the Municipal Development Project. Changes in the programme did not lead to a different design approach. The applied pattern of shortcuts and courtyards was also used by Horta to create the sort of spatial effects which Buls so appreciated in the medieval city. For example, the end of the interior street running through the Municipal Development Project which connects to the Passage de la Bibliothèque (the present Rue Baron

Horta) at a dip in the road, accentuated the view of the sloping wall of the Palais des Beaux-Arts.

As in his earlier work, Horta drew freely on his erudite knowledge of architecture, employing a combination of eclectically indulgent virtuosity which nonetheless remained neatly within the guidelines laid down: the building blocks served as enclosing figures, spatial envelopes given unity by the system of proportion borrowed from the Upper Town. Since the guidelines guaranteed uniformity of proportion (and so integration), the architecture could express great variety and employ erudite quotations. The unity of language (the system of geometrical relationships) also made it possible to provide contemporary input, to add "the spirit, the logic and the contemporary way of expression."[2] In the present context it would probably be better to read "contemporary" as signifying an eclectic accumulation of all times, neither ideologically stuck in a "golden age" nor striving for a universal language as is shown by the art deco cladding of the Municipal Development Project and the Palais des Beaux-Arts.[3] The same major-minor connection between relationships and architectural development allowed Horta to set his buildings perfectly in context. One would of course expect nothing less from the architect of the sublime Maison du Peuple.

The Palais des Beaux-Arts stood across the road from the old Hotel Ravenstein on the Rue Terarken and across the road from the ponderous former offices of the Société Générale de Belgique on the Passage de la Bibliothèque. Easy advantage was taken of both these facts, bearing in mind the old architectural truth, illustrated by many Gothic cathedrals, that adding and combining are permissible techniques of architectural composition.[4] The playfulness with which Horta applied these compositional techniques provided "an amalgam of extremes…which evokes both tension and connection between the archaic and the hypermodern."[5] The Palais des Beaux-Arts is *Aztec Airlines*, but at the same time fits smoothly into its setting, with façades and entrances along Rue Royale, Rue Villa Hermosa, Rue des Sols, Rue Ravenstein and the Passage de la Bibliothèque. The same can be said of the Municipal Development Project and the Gare Centrale, which are linked at a variety of different street levels.

2. V. Horta, o.c., p. 126.

3. For an exhaustive discussion by an art historian: J. Vandenbreeden, "Het Paleis voor Schone Kunsten. Naar een stedenbouwkundige architectuur," in F.Aubrey, J. Vandenbreeden (eds), *Horta. Van Art Nouveau tot Modernisme*, (Ghent: Ludion, 1996), pp. 209-224.

4. V. Horta, o.c., p. 128.

5. S. Jacobs, "Het Paleis van Schone Kunsten van Victor Horta," in A. Hustache, S. Jacobs, F. Boenders, *Victor Horta, Het Paleis voor Schone Kunsten van Brussel*, (Brussels: Gemeentekrediet, 1996), pp. 34-73.

While Horta's projects for the Mont des Arts could be described as additions to the proportional system of the Upper Town with the Lower Town as the source of programmatic variation, and while he applied the whole pallet of architectural techniques to integrate his work into the given context, this does not mean that Horta's projects on the Mont des Arts should be seen as a *trait d'union* (a hyphen) as Horta termed it himself. Each of Horta's projects for the Mont des Arts was an autonomous creation in itself, an independent architectonic work. But Horta also succeeded in creating something new from the way in which the systems of the Upper Town and the Lower Town merged into one another, much as a successful collage blends together elements, contradictory or not, in or out of context, combining them in strange and unexpected syntheses to form a new *Gestalt*. The Palais des Beaux-Arts, with its complicated cross-section and ground plan, symbolises a labyrinthine structure of columns in which sloping surfaces, flights of stairs and foyers give shape to an ingenious circulation system, opening up a pattern of spaces extending over different levels. Three plane figures – grid, circulation zones and rooms (openings in the grid) – are interwoven in plan and section into a single coherent, complex figure which at the same time fits perfectly into its surroundings and its setting. It is precisely this paradoxical combination of autonomy and context that shows the unsurpassed quality of Horta's urban architecture. It is a city.

The same hybrid quality is to be found not only in the Palais des Beaux-Arts' architecture, but also in the imposed programme, which includes shops, a restaurant, a bar, offices, a variety of halls for exhibitions, concerts, and theatrical performances. A microcosm which, besides all sorts of urban design and financial motives, had as its explicit purpose to put Brussels, and so Belgium, back on the world map after the First World War. What Leopold II had in mind for his Mont des Arts was a treasure chamber, an altar to Belgian art – in which that art could be consecrated and buried – to represent the nation. The attempt was to construct a Belgian identity by looking selectively at history and displaying those works of art which would justify a place in universal world civilisation. However, the Palais des Beaux-Arts was not concieved as a place to bury musty memories, but rather as an active laboratory and centre for the exchange of ideas. The Palais des Beaux-Arts was intended to provide the motive force for getting progress going – at the time art was still seen as being in the vanguard of development. After the Great War, it was art, more than ever, that would save the world. Both the exchange of ideas between disciplines (music, dance, theatre and the visual arts) and between nations found a place in the Palais des Beaux-Arts, which was seen as the platform on which Belgian artists could display themselves to the world and which conversely would give Brussels a share in international developments.

The Palais des Beaux-Arts allowed Belgium to take part once more in the internationalist tradition which caught on round the turn of the century with figures such as Otlet and Lafontaine. The Palais des Beaux-Arts was intended to restore to Brussels its status as a melting pot, a place where, in the best tradition of Belgium as the crossroads of cultures and the movement of ideas, influences from round the world would combine to form a new completely individual synthesis. It was founded not so much as somewhere to present an idea about Belgian identity but rather as a laboratory where that identity would be reinvented day by day, dealing with and absorbing high-flown material from outside, together with everything of any value found in its own history. In this sense the Palais des Beaux-Arts, as Henry Le Boeuf, the driving force behind its foundation, saw it, was in keeping with the Belgian character, whose strong points he identified as hard work, initiative and activity rather than contemplation.[6] In a special sense the Palais des Beaux-Arts took up the thread of the city as a living organism from where Buls dropped it long ago, and built on a living culture, by a continuous process of grafting on to its predecessor.

6. H. Le Boeuf, in *Cahiers de Belgique* (Brussels, June 1928), p. 4.

...re panorama qui fait le désespoir des Bruxellois : là fut l'ancien quartier de la Putterie, pittoresque dédale de rue... chèvres à la bonne saison, et à laquelle ne manque même pas sa source et son ruisseau.

passes. Aujourd'hui, c'est une petite savane, coupée de fondrières, qui a ses arbres, ses taillis, une herbe drue que p
Ketjes » des environs qui sont chez eux dans ce pays conquis depuis longtemps.

Comme en 1695

Comme en 1775

RECONSTRUIRE EN HARMONIE

La Jonction

(chanson éditée en 1913)

La jonctions'ra un'e merveille ,
Une verveille sans pareille ,
Jamais on n'aura vu nulle part
Tel assemblage de travaux d'art.
Des quatre coins de l'univers
On accourra l'été , l'hiver ,
Car dans l'monde entier la jonction
Fera notre réputation.
Les Belges , dira-t-on ,
En vlà des lurons ,
Ils savent prouver , nom d'un chien ,
Qu'ils ne reculent devant rien.
Voulant que leur capitale
Soit une ville sans égale ,
Ils n'ont pas regardé , pour le faire ,
A la foutte toute entière par terre.

Au point de vue du pittoresque ,
Bruxelles deviendra gigantesque.
Y aura plus besoin d'aller en Suisse
Pour voir tunnels et précipices.
On aura de façon journalière
Son petit tremblement de terre .
Et si les Turcs ont l'Hellespont ,
Nous aurons "Helleputte-Pont" .
Tout comme les Parigots ,
Nous aurons notre métro,
Et comme New-York , c'est entendu ,
Nous aurons des trains suspendus.
Ainsi , chose certaine ,
C'est à l'américaine.
Pour montrer que nous avons de l'étoffe ,
Nous aurons toutes nos catastrophes.

Puis nous aurons quelque chose de chic ,
Tous les trains seront électriques ,
Car , au point de vue pécuniaire ,
Çà sera une excellente affaire.
Quand aux frais qu'çà entrainera ,
Bah , c'est le voyageur qui paiera.
Mais c'qui sera le plus chic truc ,
Ca sera le viaduc
Qui dans les caisses de l'Etat
Lui apportera de l'argent en tas.
Moyennant dix centimes
Les tickets vont faire prime .
On pourra y monter : ce sera immense ,
Et... cracher , d'en haut , sur Wauwermans.

...ISIÈME FEUILLE.

LA MODERNISATION D...

Édition spéciale réalisée par l' «AGENCE ÉCONOMIQUE ET F...

JONCTION NOR...

LE COUT DE LA JONCTION

En chiffres ronds :
... milliards nominal — 9 milliards en francs actuels, soit le même montant que le Canal Albert

... calcul du coût de la Jonction n'est pas chose ... car cette opération a porté sur près de cinquante ... fertiles en incidents monétaires.

... autre part, ainsi que nous le verrons plus loin, ... grande partie du coût est représentée par des ... priations dont l'ampleur dépasse de beaucoup ... qui serait nécessaire à la Jonction proprement ... Ces expropriations assurent l'urbanisation ... zone importante de la Capitale et de ses fau... bourgs. En en laissant le coût dans le bilan d'en... semble, on charge indûment la Jonction proprement ...

... qu'on le sait, la construction de la Jonction ... étendue sur trois périodes correspondant à des ... monétaires différents qu'il y a lieu de compta... biliser à part.

PREMIERE PHASE : 1903-1914

... phase est caractérisée par d'importantes ex... propriations; celles-ci ont porté dès le début sur 16 ha., ... pratique étaient entièrement bâtis. Les travaux ... ment dits, comprenant la section allant de la ... du Midi à la Place de la Chapelle, avaient absorbé ... millions de francs-or; mais les expropriations ont ... sur 82 millions de francs-or. Le total de la ... période antérieure à la première guerre a donc été ... millions.

... est à noter que ce montant, qui est repris des ... documents parlementaires de la période 1921-1925, ne ... correspond pas aux crédits votés, et qui ne s'élevaient ... 42 millions. La différence vient vraisemblablement ... que certains paiements d'indemnités pour expro... priation ont été postérieurs à 1914.

... dépenses antérieures à 1914 doivent être multi... pliées par 30, si l'on veut les chiffres en francs actuels. ... d'avant-guerre était en effet à 750 en chiffres ..., et il doit être multiplié par 4 pour tenir compte ... index actuel, basé sur le niveau de 1936-1938. Si ... se bornait à utiliser les coefficients-or (au lieu du ... pouvoir d'achat) on arriverait à un chiffre sensible... ment moins élevé, mais on sait que ce calcul est faussé ... le maintien de l'or à sa valeur ancienne expri... mée en dollars. Ainsi calculée, la valeur-or en « francs-... actuels » revient à 6 1/2 milliards.

DEUXIEME PHASE : 1935-1944

... loi créant l'Office National de la Jonction datait ... 1 juillet 1935. En vertu de ses dispositions, l'Office ... devait recevoir une dotation totale de 400 millions; de ... il devait bénéficier du produit de la réalisation ... terrains non utilisés. Toutefois, il est apparu immé... diatement que le chiffre de 400 millions devrait être ... dépassé et qu'il ne permettrait pas d'achever le travail. ... dépenses avaient été fixées d'après le niveau des ... de 1932-1934, période de crise économique pro... fonde, alors que l'exécution se poursuivit pendant une ... période de meilleure conjoncture.

... total, il avait été dépensé non loin de 400 mil... lions, lorsque la Belgique entra dans la guerre, et le ... travail était loin d'être terminé. La conception en avait ... d'ailleurs été déjà modifiée, par l'incorporation de com... pléments coûteux, comportant notamment des abris ... anti-aériens.

... les années allant de 1941 à 1944 permirent de con... tinuer les travaux à une allure ralentie, et à un coût ... plus élevé, en raison de la pénurie de matériaux ... de la productivité réduite de la main-d'œuvre. Il ... semble que les chiffres de la période de guerre (300 ... millions) doivent être multipliés par deux, si l'on veut ... les traduire en francs actuels.

TROISIEME PHASE : 1945-1951

... jusqu'à la fin de 1951 il avait été dépensé à peu ... près 2 1/2 milliards; on doit y ajouter environ 1 1/2 ... milliard pour l'achèvement. Ici, aucun coefficient mo... nétaire n'est plus nécessaire.

Il apparaît donc ainsi que le total des dépenses actuellement envisagées, tant pour la Jonction elle-même que pour les travaux des gares du Nord et du Midi est de 4.788 millions, en francs nominaux et de 8.769 millions en francs actuels, non compris les charges financières intercalaires.

COUT DE LA JONCTION

Périodes	Coût nominal	Multiplicateur	Francs actuels
	(en millions de francs)		
1905-1914	88	30	2.640
1935-1940	374	4	1.496
1941-1944	307	2	614
1945-1951	2.418	1	2.418
A ajouter	1.601	1	1.601
Totaux	4.788		8.769

Nous arrondissons ces chiffres pour tenir compte des imprévus et des compléments que l'achèvement amènera sans doute, respectivement à 5 et à 9 milliards. Ce dernier chiffre représente approximativement le coût, en francs actuels, du Canal Albert, construit de 1930 à 1939, qui a exigé 2 milliards de francs nominaux, soit 8 milliards de francs actuels, outre plusieurs centaines de millions après 1946 (dommages de guerre non compris).

Toutefois, nous avons dit qu'une partie très considérable de ces dépenses sont relatives à des expropriations. Celles-ci étaient déjà largement pratiquées avant la première guerre mondiale, elles ont continué par la suite et on en prévoit encore pour les années 1953 et suivantes. Ces expropriations représentent environ 500 millions en francs nominaux, mais compte tenu des multiplicateurs que nous venons d'indiquer plus haut on arrive à 3.180 millions de francs actuels.

Il y a lieu de déduire du coût de la Jonction la valeur que l'on peut récupérer des terrains qui seront laissés disponibles après l'achèvement des travaux. Au début on considérait qu'il serait possible de revendre de très larges superficies. La voirie de Bruxelles ne devait pas être élargie, et l'on comptait même revendre les superficies situées au-dessus du tunnel. Mais plus tard, on a adopté des conceptions singulièrement plus larges. On envisage par exemple de ne pas réaliser des terrains de très haute valeur, pour dégager Sainte-Gudule ou pour créer des squares. Ce sont là évidemment des charges qui n'incombent pas à la Jonction.

Quoi qu'il en soit, le problème des terrains se pose actuellement comme suit :

TERRAINS DE LA JONCTION

A. Disponibles pour la vente :		
Territoire de Bruxelles (y compris l'emplacement de l'Allée Verte)	M2	120.000
Territoire de Saint-Gilles et Anderlecht (Gare du Midi)	M2	18.000
Territoire de Saint-Josse (Gare du Nord)	M2	25.000
Total des terrains libres (voirie nécessaire non comprise)	M2	163.000
B. Accroissement de la voirie (portée de 5 à 11 hectares)	M2	60.000
Total	M2	223.000

On peut estimer que la valeur de 5.000 francs le mètre carré constitue une estimation très prudente, même si l'on inclut les terrains de l'Allée Verte. Sur cette base, les terrains libres représentent 815 millions de francs, et celle des accroissements de voirie, 300 millions. Au total, l'actif de la Jonction atteint plus de 1.100 millions; en réalité, il pourrait se situer entre 1 et 2 milliards.

Fernand BAUDHUIN.

LES VALEURS DES TERRAINS A BRUXELLES DU DÉBUT DU SIÈCLE A CE JOUR

L'examen des archives relatives à la Jonction fait apparaître certaines particularités en matière de prix de terrains.

On constate, en effet, que la valeur des terrains à bâtir était extrêmement élevée à Bruxelles avant la première guerre mondiale, lors des expropriations nécessaires à la Jonction. Dans beaucoup de cas, cette valeur avait été établie par expertise judiciaire, ce qui donne une valeur objective plus grande.

Notons cependant, que dans certains cas il avait fallu payer, non seulement la valeur de l'immeuble, mais aussi une indemnité commerciale, qui est indépendante du bien ... lui-même.

Les premières estimations avaient fait apparaître que les 16 hectares, soit 160.000 m2, nécessaires pour le premier tracé, devaient coûter 27 millions, ce qui donne un chiffre moyen de 1.700 fr. le m2, pour des immeubles ..., dont les bâtiments étaient à peu près sans valeur.

En réalité, on a dépensé avant la première guerre, en expropriations, 82 millions, mais pour une superficie plus grande et pour des bâtiments ayant une valeur commerciale.

Le prix de 1.500 à 1.800 fr. le m2 avait été envisagé en 1909 pour la revente des terrains qui entouraient la Halte centrale, au Cantersteen, c'est-à-dire dans l'ancien quartier de la Putterie.

Certains immeubles commerciaux ont été payés 5.000 fr. le m2, mais ce prix comprend une certaine indemnisation pour la valeur commerciale.

Si l'on se base sur le prix de 1.500 à 1.800 fr. le m2 envisagé pour la revente des terrains de la Putterie, et en prenant le coefficient actuel de hausse des prix, qui est égal à 30, ces terrains vaudraient aujourd'hui de 45 à 54.000 fr. le m2. Or, il semble bien que leur valeur se situe actuellement entre 8 et 12.000 fr. le m2.

On peut donc en conclure, soit que le prix du début du siècle était exorbitant, soit que la valeur actuelle n'est pas encore adaptée à notre niveau des prix.

Nos calculs font délibérément abstraction de la valeur-or, qui ne donne qu'un coefficient 16, puisque, comme on le sait, cette valeur-or est artificielle, et qu'elle sera corrigée un jour. Mais même en se basant sur ce coefficient, on est à présent au-dessous des valeurs de 1909.

Signalons que, parmi les transactions les plus importantes des dernières années, le prix maximum, dans les quartiers du haut de la ville, a été de 12.000 fr. le m2 pour des immeubles à reconstruire, et de 25.000 f. pour un immeuble du Treurenberg dont les bâtiments, relativement modernes, sont encore utilisables, et ont dès lors une valeur propre, indépendante du terrain.

LA PARTICIPATION de WERKSPOOR à la réalisation de la Jonction Nord-Midi

Sur la base d'une soumission qui paraissait particulièrement intéressante, l'O.N.J. a confié à la Société WERKSPOOR d'Amsterdam, représentée en Belgique par la Soc. An. J. KAMPS & Cᵉ, Ingénieurs à Bruxelles, le montage et la fourniture de l'installation de ventilation du tunnel de la Jonction Nord-Midi.

WERKSPOOR, qui avait déjà effectué des installations semblables, notamment celle du tunnel sous la Meuse à Rotterdam, et qui dispose d'un bureau technique très spécialisé pour ce travail, a mis à la disposition de l'O.N.J. son savoir et sa longue expérience et, par une collaboration très étroite avec les services techniques de la Jonction, est parvenue à résoudre avantageusement maints problèmes d'aérodynamique qui se sont posés pendant la réalisation de cette entreprise.

L'installation effectuée par WERKSPOOR comprend trois centrales principales d'aspiration pour la ventilation longitudinale du tunnel et la ventilation transversale de la Halte Centrale, et deux centrales de soufflage, également pour la ventilation transversale.

Dans l'ensemble de ces centrales ont été fournis et installés 5 ventilateurs de 4.500 mm. de diam., 6 de 4.000 mm., 4 de 3.500 mm. et 4 de 2.700 mm.

Tous ces ventilateurs sont à très haut rendement et du système axial avec pales orientables, qui permettent de faire varier les débits pour les adapter aux nécessités résultant du réglage rationnel d'une ventilation uniforme dans le tunnel et la Halte Centrale.

Des régistres basculants ou coulissants séparent du circuit d'air les ventilateurs à l'arrêt.

Les ventilateurs et les régistres sont actionnés par des moteurs électriques et l'équipement électrique a été réalisé pour permettre la mise en service et l'arrêt, ainsi que le contrôle, depuis un poste de commande central situé au centre de la ville.

L'atmosphère dans le tunnel, ainsi que sur les quais de la Gare Centrale, est constamment contrôlée depuis le poste de commande central et la teneur en CO et CO^2 y est enregistrée sur des bandes de papier.

Ce contrôle permet de mettre à tout moment en service les ventilateurs nécessaires pour le maintien d'une atmosphère convenable.

WERKSPOOR avait conscience que la ventilation du tunnel de la Jonction Nord-Midi était d'une importance capitale et ses techniciens n'ont par conséquent épargné aucun effort pour réaliser l'installation avec le maximum de soins et de garantie.

AU moment où le public est convié à « voir » par lui-même les travaux terminés dans les différents bâtiments de la Jonction, il convient de mentionner la part non négligeable que l'Office National de la Jonction a confiée à la Société Fred. SAGE & Cie, 9-11, rue de la Senne, à BRUXELLES, les spécialistes bien connus dans les domaines de l'ébénisterie et de l'architecture en métal.

Nous relevons ainsi à la Halte Centrale, à l'extérieur, tous les montants des vitrines, les portes et les tambours d'entrées, réalisés en laiton bronzé étiré sur bois dur, sans vis apparentes, et les revêtements des deux auvents pour lesquels le même matériau a été utilisé avec grand succès.

A l'intérieur de cet imposant bâtiment, on trouvera, disséminés dans toutes des parties de l'édifice accessibles au public, portes, guichets, vitrines, cabines téléphoniques, cadres d'affiches, luminaires, en aluminium Anticorodal ton bronze, traité à l'oxydation anodique, dont le fini impeccable ne manquera pas de frapper les connaisseurs.

Dans le hall principal, nous mentionnerons également les motifs en cuivre encastré dans le pavement, évoquant d'une manière symbolique les trois principales villes du pays.

A la Halte Congrès, c'est l'auvent abritant l'entrée, d'une ligne si originale et si hardie, ce sont les batteries de portes, les guichets, les cadres de vitrines, les gaines d'éclairage des quais, les lambris, la bibliothèque, la buvette et son mobilier, comportant l'utilisation de l'aluminium Anticorodal en ton naturel et du teck poli.

C'est ensemble imposant de travaux et fournitures a été réalisé sous la direction de l'architecte Maxime BRUNFAUT, auteur des projets et des plans, et la haute surveillance des ENTREPRISES EDOUARD FRANÇOIS & FILS, agissant en qualité d'entrepreneurs généraux.

Enfin, c'est encore la firme SAGE qui est chargée du revêtement extérieur en laiton bronzé des portes et des vitrines de tous les magasins des deux quadrilatères sous voies entre l'Avenue de Stalingrad et la nouvelle gare du Midi.

FRED SAGE & Cie

CONSTRUCTEURS-SPÉCIALISTES

Agencements et Transformations de magasins.
Travaux d'architecture en bronze, aluminium, anticorodal, etc...

9/11, Rue de la SENNE
BRUXELLES
Tél. : 11.44.41 - 12.97.15

LE ...

La mise en service de la Jonction n... qu'on le sait, qu'au moyen de deux v... possible d'utiliser quatre voies, qui s... terminées, mais l'aboutissement à ... n'étant pas prêt, il a fallu se contente... du pertuis central.

Celles-ci ne peuvent évidemment p... faire passer tous les trains que l'on a...

... (Architect...

à l'entrée de la Jonction. La circul... trains à vapeur est ralentie par l'att... des tracteurs électriques qui devro... convois. D'autre part, l'alimentatio... lignes caténaires limitera à deux le ... qui peuvent se trouver simultaném... voie. Enfin, il a fallu admettre que ... moyens de secours dans les premie... que les horaires conservent une cert... ticité, afin de pouvoir remédier a... viendraient à se produire, lors de l... et du rodage.

On aurait pu se contenter de prol... Midi les trains de la ligne d'Anvers... sure de facilité, qui aurait satisfai... portante de la clientèle, représent... montant total du mouvement des v... xelles-Nord. Mais la Société Natio... pas contentée, elle a voulu répar... mesure du possible les trains dan... façon à en faire bénéficier les différ... tissant à Bruxelles.

RAIL BELGE

NCIÈRE » à l'occasion de l'Inauguration de la

MIDI

SOCIETE NATIONALE DES CHEMINS DE FER BELGE

CE A PARTIR DU 5 OCTOBRE

Un trafic déjà fort dense

t ainsi que les jours ouvrables comportent en service de 153 trains au total, soit 18 trains ionaux, 74 trains électriques d'Anvers, 46 à vapeur et 15 autorails. Ce chiffre de 153 t remarquable, et il ne pourrait être dépassé compromettre la régularité du service dans l'état de l'équipement.

eut estimer que le service des trains tel qu'il

Centrale,
r Maxime Brunfaut)

ne dès maintenant assure aux voyageurs es appréciables dans la plupart des relations vinciales qui passent par Bruxelles. C'est ainsi compte que dans les relations Anvers-Char-gain sera d'une demi-heure en moyenne; entre Ostende, Anvers et Mons et Anvers et Tour-ertaines correspondances bénéficient d'un 30 à 60 minutes. Indépendamment de cela, e ne pas devoir changer de gare, et de ne i utiliser trams ni taxis, surtout si l'on a des , constitue un avantage, qui sera certainement récié.

ement de la Halte Centrale permettra aux rs de remonter et de descendre sans fatigue, des escalators, la différence de niveau de ts qui sépare les quais de la sortie. Ils pour-llement (plus tard) gagner la rue du Marché-lets et les Galeries St Hubert.

marquera également les haut-parleurs qui à quai des trains importants et l'em-ées de toutes les particularités intéressan-rivée à quai des trains importants et l'em-des voitures de 2me classe seront indiqués.

Les modifications dans l'affectation des voies ou dans la succession des trains, les retards éventuels, la mise en marche des dédoublements, tout cela fera l'avis de communications par haut-parleurs.

Des tableaux d'annonce extrêmement rationnels donneront l'ensemble des trains au départ, plusieurs heures à l'avance. Les trains attendus seront signalés à distance en plusieurs endroits, de façon à prévenir les voyageurs qui préfèrent ne pas stationner sur le quai même.

Enfin, la Halte Centrale comportera des magasins, des salons de coiffure, échoppes de fleuristes, buvettes, etc.

* * *

La première phase de la mise en service de la Jonction utilise les deux voies du pertuis central du tunnel reliées à Bruxelles-Nord aux voies 6 à 12, et à Bruxelles-Midi aux voies 4 à 9.

A partir de maintenant le terminus de la ligne électrique d'Anvers à Bruxelles est reporté de Bruxelles-Nord à Bruxelles-Midi, pour une partie du trafic de cette ligne, comportant au minimum deux trains directs par heure et par sens de la marche.

Les trains à vapeur traverseront la Jonction avec leur locomotive à vapeur, la traction étant assurée par des locomotives électriques. Cette catégorie de trains comportera des internationaux d'Ostende-Bâle,

Ostende-Cologne, Bruxelles-Bâle, Bruxelles-Cologne et Bruxelles-Paris.

Provisoirement, les trains de Bruxelles-Amsterdam continueront à employer la ceinture ouest de Bruxelles en attendant l'achèvement des voies entre Schaerbeek et Bruxelles-Nord.

Les trains express d'Ostende à Liège passeront également par la Jonction, et dans la mesure du possible les trains directs et semi-directs de diverses lignes atteignant Bruxelles-Nord et Bruxelles-Midi. La plupart de ces convois s'arrêteront à Bruxelles-Nord, à la Halte Centrale et à Bruxelles-Midi. Un certain nombre pourront s'arrêter à la Halte Congrès.

Voici le trafic qui est effectif depuis le 5 octobre :

Electriques : 74 trains direction Anvers.

Internationaux : 18 trains des directions Bâle, Cologne, Ostende, Paris et Lille.

Service intérieur : 46 trains des directions Alost, Blankenberge, Courtrai, Poperinghe, Hasselt, Mons, Piéton, Haine-St-Pierre, Erquelinnes et Quiévrain. Des autorails (15) sont prévus dans les directions Hasselt, St Nicolas, Grammont, Ottignies, Alost, Manage, Burst et Gand.

Bon voyage !

La salle des pas perdus, avec vue sur les escaliers d'accès à partir de l'entrée secondaire de la Halte vers le Cantersteen.

L' AGENCE ÉCONOMIQUE & FINANCIÈRE

est un organe de dépêches originales transmises par des bureaux et correspondants qualifiés et publiées chaque jour ouvrable à l'intention des d'entreprises et d'administrations et de tous les hommes d'affaires en géné soucieux d'être parfaitement informés. Les consignes données à ses correspondants belges et étrangers sont :

CELERITE
PRECISION
CONCISI

Des éditions spéciales sont consacrées à tous les événements ma de la vie économique belge.

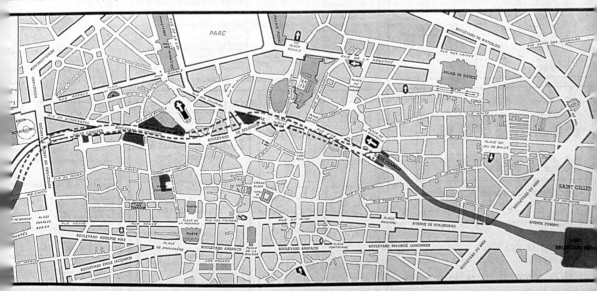

THE CARREFOUR DE L'EUROPE

RECENT ARCHITECTURAL DESIGNS
IN THE REAR VIEW MIRROR

Bruno De Meulder

The Boulevard de l'Impératrice is an outsize boulevard running over the north-south underground railway link. While one might say that it was constructed rather foolishly – it does not really lead anywhere, and it seems ridiculously wide – after the event, now that the possession of a car has been democratised, it seems to have come into its own. Not so much as a connective element but as a piece of theatre. Where better to show off your new freedom and status – an ancient custom in a public forum – than in the centre of the city? See, and be seen. *En voiture! Voyez, c'est une Simca 1.000!* The new god of prosperity was able to take over the centre of the city without a single blow being struck. The Boulevard de l'Impératrice can best be compared with a number of useless and now superfluous elements of infrastructure in the urban corpus which have mutated to become an accepted part of the urban structure. Foreign bodies which have managed to become incorporated: the drained creek or dock, which has become a boulevard or a market, the disused churchyard or urban fortification which has become a park. All of these frequently become highly valuable public places with a very special and highly individual character transcending their utilitarian nature. The loss of the original function evokes a sense of deprivation but at the same time has a liberating effect. The site, the relic, suddenly becomes a charming refuge – not infrequently remaining a public place – where suddenly all sorts of things become possible, for which there was previously no space (and for which no town planner would ever provide space). Like the jolly parade of cars in the 1950s and 1960s, with their chrome highly polished and drivers with brilliantine in their hair.

The section of the Boulevard de l'Impératrice that interests us crosses the historical east-west route between the Upper and the Lower Town, the age-old trade route, in fact the definition of the city: the "bridge" over the valley of the Senne. The Boulevard de

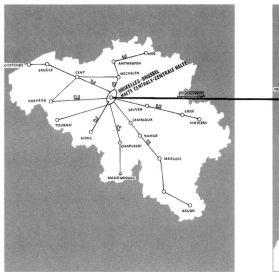

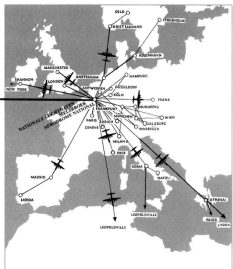

l'Impératrice cuts off the foot of the Mont des Arts, just at the point where the Gare Centrale is located, that pumping station that daily sucks in and spews out tens of thousands of commuters. On this site, the over-dimensional Boulevard de l'Impératrice is both Upper and Lower Town, north-south link and east-west route, oversized turntable and pump, transitional zone and point of departure, even a market. This must be the essence of Belgium, *Carrefour de l'Occident* as Vanaudenhove called Brussels in 1958 – or was it *accident*?

The area in front of the Gare Centrale was named the Carrefour de l'Europe. It was just about everything at once, yet till the mid-1980s it really was nothing at all. An urban void *avant-la-lettre*. The demolition that took place in the wake of the old agreement between city and state to combine the north-south link, the Maquet Curve, the siting of the Gare Centrale and the redevelopment of the Putterie district left space that was not in fact used. A practically-minded fellow with good connections set up a barrier, collected parking fees and installed a petrol station. It could only happen in Belgium. It did however shock many right-minded and sensitive cit-izens – not least architects on the lookout for a commission or those seeking to prove themselves right. Not surprisingly, the Carrefour de l'Europe was the subject of many discussions on architecture and urban design. At first sight, the yawning gap offered a superb exercise

PLATES PP. 180-181

ground for doctrinal architectural designs. A.R.A.U. (*Atelier de Recherche et d'Action Urbaines*), Deleu, Groep Planning, Baines, Terlinden, Birkiye, Busieau & Neirinck, Crépain, Daems and so many others with a name, fame or ambitions, tried to refill this city location with their own paradigms for the city: critical reconstruction, late modernism, structuralism; practically everything that had had any success as an approach in the world of architecture since 1950 was tried out there. André Loeckx has already written a detailed review of this subject, painstakingly weighing up the pros and cons, so all we need to do here is to make sure we get back to it promptly.[1] Anyhow the discussion fell silent when, in the mid-1980s, jumbo hotels in neo-Flemish renaissance style and other fake packaging were rudely plumped down on the site. Practically-minded fellows with even better connections had realised that there was even more money to be made out of putting up tourists than out of putting up cars. Money. Money. A.R.A.U. found it all rather better than might have been expected. After all, the project presented itself as a "reconstruction of a European city," though in this case the morphological and typological basis for this method of approach, as much advocated by A.R.A.U., was reduced to the most elementary ABC, far beyond the point of coherence.

Carrefour de l'Europe, building site
(Pauwels, 1985)

There had been nonetheless no lack of extremely interesting designs which were advocating a morphological and typological approach (Birkiye, Busieau & Neirinck, Baines and Crépain), which made its dull recycling and scandalous reduction by the world of promoters all the more painful. The architectural community, which from time immemorial has believed it held exclusive rights to the truth on everything concerned with the making of "the city," screamed blue murder. Probably partly because of this, scarcely three years ago this *coup manqué* (lost opportunity) by the Brussels city council was again selected as the site for a competition. The city council had a bit of beautification in mind, and asked for a handsome boulevard with trees, greenery and comfortable street furniture. In fact the point of the exercise was to help the incapacity of the hotels concerned to organise their open space.

The competition ended up with the first place shared by designs from Alain Sarfati and Xaveer De Geyter. The execution of Sarfati's design is now in view. After the election, as they say. Sarfati foresees, as required by the programme specification, trees up above on the north-south link, little lights and probably even benches. There will in any event be a "tiny creek" worked through it!?! A bombastic gold floating ring (a thousand bombs and grenades?!?) is to be installed above the roundabout in front of the Gare Centrale. The Place de l'Albertine will be spanned by wooden bridging.

The design recreates an "urban" boulevard, where presumably what had been in mind was a sentimentalised middle-class cliché image of what a boulevard should be like in a provincial city. In this sense, the design provides the perfect complement to the A.R.A.U. doctrine on public space. The design introduces the concept of a middle-class boulevard, the sort of boulevard that never was, but a place where Aunt Jeannot and Uncle Jean-Jean – fictional characters representing the real *Bruxellette* and *Brusseleir* – can take a peaceful stroll. A dream boulevard (lying next to a battery of dream hotels). It rather resembles the rediscovery of the *Belle Epoque* or even earlier, when Auntie thought that everything was still authentic. It is the Brussels of the good old days that A.R.A.U. and A.A.M. (*Archives d'Architecture Moderne*) manage to evoke so strikingly, over and over again, in fragile black and white drawings.

The outsize Boulevard de l'Impératrice – though God knows how this is to be done above the north-south link – is quietly reduced to a proper size by neat rows of trees, making it a boulevard for the Brussels citizen and his lapdog. It is a rather annoying reduction, immoderately reducing the contemporary problem of public space into an image. It is offensive because it reeks of the notion of exclusivity and purity, and this at a location where everything combines, a place which is really a metropolitan mix of commuters – eternally in transit along endless metro corridors – tramps and the homeless – constantly being chased away but nonetheless always present – skaters and breakdancers selling the commuters free, mildly provocative theatre, and yes, even a sullen Aunt Jeannot and a shocked Uncle Jean-Jean.

The majority of public events on this site take place underground: in flows and turbulent lines of flow, in dawdling on the platform and chasing after the bus, in playing music in metro corridors, the crowd at the paper kiosk and the smell at the hot dog stand, the aberrant disco atmosphere in the adjoining Galerie Ravenstein. The

1. A. Loeckx, "The Eloquence and Silence of An Urban Fragment," in *B. Architectural Magazine* 51 (1994), p. 98-109.

pallet is infinitely richer than the monotonous, rather seedy stroll of Aunt, Uncle and FiFi. In short, a public is created for the, by now, dilapidated site through its congested function as a place to change from one form of transport to another. The public is mainly to be found in the belly of the city, its metro corridors and station halls.

PLATES PP. 186-188 All this is treated quite differently in the design by Xaveer De Geyter, who completely disregarded the programme set for the competition. Not surprisingly, De Geyter does not re-equip the Boulevard de l'Impératrice, but swallows it up in one great superblock, which does, however, include the monster hotels already mentioned. The answer to the speculative exodus from Brussels is speculation of the most extreme kind, the speculation of a project developer who has blown his top and gone into overdrive. Bingo! Cash! Cash squared! As envisaged, the megalomaniac superblock will function on various levels. A useless piece of infrastructure, partly a superfluous boulevard, partly a piece of underground space presenting itself as a "cathedral along the tracks," is to be recycled, made productive and linked to the city's various networks. De Geyter has jumped on to the bandwagon of privatisation and hyperdevelopment. So-called public space, the holy cow of the contemporary planning debate, will just have to accept it. Big sales, now. The massive building works and an injection of activities, combined with limited public space, will inevitably create a congested atmosphere. The resurrection of a vital city, itself invented.

PLATES PP. 184-185 For their entry to the 1983 Bonduelle competition, De Geyter and Team Hoogpoort (S. Beel, X. De Geyter, A. Karsenberg and W.J. Neutelings) froze the void of the Boulevard de l'Impératrice. Hoogpoort, like Marcel Schmitz in the mid 1940s and Tekhne 20 years later, recognised the latent force of the void. Their proposed designs added practically nothing, except perhaps in the margin. They left the metropolitan open space free to sparkle and to make the best of itself, to develop into a forum for urban confrontation. Not for nothing was the approach in the last three designs described as "adoctrinal;" they were not "applications" of a paradigm to the empty site – however "right," "wise" or "hip" that might be – but designs which interpreted the site themselves. Designs which discovered the void not as an empty receiver and so something to be filled, but as a surface, a screen revealing the metropolitan character of the site, and lighting

Brussels' forum (Marcel Schmitz, 1940s)

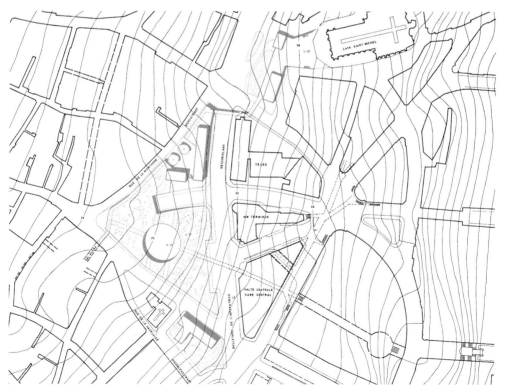

Proposal for a new link between the Grand'Place and the Cathédrale Saint Michel (Tekhne, 1969)

up the criss-cross of flows above and below ground. Finally, the empty space as potential, inviting individual use, providing an opportunity for compensation, a free haven for unscheduled alternatives, which can not or may not flourish anywhere else. A heterotopia. A juvenile show of power, with cars, an underground rave, whatever.

What is done cannot be undone. Meanwhile the notorious hotels have been plumped down. The void is no longer void in the literal sense of the word, but rather an overcrowded void of surplus, so loaded and emotionally charged that any expressiveness is swept away, wiped out. It is empty. Without meaning. *Le degré zéro.* De Geyter's new design appears to explore and exploit this bipolar notion of the void. Ostensibly his approach has been inverted, but in fact it is probably the same. Once again, he takes as his starting point a reading of the crowded site which he then systematically bombards with further volume. The Carrefour de l'Europe has become a gigantic wedding cake of a building. In this way, unallocated space – given all these oversize roads, is mainly a surplus of infra-

Project for the layout of the Carrefour de l'Europe
(Xaveer De Geyter Architecten, 1997)

structure, but even the unallocated remnants of space between the collection of new 1980s hotels – are drastically reduced and individual buildings are clicked together into a single urban superblock. The superblock will provide housing (even – by way of excess – inside the Gare Centrale), a conference centre (in synergy with the existing Palais des Congrès and the facilities provided by the hotels), a bus station (for scheduled service and tourist buses, 600 a day), hotels, offices, commercial space. The existing buildings are kept intact and carefully filled in. The superblock is therefore in the first place an extremely complicated spatial puzzle, with re-use, additions, adjustments, private, semiprivate and public sections. As manipulator of all kinds of activities and patterns of circulation, both above and below ground, it will house a city within a city, with the whole spectrum of publics that such a thing brings with it: conference goers, commuters, students and shoppers, tramps and the homeless, tourists and business people, European civil servants, concert goers and museum visitors. All are brought together in the congested melting pot of the megablock, which therefore becomes a setting for unusual confrontations and improving exchanges. The station megablock, the last great public space where all kinds of people really do come together, is the last bastion of traditional metropolitan urbanism; a piling up and combination of differences. De Geyter turns the conventional notion of public space, which is what the competition was all about, inside out and upside down. In a word, the Gare Centrale as mall. Unasked, De Geyter is dropping, *deus ex machina*, an outsize pacemaker into Brussels Central.

De Geyter's design is a collage. No longer the collage that it was in the design by Team Hoogpoort, where a limited number of figures were placed on the margin of the empty white field (so accentuating the white field), but a collage in which everything runs together. De Geyter's design deconstructs the historic stratification of the site and then, in an unexpected way, piles it all back and links it all together. In the course of this piling up the layers suddenly melt and flow together to form a new figure, a different and new kind of hybrid figure. The emptiness in the collage turns into volume. As a complex, hybrid figure, the collage absorbs all the characteristics of the site into a new "inn" of differences. In urbanism, of course.[2]

2. See also: T. Avermaete, B. De Meulder, *Fra|cture. Brussels urbanism at Europe's Crossroads* (Copenhague: Dansk Arkitektur Center, 2000); K. Borret, M. Delbeke, S. Jacobs, K. Vandermarliere, *Homeward. Contemporary architecture in Flanders* (Antwerp: deSingel, 1998), p. 91-108; B. De Meulder, "The Boulevard de l'Impératrice: an arena for Brussels urbanism," in *Archis* 6 (1998), p. 52-57.

BRUXELLES 1962
Triomphe du Style Bric-à-Brac

B RUXELLES vit dans une ambiance de série noire.
Depuis quelques années, on ne compte plus les attentats perpétrés en plein cœur de la capitale. Ils se trament derrière d'énormes palissades placardées d'affiches multicolores. Froidement, on y abat, dans l'indifférence de tout un peuple, maisons bourgeoises et vieux hôtels. On coupe en pleine chair du passé, on fait table rase de l'histoire, de la petite comme de la grande. La ville se couvre de blessures béantes que l'on cicatrise au petit bonheur à grand renfort d'échafaudages et de blockhaus en béton.

Un jour, enfin, les palissades tombent. Le convalescent montre au grand jour ses plaies et ses cataplasmes. Les chirurgiens ès urbanisme attendent le verdict, assurés d'être applaudis pour une telle série d'opérations si rondement menée. Bruxelles, arguent-ils, a pris le grand visage : son visage rajeuni est celui d'une capitale qui marche avec son temps!

Hélas, trois fois hélas : après cette cure de cheval, la ville ne se reconnaît plus. Ses amis, ses admirateurs crient à l'attentat prémédité. C'est le triomphe du style bric-à-brac! La collégiale Saints-Michel-et-Gudule se retrouve emprisonnée dans un carcan de béton armé. Un large immeuble ne craint pas de barrer la perspective (ou ce qu'il en reste!) de sa masse fonctionnelle en forme de radiateur de chauffage central. Et pour corser le tout, un hôtel en construction hisse sa carcasse à 85 mètres de hauteur, « agrémentant » encore ce décor urbain incohérent, et laid.

Bruxelles se travestit en Brussels City.

vant un tel désastre, il semble que
pinion publique prenne enfin con-
nce de la faillite de la vaste
ération qui a bouleversé et remo-
é, entre Sainte-Gudule et la
and-Place, tout un vaste secteur
la capitale. Il faut dire que l'effa-
t décor s'étale avec complaisance
vant les yeux ahuris du flâneur
chercherait en vain ici un peu
armonie, un peu de chaleur hu-
ine. L'échec est flagrant.

pinion, la grande presse, les ligues
défense de la capitale, des manda-
es communaux crient à la cata-
ophe. La réaction est tardive, mais
est heureux qu'elle intervienne
nt que l'irrémédiable ne soit
asommé.

Touring Club qui n'a cessé,
uis sa fondation, de défendre le
rimoine de nos monuments et de
sites, se réjouit de cette prise
lective de conscience. Elle vient
lleurs de se révéler, vigoureuse,
de la décision récente d'un
nistre de s'attaquer aux arbres
avenue de Tervueren, cette parure
la capitale.

doute que désormais les atten-
contre la beauté de Bruxelles
commettront avec moins d'im-
ité que naguère.

endons-nous bien. Il ne s'agit
de figer le *Bruxelles de papa*
s un immobilisme stérile. Une
est une vaste cellule vivante.
doit s'adapter aux exigences
velles sous peine de sclérose
d'étouffement.

s vivre avec son temps, cela ne
pas signifier un carnage incon-
é du patrimoine du passé, cela
ignifie pas improviser fébrilement
nouveau visage de ville où s'op-
nt toutes les audaces, toutes les
atures.

train-là, les touristes qui, dans
ans, passeront encore par Bru-
n'y feront plus qu'une courte
pour contempler ce qu'en
ère d'urbanisme, il ne faut à
n prix, imiter.

C. B.

On croyait la Grand-Place à l'abri des aventures architecturales de notre temps. Il n'en est rien puisque les travaux d'un building en construction près de la gare centrale ont dû être arrêtés par le Conseil échevinal, la tour s'inscrivant malencontreusement dans la perspective des vieilles façades à l'espagnole.
(Photos A. Turpin - T.C.B.)

Des voisinages
contre-nature...

THE "INVISIBLE" MUSEUM OF MODERN ART: THE PEAK OF MODESTY?

Johan Lagae

Luckily the architects of that museum were not allowed to implement their design – it would have been a kind of colossal, concrete grand piano. Now there is nothing there, and isn't that the peak of modesty in architecture; there is just a low parapet and a sunken well in an old-fashioned, quiet square.

GEERT VAN ISTENDAEL, Arm Brussel [Poor Brussels], 1992, p. 237.

Tackling the historic city

9 May 1973. The public presentation of architect Roger Bastin's design for the Musée d'Art Moderne on the Mont des Arts sparked off an unusually bitter controversy in Belgian architectural circles.[1] Of course, it was more or less a foregone conclusion that there could be no consensus on the design for a public building on a potentially prolific historic site in the heart of the city and under the supervision of a wide group of clients and commissions. However, the demolition of a block of houses to make room for a "modern" building that was expressly intended as a signal of the new museum in the public space is regarded by many as yet another example of the unacceptable modernist stripping of the inner city of Brussels. The minds behind the *Archives d'Architecture Moderne* (A.A.M.) devote their first dossier to the museum design, and the *Atelier de Recherche et d'Action Urbaines* (A.R.A.U.), founded in 1969, designs a thoroughly elaborated counter-proposal.

An analysis of the design process, however, reveals that the allegation that Bastin's design was an ill-considered *tabula rasa* is debatable, to say the least. The main lines of the design process are reconstructed here, not to rehabilitate the original design, but to show how Roger Bastin tried to cope with the historic centre of Brussels in a contemporary way, devoid of any misplaced nostalgia. After all, it is the topical issue of the "incorporation" of new architecture in the historic city that is brought out very clearly in the history of the design of the Musée d'Art Moderne.

"The sole law of correct proportions"
Designs 1967-1968

Although various sites were mentioned as possible locations for the new Musée d'Art Moderne in the course of the 1960s, the Mont des Arts seemed to be the obvious site. In 1966 Roland Delers and Jacques Bellemans, the architects who had completed the Bibliothèque Royale, tried to find a way of integrating the future museum in the original master plan for the Mont des Arts drawn up by Jules Ghobert and Maurice Houyoux.

At the instigation of the *Amis des Musées* they consulted Roger Bastin, who had been responsible for the strikingly contextual architecture of the Musée de Mariemont shortly before. Faced with the retrograde master plan for the Mont des Arts, Bastin marked out the lines of an alternative approach at the end of 1967. Instead of the stepped façade along the Montagne de la Cour in Ghobert's plan – whose style matched the architecture of his Palais des Congrès – Bastin envisaged a simple composition of two sober units: a low block, adjacent to the Hôtel Altenloh, following the walls of the existing row of houses that were to be demolished, and a high unit with a square ground plan and an internal patio. This second unit is inserted in such a way that the Place du Musée acquires the dimensions of a square *à l'italienne*, a scale already suggested by the 19th century Balustrade Leopold II.

This first version of the design shows that Bastin was by no means determined to "rip open" the closed nature of the Place du Musée, as the A.A.M. would later claim, but to link the square visually with the Mont des Arts. However, the fact that this proposal blocked the view of the semicircular entrance to the Palace of Charles de Lorraine was the crucial objection raised by *La Ligue Esthétique Belge*.[2] The preservation of that view was therefore to become the decisive limiting condition in the following designs: Bastin first reversed the height of the two blocks, before leaving the view entirely free in his second (1968) and subsequent designs. The earliest designs illustrate that for Bastin the challenge of building in a historic urban context lay primarily in adapting the new construction as accurately as possible to the existing architectural fabric. By observing strict volumetric proportions, Bastin wanted to respond to the compositional lines that were already there and to create new visual relations.

1. Claire-Anne Delvaux, *Le Musée d'art moderne au cœur de Bruxelles: un problème d'intégration* (unpublished dissertation, U.C.L., 1984) and Thierry Demey, *Bruxelles. Chronique d'une capitale en chantier* (Brussels: Legrain, 1990), p. 292-313. Officially, the name of the architect Leo Beeck should also be mentioned, even though he did not play any significant role in the design process.

2. This entrance is interesting in art historical terms for the way in which the modulation of open and closed parts of the façade makes use of trompe-l'oeil to play on the change of orientation between the actual symmetrical axis of the entrance itself, on the one hand, and the visual axis of the view of it from the Place Royale, on the other.

Second design, 1968, bird's-eye view

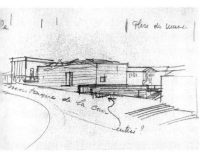

Second design, 1968,
view from the Montagne de la Cour

Musée de Mariemont

PLATES PP. 175-177

A sketch from the second design (1968) shows the resumption of several themes from the Musée de Mariemont:[3] the powerful and monumental force of the building itself, the carefully chosen orientation towards the outer surroundings from a closed interior, and the role of a stretch of water to link the existing and the new architecture. This design indicates that Bastin considered his contextual approach to the park landscape of Mariemont applicable in the centre of Brussels. The proposal was also completely in line with the vision of the curator of the Musées Royaux des Beaux-Arts at the time, Philippe Roberts-Jones, for whom a contemporary museum should manifest itself as a "classical construction of the 20th century" constructed from correctly proportioned volumes, while the interior should be a self-enclosed world that afforded an occasional glimpse through carefully placed windows of "the common everyday world."[4]

A relation of this kind between city and museum is reminiscent of Marcel Breuer's Whitney Museum of American Art in New York (1963-1965). The way in which Bastin incorporated the Place du Musée and its garden of sculptures into the pedestrian route through the city also bears comparison to the way in which Breuer allows the passer-by a view of a sunken sculptural garden from Madison Avenue.

An "echo of the surroundings." Designs 1969-1973

The intentions of the first designs continued to influence the later stages. The actual exhibition rooms were now planned for the most part underground so as not to block the view of the entrance to the Palace of Charles de Lorraine. Some designs show no less than six subterranean strata below the Place du Musée, including car parks accessible from the Montagne de la Cour. Light shafts and sunken patios in the square convey natural light deep down into the interior. The only parts of the museum above the ground are the Hôtel Altenloh (due for renovation) and a new building to give access to the exhibition rooms. This new volume was the only opportunity to give the Musée d'Art Moderne on the Mont des Arts a face of its own, and Bastin was resolute in choosing to set it as a contemporary signal in the setting. The brochure for the design presented in 1973 described this measure as an "incisive and bold integration," justifying it as the answer to the clients' request for a museum that is an "image of its epoch."[5]

In the design dating from January 1969, this volume is constructed by means of two curved concrete walls out of alignment with one another, separated by large windows. The complexity of the organisational structure increased in successive stages. First one of the outer walls was given a serrated contour. After March 1971 the same walls are composed of different segments, referring to the directions present on the site. According to Bastin, these "free and sinuous forms," combined with the height, which is attuned to the buildings surrounding the Place du Musée, and the choice of material – elegant, vertical prefab elements in white decorative concrete – would ensure that this abstract volume could be understood as an "echo of the surroundings."[6]

The interior of this new building is dynamically constructed around a well with ramps – certain designs are reminiscent of Frank Lloyd Wright's Guggenheim – and topped with a floating roof that admitted indirect light. The relation with the site is achieved from the interior by two ample windows with a view of the direct surroundings of the Montagne de la Cour and the Place du Musée.

The placing of the part of the museum that was visible above the ground as a free-standing block fulfilled the promise to create views of the Place du Musée from the Coudenberg and the Place Royale. Sketches show how Bastin wanted to divert the pedestrian route up the Mont des Arts towards the Place du Musée in order to make it a more intensively used urban square. Perspective drawings are populated with figures walking around or seated on benches, while the sunken patios set apart in the square allow for visual interaction between the museum visitors and the urban passers-by.

Toward an "invisible" museum. Designs 1973-1974

A large part of the criticisms of Bastin's project in 1973 was directed at the most visible intervention: the new building was regarded as a *Fremdkörper* (an intruder) that had no relation with the surroundings. A.A.M. and A.R.A.U. argued that abandoning the closed nature of the Place du Musée was deplorable. The busy traffic along the Rue Montagne de la Cour would totally destroy the "calm and serenity" of the square. Besides, they regarded the access to the car park as an unacceptable short-circuit of the pedestrian route on the Mont des Arts.[7] They also feared that the site would become a lifeless spot

3. *La Maison* 8 (1966). Special issue on Roger Bastin.

4. Philippe Roberts-Jones, "Grandeur et servitude de l'architecte," in *Rythme* 44 (December 1967), p. 23. Special issue "Pour le Musée d'Art Moderne".

5. Service des Relations Publiques du Ministère des Travaux Publics, *Le Musée d'Art Moderne à Bruxelles* (Brussels, May 1973), p. 23.

6. Roger Bastin, "Les projets pour le Musée d'Art Moderne à Bruxelles 1973-1978 ou l'architecture entravée," in *Bulletin de la Classe des Beaux-Arts* Vol. LXI (1979), p. 57.

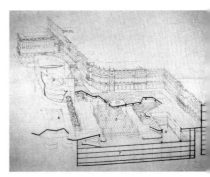

Design May 1969, axonometric projection

7. Archives d'Architecture Moderne, *Dossier n° 1* (Brussels, 28 May 1973). This criticism ignores the fact that Bastin actually wanted to divert this route towards the Place du Musée, even though the architect himself was not happy with the imposition of the entrance and exit to the car park.

Design November 1974, bird's-eye view

because of the uniformity of the building programme. This was precisely the reason for the objections to the demolition of the existing row of houses, with their lively, typically urban programmatic mixture. There is however some substance in the criticism by A.A.M. and A.R.A.U. Without prior knowledge, for instance, it is by no means immediately obvious that the building above the ground is to be understood as an "echo of the surroundings." But their criticism was too blunt to generate a meaningful and fruitful dialogue: the new building was simply characterised as a "concrete bunker."

In October 1973 Bastin presented another alternative project in which a commercial gallery was appended to the museum on the Montagne de la Cour side, but in July 1974 a compromise solution was thought up of the kind to which Belgium seems to hold the patent: the new building above ground level was definitively scrapped to preserve the existing row of houses (though it is an irony of history that after years of neglect most of them were eventually demolished). In other words, the Musée d'Art Moderne became an "invisible" museum.

In October of the same year Bastin came up with a design which meets this new condition in a simple but intelligent way. He created a funnel-shaped semicircular well in the Place du Musée, an intervention that recalls the empty space in one of his previous projects. The result was a well of light which not only eliminated the risk that the space might be felt to be claustrophobic, but also, thanks to its carefully conceived form, immediately produced an efficient orientation point along the underground exhibition route. One can follow Van Istendael's rather moralising tone in regarding this design solution as a "peak of modesty," but in all its stillness, it undeniably forms a powerful response by an honest modernist to a debate that fell on deaf ears and quashed any opportunity for contemporary architecture in the historic city. At a time when the scope for intelligent architecture in Brussels still seems to be minimal, when the museum is regarded as the ultimate architectural commission and it seems natural to design museums as urban landmarks, it is important to put the "invisible" Musée d'Art Moderne and its turbulent design history back on the agenda.

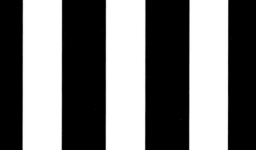

III

ARCHITECTURAL ARCHIVES DISC

From the time of the fire in the Ducal Palace in 1731 and the subsequent construction of the Place Royale and the Parc de Bruxelles at the end of the 18th century, a vast flood of projects was drawn up and still continues to pour out. The majority of these projects revolve around the restructuring of the Montagne de la Cour: Henri Maquet's project for a connecting road between the Upper and Lower Towns; Leopold II and his architect Alphonse Balat's plans for the transformation of the hill into an enormous museum complex, to transform the Montagne de la Cour into the Mont des Arts; designs by architects, such as Victor Bourgeois and Victor Horta, for the Musées Royaux, etc. The project current could not be repressed. The whole hillside, from the Place Royale in the Upper Town, down to the Marché aux Herbes in the Lower Town was flooded by consecutive waves of pent-up design activity, which may possibly be unique, both due to the magnitude as well as the diversity and perpetuity. Architectural and urban history knows of few places which have been exposed to such a phenomenal and continual flow of investment in design.

This is undoubtedly due to the distinct quality of the location. Unfortunately, in spite of all the interventions, the hillside between the Lower and Upper Towns never became part of the latter, but remained in its shadow. The hill was perceived as a stepping stone to the Upper Town, as a step up towards power, money and its manifestations. In the undefined area between the Upper Town, where the power came from above and the Lower Town, where diligent citizens enforced their authority, the Montagne de la Cour was transformed from a transition zone into an ambivalent zone – neither the one nor the other – and into an area of altercation in which the changing power relations were physically manifested. Therefore projects invariably generate counter-projects – a means of action in the *luttes urbaines* which are a trademark of Brussels.

The Montagne de la Cour was a division but also a link between the two civil realms. Nothing was ever completely unambiguous there. Nor was anything definitively permanent, one of the reasons being that the radical transformations which took place there only came to pass after lengthy tugs-of-war, and extensive means were required to such an extent that prolongations almost constantly became part of the facts. Due to these reassessments, work which was carried out was questioned. Because of all this, flexibility still existed to redefine the future and the objective of the area. The countless architectural and urban development projects demonstrate this clearly. The convention between the Belgian state and the city of Brussels in 1903 for example legally ratified a "definitive master plan"– the most unambiguous ever made for this location. However, this did not prevent undisciplined reality from unsettling everything from the outset and creating margins, possibilities to manoeuvre, which were continually explored and which architects and urbanists increasingly attempted to expand.

Almost every famous name in the history of Belgian architecture has got his teeth into the Montagne de la Cour or the surrounding area, but also various thrill-seekers and just as many active or enterprising citizens came with all sorts of proposals. The most diverse architectural currents went into battle against each other and with reality, took their positions in the tension areas of contrasts such as identity and interaction, restoration and modernisation, preservation and progress, utopia and reality. The Montagne de la Cour can thus justifiably be known as a training ground for architecture and urbanism. Hundreds of projects were tested for their viability: grandiose vision confronted with day-to-day reality. Boundaries between architecture and urbanism were stretched to the point where they disappear. In contrast, architecture took the position of an autonomous discipline in opposition to urbanism, while at the same time the infrastructure infiltrated and undermined the disciplines of architecture and urbanism. However, the most fascinating project which was created from this briefly outlined instability was not derived from the world of architecture, but from Paul Otlet. The concept of his Mundaneum was conceived as a synthesis of different elements which he was working on at this selfsame location: the idea of the museum, the *Office Internationale de la Bibliographie* and the *Union des Associations Internationales* for which the Belgian government intended to provide a seat on the Mont des Arts. This can be seen as an embryo of Otlet's Mundaneum. Otlet, who can be considered as the "godfather" of the programmers, will be discussed in the contribution of Karina Van Herck and Hilde Heynen.

Contemporary design work which is presented in the last section (*Laboratory for the city of tomorrow*) and complements the programmatic investigations, engulfs the Mont des

Arts with a new, and for the first time, wholly international design surge. It forms an attempt to explore the possible destination of the Mont des Arts in the post-national era, thus commemorating the 19th and 20th century urban utopias. Here, the project archives are not only implemented as a commemoration of the site, but also as the memory of the disciplines of architecture and urbanism. This provides data for a meaningful and *contemporary* discussion about architecture and urbanism, about infrastructure and programmes, about the paradoxical conditions of modernisation and preservation, about erasure and accumulation. Material for a discussion about the Mont des Arts as an intermediate zone between Upper and Lower Town, about Brussels, about city life *tout court*.

The Mont des Arts' architectural archives (compiled by Maureen Heyns) are not strictly chronologically presented, but constructed around a few pivotal points which have had a decisive influence on the restructuring proces of the Mont des Arts and the surrounding area, either conceptual or executed. At the same time, the focus is moved from the royal Upper Town, to regarding the Mont des Arts as a link between Upper and Lower Towns, to the Mont des Arts as a museum site, ultimately to end at the Carrefour de l'Europe at the base of the hillside. The chain of projects flows like a meandering *roman fleuve* over the various chapters from Upper to Lower Town, from the 18th century to the present day, and contains global urban design projects as well as limited architectural interventions. They present alternating themes from various approaches.

FROM DUCAL PALACE TO QUARTIER ROYAL

Medieval incremental urban growth resulted in an organic and layered structure, which can be considered as a *Gesamtkunstwerk*: the European town as the crystallised form, as a tangible result of civilisation. The painting of the palace fire couples perfect coherence with immediate transience. The fire was the starting signal for a continuous flow of projects for reconstruction, restructuring, renewal, transformation which resulted in the current situation of the Mont des Arts: a complex, layered structure of which the ruin will become nothing less than the foundation for the subsequent *Gesamtkunstwerk* (which the city actually is).

After various design series, Guimard's project for the reconstruction and transformation of the Upper Town was carried out. The Parc de Bruxelles and the Place Royale were built on top of the existing ruins of the Ducal Palace as complete autonomous architectural forms. The former texture has been swept away, and can only be seen at the edges of the site and below ground. The contrast with the medieval Lower Town is so strongly brought out that a cascade of projects for the transformation of the whole area came into action. The starting signal for modern urbanism had now been given.

1. Fire at the Ducal Palace (Gillis van Auwerkercke, 1674)

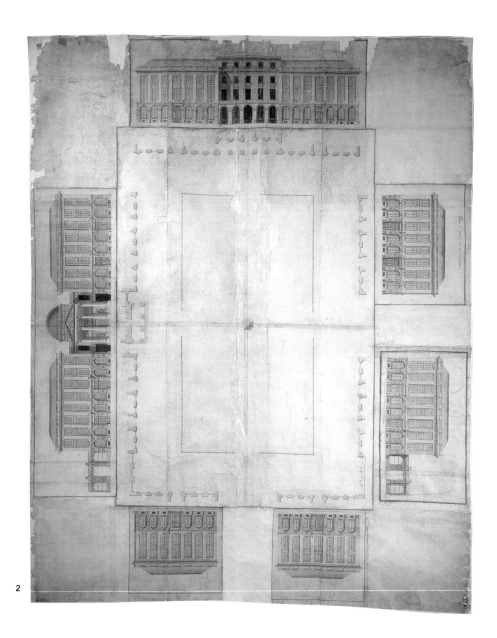

2

114

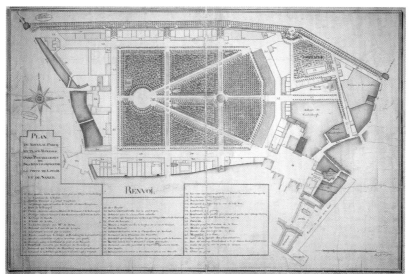

3

4

2. Project for the Place Royale (Jean-Benoît-Vincent Barré – after the project by Gilles-Barnabé Guimard, circa 1775)   **3.** Project for the new Parc and the Place Royale (Joachim Zinner, circa 1780)   **4.** Place Royale, view of the Lower Town (Thomas Sidney Cooper, 1828)

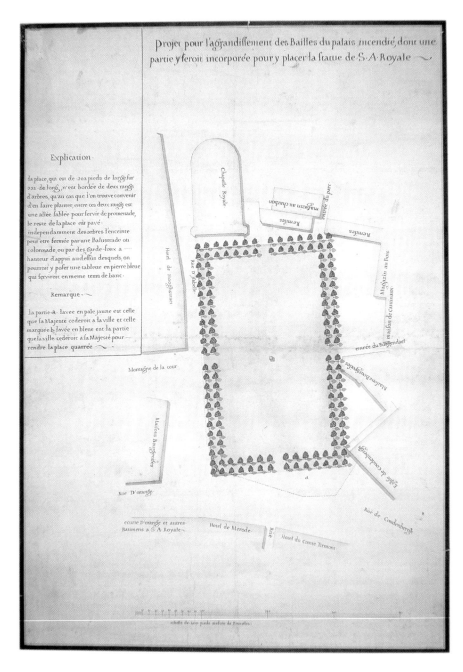

5. Project for the enlargement of the Place des Bailles on the site of the burnt out palace (Landelin-Louis-Joseph Baudour, 1774)

THE RESTRUCTURING OF THE MONTAGNE DE LA COUR

Two opposing but contemporary 19th century modernisation concepts come face to face here: the modernisation which develops from a *tabula rasa* and introduced a new townscape on top of the existing one and the concept of modernisation which channels the renewal into a mutation and transformation process based upon the existing one. Both approaches are brought into play in order to solve the "problem of the Montagne de la Cour" and as such improve the connection between Upper and Lower Towns. Both of these fundamental approaches are on the Mont des Arts/Montagne de la Cour, strikingly illustrated by Henri Maquet's projects (various plans since 1876) and the response of the Mayor Charles Buls (1893), "father" of the *Esthétique des Villes* movement.

Maquet's plans apply Haussmann's methods to the specific Brussels' topographical situation with its difficult east-west connections. On the other hand, Charles Buls' ideas rest on the basis of a reconstruction of the traditional European city, whereby the notions such as the picturesque, the individual and the nation are linked to the locus on the one hand, and on the other hand to the urban texture (housing typology, bourgeois culture) which could be interpreted in terms of identity. They form the opposite ends of a spectrum regarding approach methods in the design current which commenced with Trappeniers' project (1856) and was followed by De La Roche and Arveuf's proposal for a Palais du Commerce (commercial exchange, 1854), and De Curte's project (1858) etc. In this design current, the architectural approaches alternate with proposals for infrastructural interventions, such as those of Buls and Maquet.

1

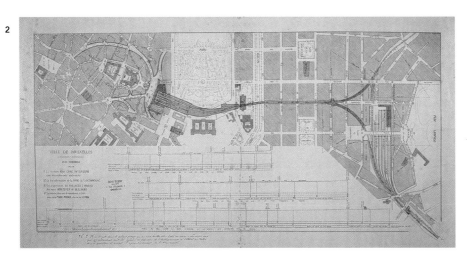

2

1. Project for a major thoroughfare linking the Upper and Lower Towns (Henri Maquet, 1876)
2. Overall view with a central station and a curved street between the Place Royale and the Rue de Loxum (Henri Maquet, undated)
3. Project for the construction of a central station and a curved street between the Place Royale and the Marché aux Herbes (Henri Maquet, 1887)

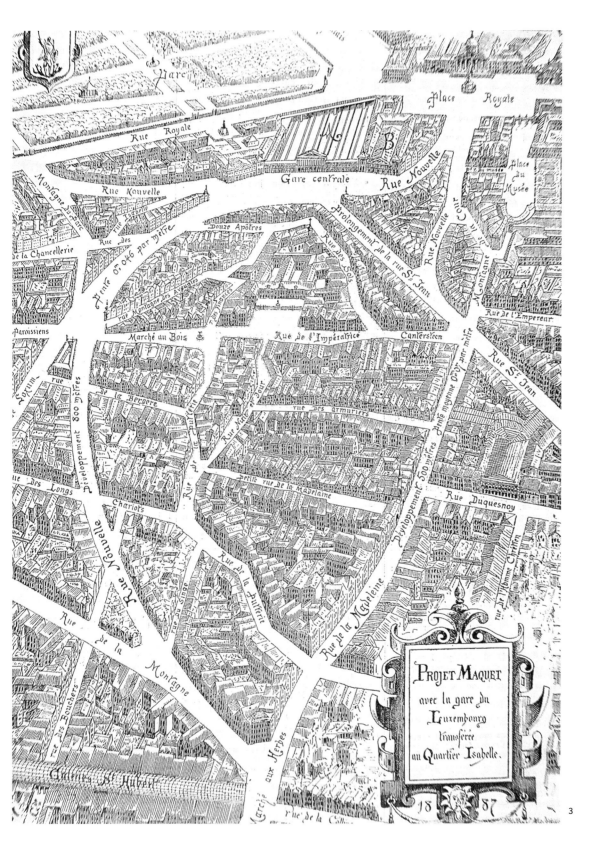

PROJET MAQUET
avec la gare du
Luxembourg
transférée
au Quartier Isabelle.

18 87

3

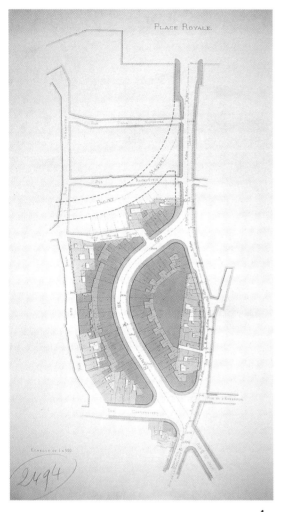

PLACE ROYALE.

ECHELLE DE 1 A 500

4

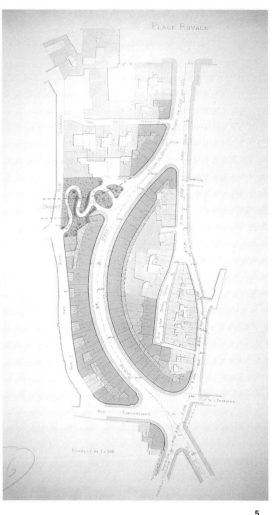

PLACE ROYALE

ECHELLE DE 1 A 500

5

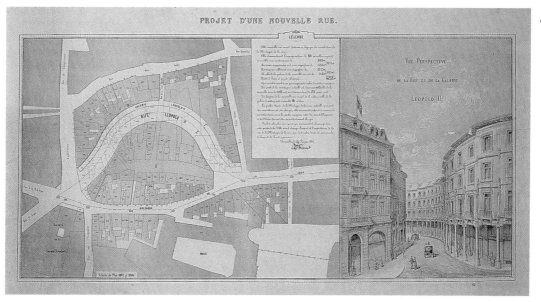

4. Project for the redevelopment of the Quartier St. Roch
(Collège échevinal de Bruxelles, 1893)

5. Project for the redevelopment of the Quartier St. Roch - Rue Coudenberg
(Heyvaert - implementing the small Maquet curve, 1894)

6. Project for a new street designed to relieve traffic congestion on the Montagne de la Cour
(Vincard, 1884)

7. Project for the restructuring of the Montagne de la Cour, with roundabout and covered galleries (Antoine Trappeniers, 1856)   **8 & 9.** Project for the restructuring of the Montagne de la Cour, with Galerie Marchande and Palais des Beaux-Arts (L. De Curte, 1858)

8

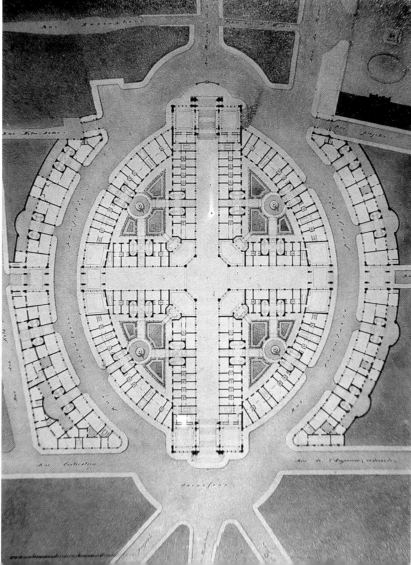

9

PROJET
D'UN PALAIS DU COMMERCE
à exécuter
POUR LA VILLE DE BRUXELLES
sur l'Emplacement de la Montagne de la Cour
et présenté à l'Administration communale

PAR M.M. DE LA ROCHE ET ARVEUF ARCH.

le 23 Mars 1854.

10. Project for a Palais du Commerce (commercial exchange) to be built on the site of the Montagne de la Cour (De La Roche & Arveuf, 1854)   **11.** Project for a set of streets designed to facilitate communications between the Upper and Lower Towns (Henri Beyaert, 1864)

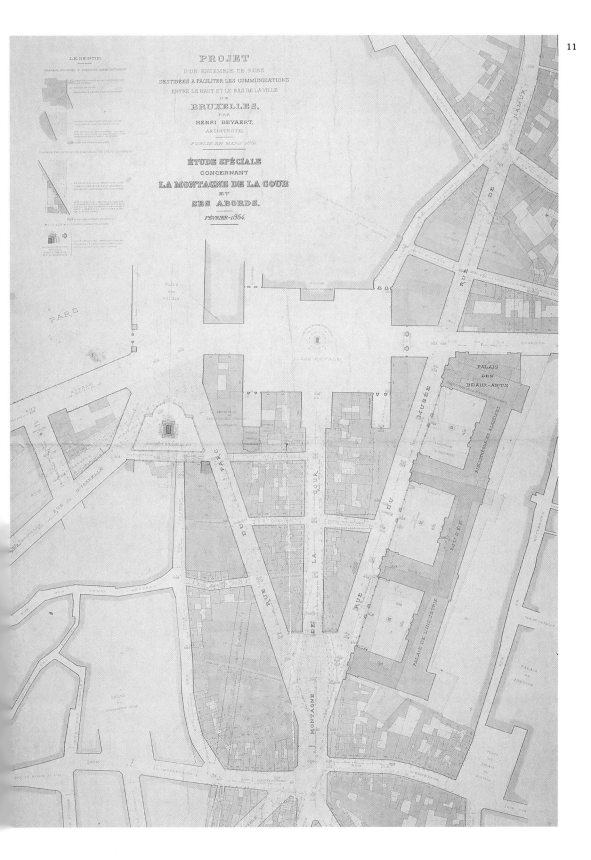

PROJET

D'UN ENSEMBLE DE RUES

DESTINÉES A FACILITER LES COMMUNICATIONS

ENTRE LE HAUT ET LE BAS DE LA VILLE

DE

BRUXELLES.

PAR

HENRI BEYAERT,

ARCHITECTE.

PUBLIÉ EN MARS 1861

ÉTUDE SPÉCIALE

CONCERNANT

LA MONTAGNE DE LA COUR

ET

SES ABORDS.

FÉVRIER-1864.

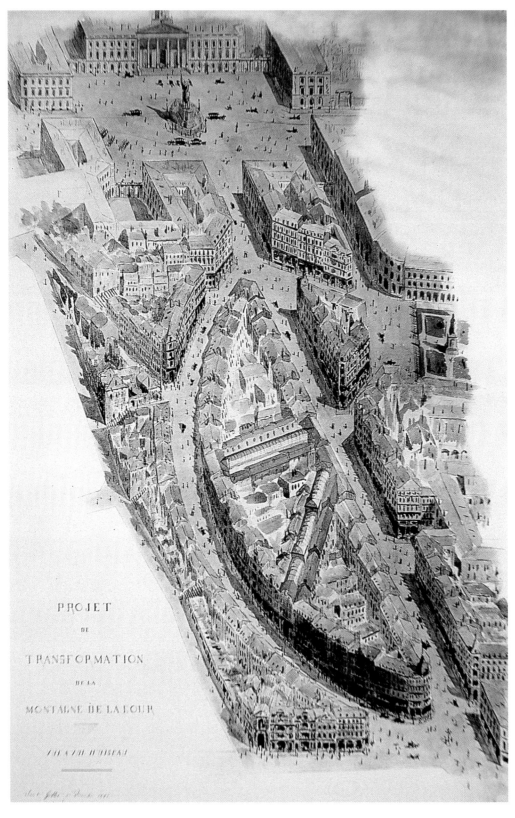

PROJET
DE
TRANSFORMATION
DE LA
MONTAGNE DE LA COUR

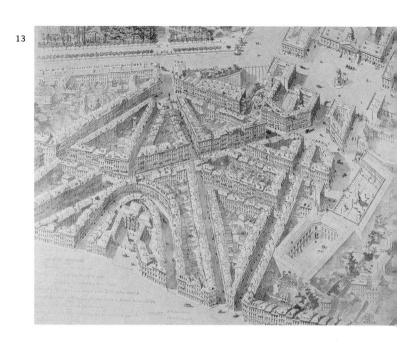

12. Project for the transformation of the Montagne de la Cour (S. Vermont, 1885)
13. Project for the transformation of the Montagne de la Cour (Peeters, Kennis & Alleweireldt, 1870)
14. Project for the straightening and levelling of the Montagne de la Cour (Vander Plaetsen, 1875)

15. Project for the restructuring of the Montagne de la Cour (Inghels, undated)

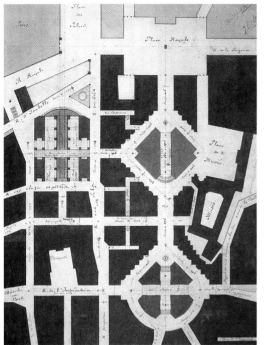

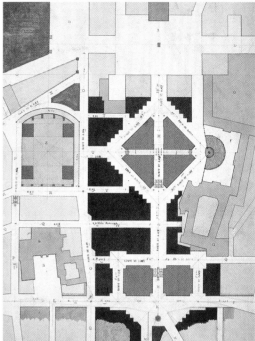

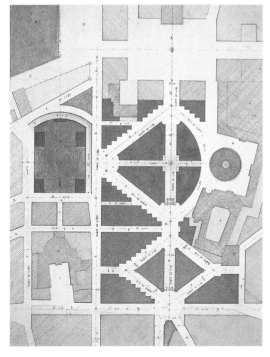

16. Project for the transformation of the Montagne de la Cour (I.-J. Culot, 1887)

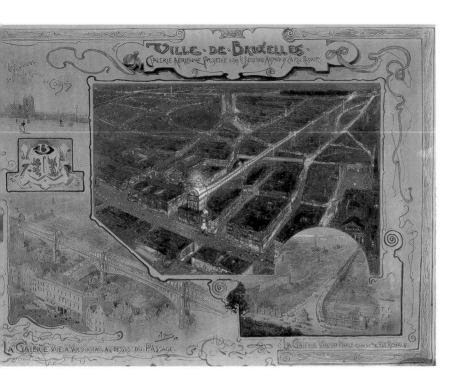

17. Project for an overhead gallery between the Boulevard Anspach and
the Rue Royale (A. Heins, 1898)

18. Project for a funicular connecting the Upper and Lower Towns (Wellens, 1890)

FROM MUSEE ROYAL TO MUNDANEUM

The infrastructural interventions, which were central in the previous episode, created the leeway for a new programmatic interpretation of the Montagne de la Cour. Leopold II's intention to reshape the Montagne de la Cour into the Mont des Arts was, of course, placed in the foreground. The Musées Royaux des Beaux-Arts would be (on paper at least) expanded and supplemented with numerous institutions (industry palace, national archives, the national library), with which a cultural pool would be created on the Montagne de la Cour. It is a consistent attempt to construct a national identity with regional art treasures from the past. The personal contribution to universal civilisation was placed in a shrine, which then became the altar of national identity. Balat's design was the first in this series of expansion projects which have the museum as main theme and wherein later on Maquet, Chambon, Caluwaers, etc. also play a role. The projects, due to their vastness (in some cases accentuated by the use of a plinth), can only broach a limited affinity with the sloping site. In this way, the city is created using architecture, with the building occupying the slope. Here architecture is placed in juxtaposition to urbanism, a contradiction which also came into question in the previous episode.

With Paul Otlet's project for the Mundaneum, the notion of a "Mont des Arts" undergoes a total metamorphosis and becomes a grandiose utopia. Here the national identity is no longer on the agenda, but is replaced by internationalism and pacifism, knowledge and progress. Since the Mont des Arts (where Otlet had his secretarial building/offices in the former Bibliothèque Royale) the Mundaneum created a movement, first in Brussels, later throughout the whole world, the pinnacle of which was Le Corbusier's designs for Geneva and Antwerp. On the Mont des Arts itself, the Palais Mondial was crystallised through Victor Bourgeois' Urbaneum (1928), a documentation and information centre for urban development in Brussels. Under the form of the metaphor of the "museum of the 21st century," the current project *Vacant City* takes the Mundaneum back to its birthplace – the Mont des Arts.

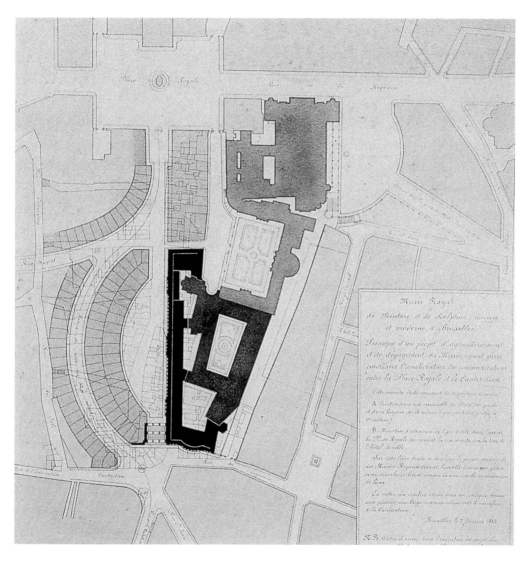

1. Project for the Mont des Arts (the enlargement and clearing of the Musées Royaux) (Alphonse Balat, 1882)

2

2. Musée d'Art Ancien (Balat, 1875), main façade, circa 1909   **3.** Sculpture hall, circa 1909
4. Entrance hall, circa 1909

3

4

5

PROJET MAQUET POUR LE DÉGAGEMENT DES MUSÉES ROYAUX

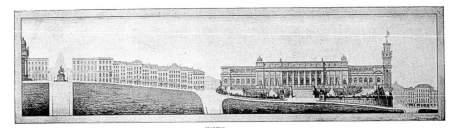

Plan en élévation.

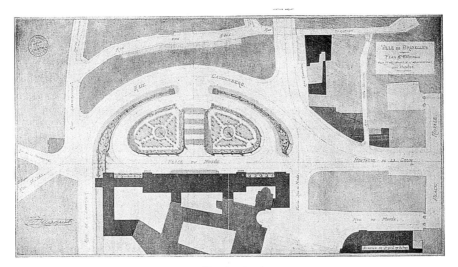

Plan terrier.

Panorama résultant de l'exécution du projet.

(Vue de la Place Royale.)

6

5. Project for the Mont des Arts (the enlargement and clearing of the Musées Royaux) (Henri Maquet, 1898) **6.** Model of the Maquet project (1908)

7

7. Project for the layout of the Mont des Arts (Joseph Caluwaers, 1921) 8. Mont des Arts project (Paul Hermanus, 1908) 9. Project for the layout of the Mont des Arts (Alban Chambon, 1909)

8

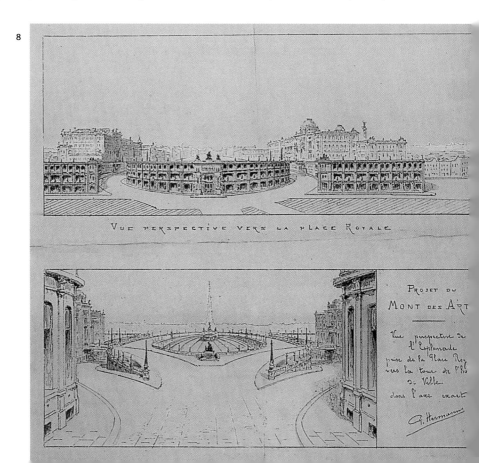

VUE PERSPECTIVE VERS LA PLACE ROYALE

PROJET DU
MONT DES ART

Vue perspective de
l'Esplanade
prise de la Place Roy
vers la tour de l'Hô
de Ville
dans l'axe exact

G. Hermanus

9

COVPE SVR L'ENTRÉE DV MVSÉE

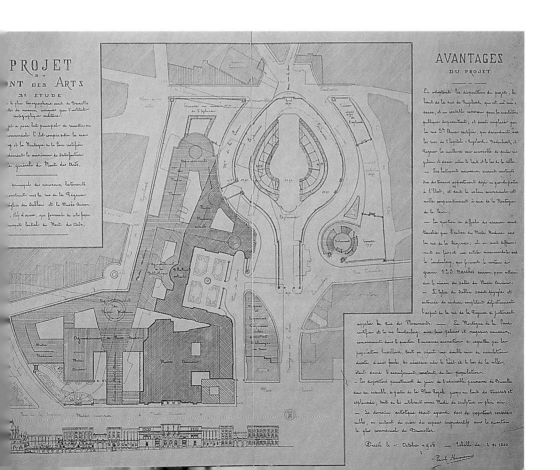

LE MONT DES ARTS - BRUXELLES

V. BOURGEOIS - ARCHITECTE

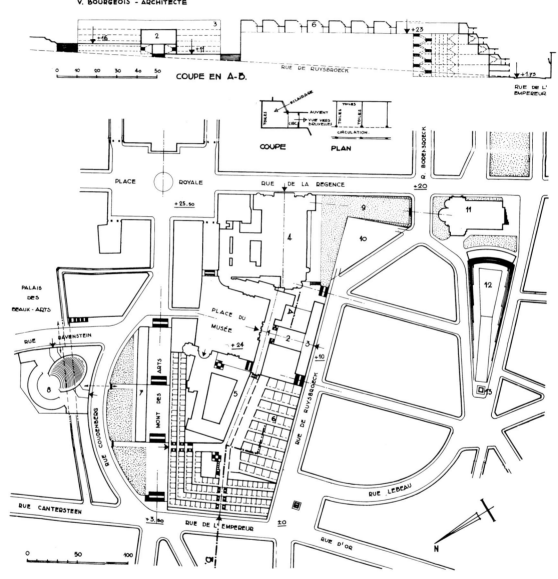

COUPE EN A-B.

RUE DE RUYSBROECK

RUE DE L' EMPEREUR

ECLAIRAGE
TOILES
TOILES
AUVENT
TOILES
VUE VERS BRUXELLES
CIRC
CIRCULATION.

COUPE

PLAN

PLACE ROYALE

RUE DE LA REGENCE

R. BODENBROECK

PALAIS DES BEAUX-ARTS

RUE RAVENSTEIN

PLACE DU MUSÉE

RUE COUDENBERG

MONT DES ARTS

RUE DE RUYSBROECK

RUE LEBEAU

RUE CANTERSTEEN

RUE DE L'EMPEREUR

RUE D'OR

N

10 & 11. Project for the enlargement of the Musées Royaux (Victor Bourgeois, 1931)

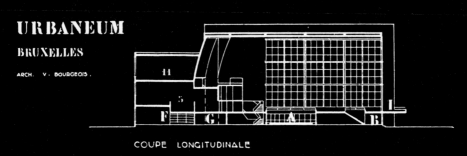

12

URBANEUM

BRUXELLES

ARCH. V · BOURGEOIS .

COUPE LONGITUDINALE

LE REZ · DE · CHAUSSEE   L'ETAGE   LA GALERIE

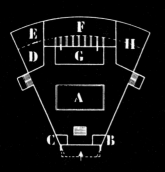 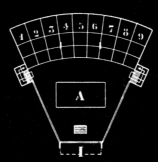 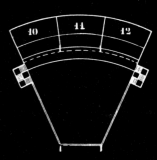

Plans de l'Urbaneum.

A. Maquette du Grand Bruxelles.   **B.** Huissiers.   **C.** Vestiaire.   **D.** Toilette.   **E.** Services généraux.

F. Bibliothèque.   **G.** Réserve.   **H.** Salle d'étude, avec 12 compartiments de documentation.

12, 13 & 14. Project for an Urbaneum on the Mont des Arts (Victor Bourgeois, 1928)

13

14

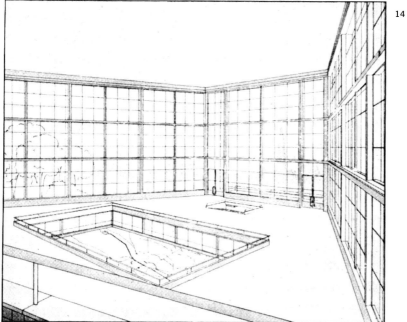

HORTA ON THE MONT DES ARTS

Horta demonstrates, in various architectural designs which he created of the Mont des Arts site and which are extensively documented here, an astounding expertise in working with programmes, structures and circulation within the limitations stipulated by an exceptionally predetermined urban form. Merged together, the various projects by Horta form a virtual master plan for the whole Mont des Arts area: the Palais des Beaux-Arts, the Gare Centrale, the Musées Royaux des Beaux-Arts and the Municipal Development Project (the whole building block between Rue Ravenstein and Cantersteen) appear to be haphazard puzzle pieces which can be fitted together. In reality the building block between the Rue Ravenstein and Cantersteen was split into various lots and worked on by various architects, producing, among others, the unfinished Shell building and the flamboyant Galerie Ravenstein, both of which architect Dumont provided.

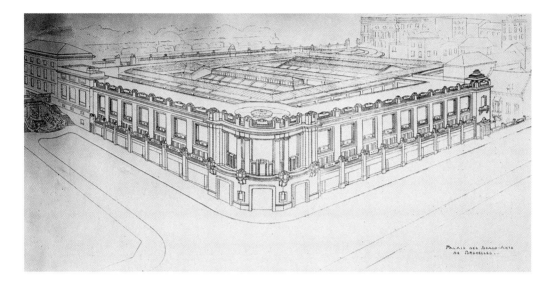

1. Project for the Palais des Beaux-Arts (Victor Horta, circa 1922)

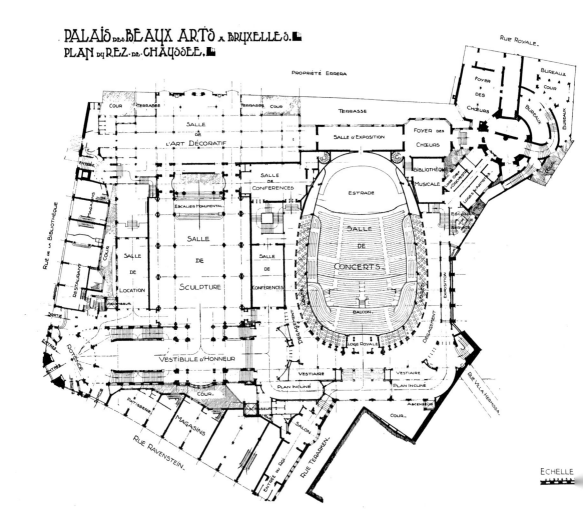

PALAIS des BEAUX ARTS a BRUXELLES.
PLAN du REZ-de-CHAUSSEE.

PROPRIÉTÉ ERRERA

RUE ROYALE.

BUREAUX

FOYER
DES
CHŒURS

COUR

BUREAUX

BUREAUX

COUR TERRASSE

TERRASSE COUR

TERRASSE

SALLE
DE
L'ART DÉCORATIF

SALLE D'EXPOSITION

FOYER DES
CHŒURS

BIBLIOTHÈQUE
MUSICALE

ENTRÉE

MAGASINS

RUE DE LA BIBLIOTHÈQUE

SALLE
DE
CONFÉRENCES

ESCALIER MONUMENTAL

SALLE
DE
SCULPTURE

SALLE
DE
CONFÉRENCES

ESTRADE

SALLE
DE
CONCERTS

LOGE DE L'ORCHESTRE

ESCALIER
DE
SERVICE

COUR

RESTAURANT

SALLE
DE
LOCATION

ASCENSEUR

SORTIE

ROTONDE

ENTRÉE

VESTIBULE D'HONNEUR

BALCON.

LOGE ROYALE.

DÉGAGEMENT

EXPOSITION

DÉGAGEMENT

ENTRÉE

COUR.

PATISSERIE

MAGASINS

ASCENSEUR

SALON

VESTIAIRE

PLAN INCLINÉ

VESTIAIRE

PLAN INCLINÉ

ASCENSEUR

COUR.

RUE VILLA HERMOSA.

ENTRÉE DU ROI

RUE TERARKEN.

RUE RAVENSTEIN.

ECHELLE

2. Project for the Palais des Beaux-Arts (Victor Horta, circa 1922)

4

3. Palais des Beaux-Arts, main façade (Mansy, circa 1928)
4. Sculpture hall (Mansy, circa 1928)

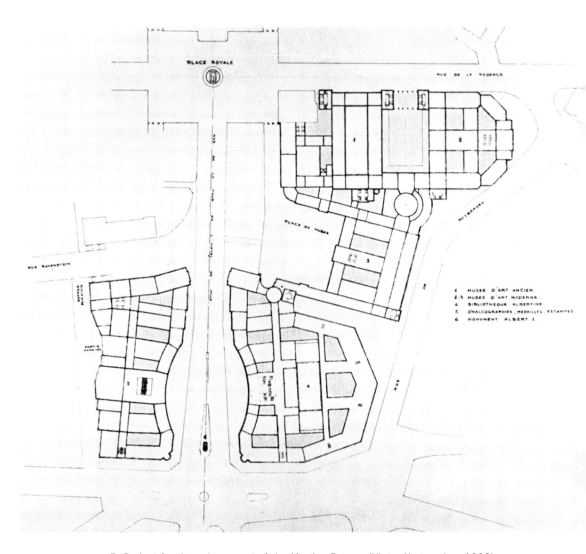

5. Project for the enlargement of the Musées Royaux (Victor Horta, circa 1938)

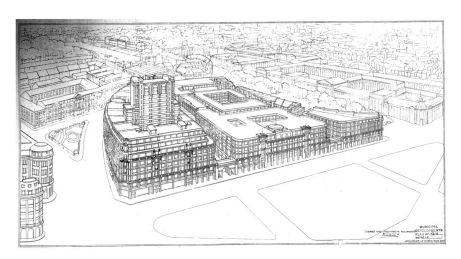

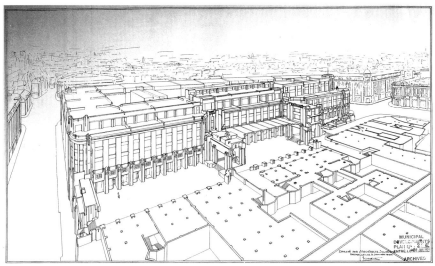

6. Municipal Development Project (Victor Horta, 1928)

7 & 8. Project for the Gare Centrale (Victor Horta & Maxime Brunfaut, 1938)
9. Ticket hall (Albert Demesmaeker, 1940)   **10.** Platform access hall (Albert Demesmaeker, 1940)

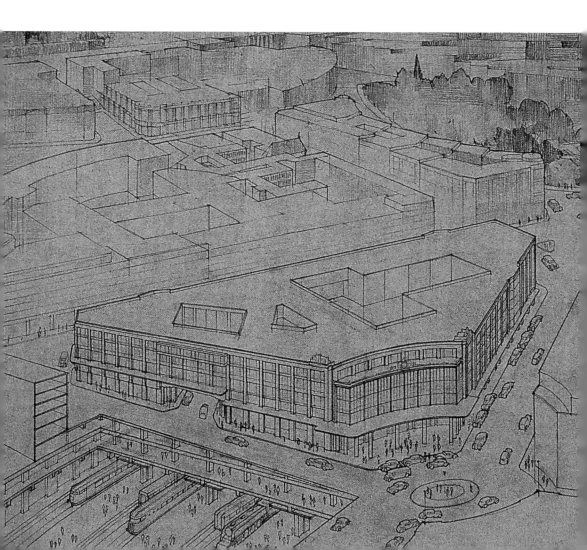

HALTE
CENTRAL
PERSPECTIVE AXONOMÉTRIC
AUX NIVEAUX DU CARREFOUR
ELLIPTIQUE ET DE LA RUE
CANTERSTEEN.

7 | 8

9

10

11. Gare Centrale, main façade, circa 1950

12. Ticket hall, circa 1952   **13.** Platforms, circa 1952

14

15

156

14. Shell building project (Alexis Dumont, 1931) **15.** Design for a tower (Alexis Dumont, 1937)
16. Design for a tower (Philippe Dumont, 1962)

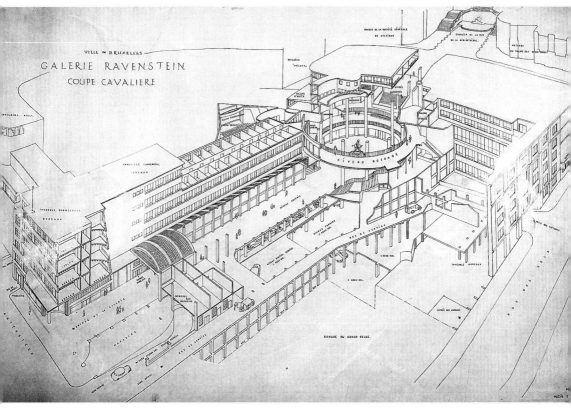

17. Project for the Galerie Ravenstein (Philippe Dumont, 1954)
18. Galerie Ravenstein, rotunda (Haine, circa 1958)

19. Project for the Galerie Ravenstein
(Philippe Dumont, 1954)

ALONG THE NORTH-SOUTH BOULEVARD

After the second world war the Belgian state, at the pinnacle of its coherence and due to an impetus for affirmation after the black war years, carried out heavyweight government investments in the north-south railway line area. The Belgian state, in a manner of speaking, took control of the area. Two modes of modernisation seemed to have arisen.

A visionary and extraordinarily daring construction above the railway tracks, with the Telex building, the Sabena Air Terminus and the large open-air car park opposite the Boulevard de l'Impératrice, shows a surge in the aspirations for progress. A parade of modernity which is concerned with everything that has to do with communication which the north-south connection proudly wears on its lapel: train, aeroplane, telephony, telegraphy, and last but not least: the car. This Euralille *avant-la-lettre* – the Carrefour de l'Europe thus – appears to be modernity itself.

This is in glaring contrast to the almost canonised modernism, which had become static due to its incapacity to deal with monumentalism, as illustrated by the Bibliothèque Royale and the vast Jardin de l'Albertine just next to the series of icons of modernity which were previously touched upon. The knowledge centre was closed off to the town like a fortress. The Mont des Arts architecture – executed fast for the World's Fair 1958 – cannot break free from the form idioms of the 1930s. In this way the post-war realisation can couple seamlessly with the competition designs for the Bibliothèque Royale and for the Mont des Arts from the 1930s.

1. Draft project for the Sabena Air Terminus (Maxime Brunfaut, 1952)
2. Draft project for the Telex building (Léon Stynen & Paul De Meyer, 1956)

HOTEL Westbury
BRUXELLES

The Westbury Hotel is part of the Knott Hotel chain in the U. S. A.; this skyscraper is situated at the vantage point of Brussels opposite the Sabena Air Terminal, and the Central Station and is within five minutes' walk of the shopping centre, theatres, la Grand'Place, the museums, the Royal Palace and the Palais des Congrès.
With 24 floors, the hotel is one of the tallest in Europe and gives you the best of service, food and comfort.

L'hôtel Westbury fait partie de la chaîne américaine Knott; ce gratte-ciel jouit d'une situation particulièrement avantageuse au centre de Bruxelles, face à l'Air Terminus et à la Gare Centrale, et à cinq minutes de marche du centre commercial, des théâtres, de la Grand'Place, des musées, du Palais Royal et du Palais des Congrès. Avec ses 24 étages, l'hôtel est un des plus hauts d'Europe; par la qualité de son service et de sa cuisine et le raffinement de son confort, il se veut aussi le meilleur...

Het Westbury Hotel behoort tot de Amerikaanse Knott organisatie. Deze wolkenkrabber is gelegen op een zeer gunstig punt in de stad Brussel, tegenover de Sabena Air Terminal en het Centraal station. Vanuit het hotel bereikt men te voet binnen vijf minuten de winkelcentra, theaters, la Grand'Place, musea, het Koninklijk Paleis en het Paleis voor Congressen.
Met zijn 24 verdiepingen is het hotel, dat de gasten het grootste comfort, de meest uitgebreide service en een bijzonder verfijnde keuken biedt, een van de hoogste in Europa.

*Das Westbury Hotel gehört zur amerikanischen Hotelkette Knott. Dieser Wolkenkratzer erfreut sich einer besonders günstigen Lage im Stadtkern von Brüssel, gegenüber dem Sabenagebäude und dem Zentralbahnhof, und nur fünf Minuten zu Fuss vom Geschäftszentrum, den Theatern, dem Rathausplatz, den Museen, dem Königlichen Schloss und dem Kongresspalast, entfernt.
Mit seinen 24 Stockwerken ist es eines der höchsten Hotels Europas; durch die Qualität seiner Bedienung und seiner Verpflegung, und des ausgeklügelten Komfortes, will es auch das Beste sein...*

Téléphone: 13.64.80   Telex: 22062
Cable: Westburyotel
General Manager: William F. GRELL
Resident Manager: H. Nelson VICKERS
6, rue Cardinal Mercier BRUXELLES I

Hotel
WESTB
Bruxel

OUSE CLUB
2nd floor, this private club offers a magnificent
he city whilst one can enjoy a cocktail or a meal
eisure.

22e étage, ce club privé d'où l'on jouit d'un magni-
d'œil sur la ville, permet de prendre un cocktail
un tout à loisir.

ste verdieping biedt de intieme club een impo-
cht over de stad, terwijl men er geniet van een
of een uitgelezen diner.

tockwerk gelegen, bietet dieser private Klub, von
man einen wunderbaren Gesamtblick auf die Stadt
Gelegenheit in einem vornehmen Rahmen ein Ge-
r ein Mahl einzunehmen.

AR
al floor. Renowned for its « Polo » murals, as
her major cities where the name « Westbury »

Rez de Chaussée. Là où existe un hôtel « West-
a un Polo Bar qui se distingue par sa décora-
le.

elijkvloers. Vermaard om zijn « Polo » muur-
en als in alle belangrijke steden, waar de
estbury » bestaat.

hoss. Berühmt für ihre wunderbare Wanddeko-
in allen anderen grossen Städten wie ein « West-
eht.

MS - CHAMBRES - KAMERS - ZIMMER
has 252 rooms giving every comfort possible:
its own private bathroom and shower, fully air-
d and radio.

de 252, elles sont toutes dotées du confort le plus
ain et douche privés, conditionnement d'air, radio.

heeft 252 airconditioned kamers, die de gasten
ste comfort bieden. Elk appartement is onder
ien van een badkamer en van een radiotoestel.

Zahl, alle mit dem allermodernsten Komfort
: Privat-Bad-und Brause, Luftkonditionierung.

APPARTEMENTS
numerous suites including two Presidential
igned to accommodate the most fastidious
evision and Radio.

ide plusieurs suites, dont deux suites présiden-
ues pour satisfaire les hôtes les plus exigents.
+ Radio.

ke suites, waaronder twee suites ingericht voor
van vorstelijke personen en staatshoofden. De
odanig ingericht, dat zij aan de eisen van de
ende gasten beantwoorden. Televisie en Radio.

besitzt mehrere Appartements darunter zwei
Appartements, mit allem ausgestattet was die
sten Gäste verlangen könnten. Fernsehen und

HOTEL Westbury
BRUXELLES

LOBBY
On the street level of the hotel opposite the Sabena Air
Terminal

Au rez-de-chaussée, et face à l'Air Terminus Sabena.

Gelijkvloers, tegenover de Sabena Air Terminal.

Im Erdgeschoss und genau gegenüber der Flugzeug-Endsta-
tion.

PANORAMA ROOM
The restaurant of the hotel, on 23rd floor styled in Louis
XVI by Dorothy Draper & Company Inc. of New York,
giving an unsurpassed panoramic view of Brussels.

Le restaurant de l'hôtel, situé au 23me étage entièrement
décoré et meublé en style Louis XVI par Dorothy Draper
& Cie, Inc. de New-York, offre un incomparable panorama
de Bruxelles.

Vanuit het restaurant van het hotel, op de 23e verdieping
en door Dorothy Draper & Cie, Inc. uit New-York uit-
gevoerd in Louis XVI stijl, kijken de gasten over geheel
Brussel uit.

L'on aus Fenstern des im 23. Stock gelegenen Restaurants,
vollständig von Dorothy Draper & Cie, Inc. aus New York
im Louis XVI Stil dekoriert und möbliert, geniesst man
das unvergleichbare Panorama der Stadt Brüssel.

3. Project for the Westbury Tower (R. Goffaux & C. Heywang, 1961)

4

ALBERTINA

4. Project for the Bibliothèque Royale (Renaat Braem, 1935)
5. "Sérénité, Ordre, Expression," Urbanism and Architecture Competition for the layout of the Mont des Arts (Jules Ghobert, 1937)
6. Project for the layout of the Mont des Arts (Jules Ghobert, 1942)

5

6

167

7

8

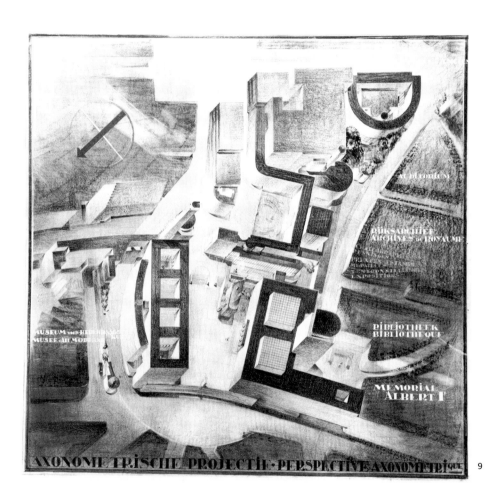

9

7, 8 & 9. "Akropolis," Urbanism and Architecture Competition for the layout of the Mont des Arts
(Eduard Van Steenbergen, 1937)

10. "Stat Magni Nominis Umbra," Urbanism and Architecture Competition for the layout of the Mont des Arts (Stanislas Jasinski, 1937)
11, 12 & 13. "Ars Scientia," Urbanism and Architecture Competition for the layout of the Mont des Arts (Jos Smolderen, 1937)

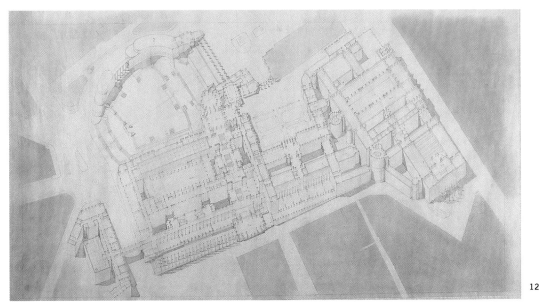

11

12

13

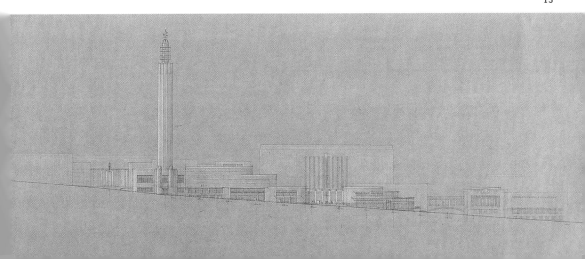

14

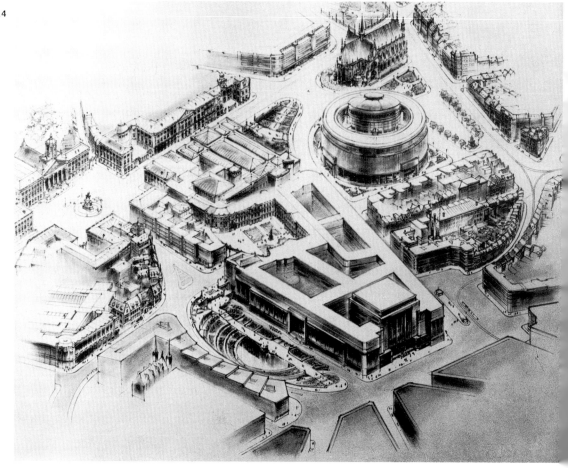

14. "Dé," Urbanism and Architecture competition for the layout of the Mont des Arts
(Alfred Chambon, 1937)
15 & 16. "D.36.37.38," Urbanism and Architecture Competition for the layout of the Mont des Arts
(Gaston Brunfaut, 1937)

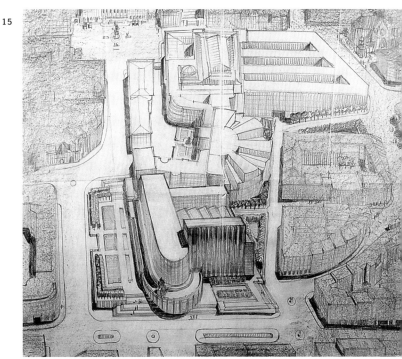

15

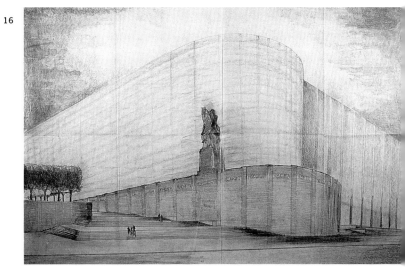

16

THE MUSÉE D'ART MODERNE

In this episode, the architect Bastin's original project for the expansion of the Musées Royaux with a Musée d'Art Moderne on the Coudenberg is reinstated as an intelligent architectural project. The project exhibits a withered, but nonetheless authentic and fulfilled modernism, but caused clashes of virulent opposition. In the wake of this, numerous opposing projects surfaced. The first brochure produced by the *Archives d'Architecture Moderne* (A.A.M.) linked criticism for Bastin's design to "alternatives" which set their sights more on the "city for the inhabitant" and the "human scale." This alternative stream gradually took shape during the critical reconstruction of the European city. In practice the Musée d'Art Moderne disappeared underneath the Place du Musée and the site between the Montagne de la Cour and the Place du Musée remains a void. The *Atelier de Recherche et d'Action Urbaines* (A.R.A.U.) is demanding, to this day, the reconstruction of this site with housing, considered as the basic ingredient of the European city.

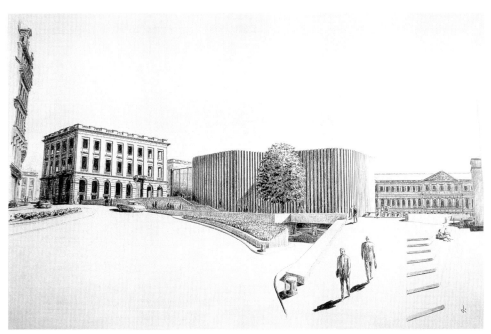

1. Project for the Musée d'Art Moderne (Roger Bastin & Pierre Lamby, 1973)

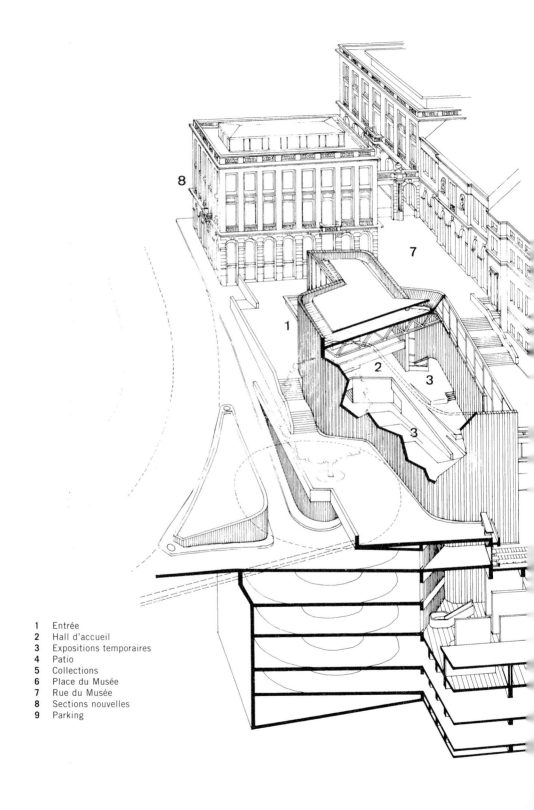

1   Entrée
2   Hall d'accueil
3   Expositions temporaires
4   Patio
5   Collections
6   Place du Musée
7   Rue du Musée
8   Sections nouvelles
9   Parking

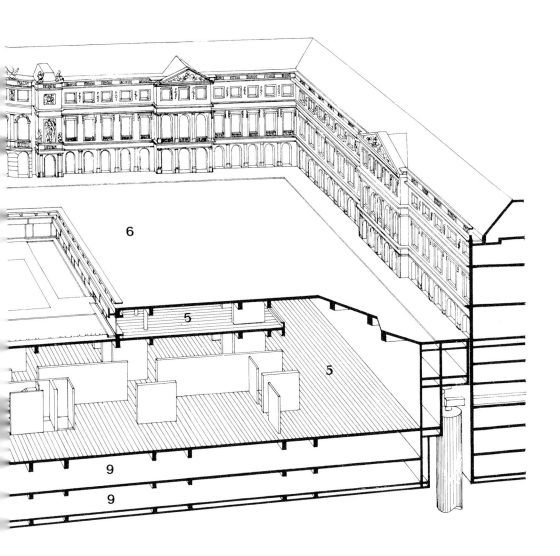

2. Project for the Musée d'Art Moderne (Roger Bastin & Pierre Lamby, 1973)

3. Counter-proposal for the Musée d'Art Moderne (1973)

THE CARREFOUR DE L'EUROPE

On the Carrefour de l'Europe, in the clash between architecture paradigms, late modern is exchanged for neo-modernism. The design source for this location took hold in the forties with Marcel Schmitz' plan for an urban forum (see p. 89). The A.R.A.U. made its debut on this scene in the late sixties. A competition organised by the city of Brussels (1970) and the Bonduelle competition (1983) cause the design current to swell. In the 1980s and 1990s, the architectural debate was brought to a head by the antagonistic positions taken by neo-modernistic architecture (as expressed by the Hoogpoort project and De Geyter's project) on the one hand, and the neo-rationalistic approach on the other. The latter builds on the Italian and French morphotypological tradition, as expressed in later designs by A.R.A.U. The experience of the modern, in this design series, clashes with a yearning for a "normal" town.

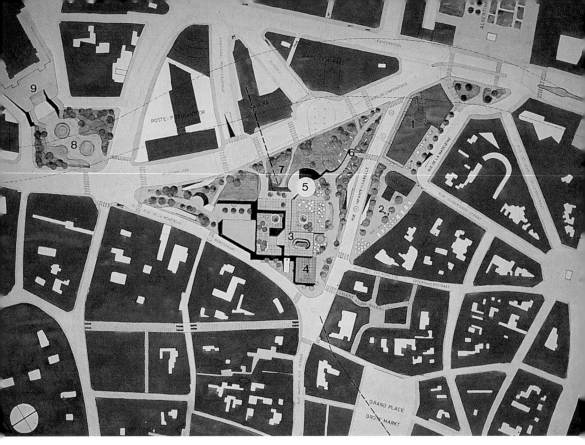

1

2

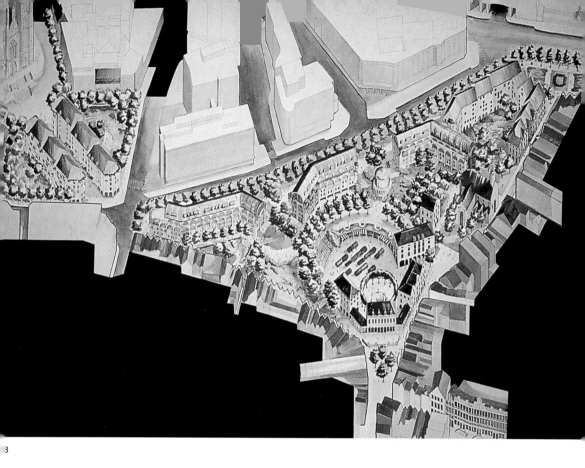

3

1 & 2. Project for the layout of the Carrefour de l'Europe (A.R.A.U., 1969)
3. Project for the layout of the Carrefour de l'Europe (A.R.A.U., 1976)

4

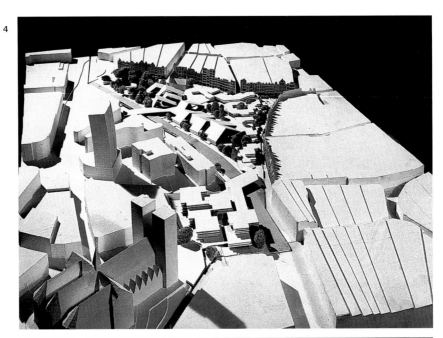

5

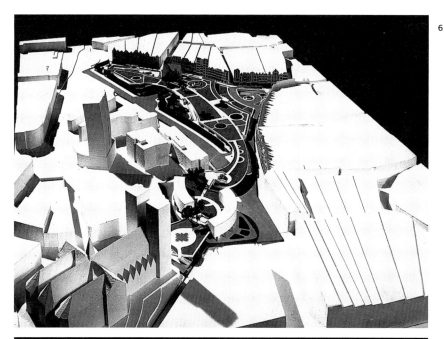

6

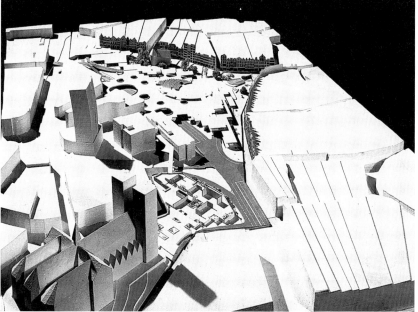

7

Project for the layout of the Carrefour de l'Europe, competition of the City of Brussels, 1970 **4.** Ausia **5.** Group Planning **6.** Jacques Dupuis **7.** Bizet

8 & 9. Project for the layout of the Carrefour de l'Europe, Bonduelle Competition (Team Hoogpoort: Stéphane Beel, Xaveer De Geyter, Willem-Jan Neutelings & Arjan Karsenberg, 1983)

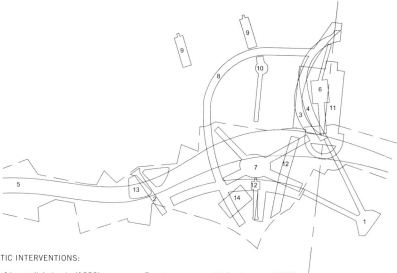

SUPERPOSITION OF URBANISTIC INTERVENTIONS:

1. Place St. Jean and layout of two radial streets (1850)
2. axis in front of cathedral (1894)
3. project for junction by Maquet (1889)
4. layout of Rue Coudenberg
   (project by Maquet partly reduced) (1890)
5. construction of north-south railway junction (1903-1954)
   with accompanying demolitions
6. temporary layout of Mont des Arts garden by Vacherot (1905)

7. temporary road infrastructure (1910)
8. realisation of Maquet junction between upper and lower city
9. continuation of park grid (1911)
10. Galerie Ravenstein (1954)
11. Mont des Arts layout (1954)
12. temporary layout of Carrefour de l'Europe (1958)
13. Place St. Gudule (1960)
14. layout of Place d'Espagne (1986)

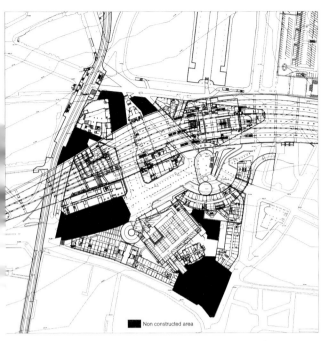

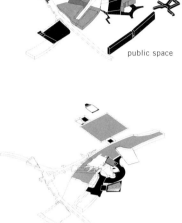

public space

congress

x-ray of existing situation (black = non-constructed area)

n our proposal the solitary, existing buildings and the unexploited underground melt together with new program and infrastructure into a super block, with the Central Station as a pounding heart. Inside the block, we reduce the public space to a chain of - both existing and new - urban rooms.

The transformation bases on hyper-realistic starting points:
  Keeping all the built elements intact, regardless of their architectural quality or style, and accept them as an economic reality. They will be recycled n the conglomerate.
  A series of archaic urban prescriptions about protected views - for example view from the royal palace – determine the possible building envelope.

The project is a big-scale but limited intervention; we add a new object to the city. Around the block, we propose three new gardens, horizontal surfaces that cut in the sloping plane and thus give additional access to the infrastructure below it.

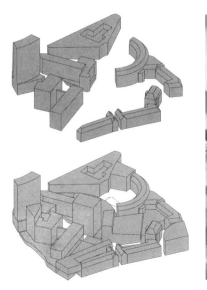

). Project for the Carrefour de l'Europe, competition of the City of Brussels (Xaveer De Geyter Architecten, 1997)

Rotunda, Gare Cer

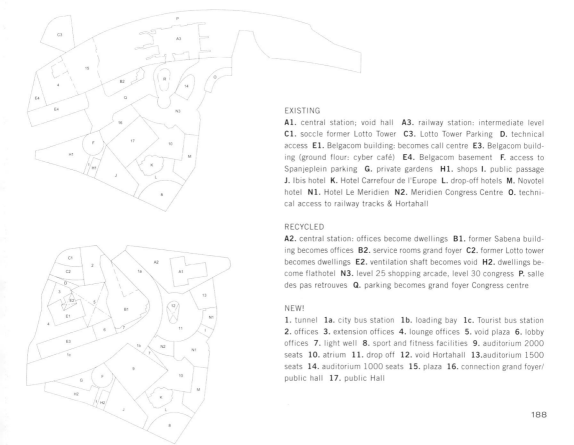

EXISTING

A1. central station; void hall   **A3.** railway station: intermediate level
C1. soccle former Lotto Tower   **C3.** Lotto Tower Parking   **D.** technical
access   **E1.** Belgacom building: becomes call centre   **E3.** Belgacom building (ground flour: cyber café)   **E4.** Belgacom basement   **F.** access to
Spanjeplein parking   **G.** private gardens   **H1.** shops   **I.** public passage
J. Ibis hotel   **K.** Hotel Carrefour de l'Europe   **L.** drop-off hotels   **M.** Novotel
hotel   **N1.** Hotel Le Meridien   **N2.** Meridien Congress Centre   **O.** technical access to railway tracks & Hortahall

RECYCLED

A2. central station: offices become dwellings   **B1.** former Sabena building becomes offices   **B2.** service rooms grand foyer   **C2.** former Lotto tower
becomes dwellings   **E2.** ventilation shaft becomes void   **H2.** dwellings become flathotel   **N3.** level 25 shopping arcade, level 30 congress   **P.** salle
des pas retrouves   **Q.** parking becomes grand foyer Congress centre

NEW!

1. tunnel   **1a.** city bus station   **1b.** loading bay   **1c.** Tourist bus station
2. offices   **3.** extension offices   **4.** lounge offices   **5.** void plaza   **6.** lobby
offices   **7.** light well   **8.** sport and fitness facilities   **9.** auditorium 2000
seats   **10.** atrium   **11.** drop off   **12.** void Hortahall   **13.** auditorium 1500
seats   **14.** auditorium 1000 seats   **15.** plaza   **16.** connection grand foyer/
public hall   **17.** public Hall

THE STATE OF THE ARTS

THE MONT DES ARTS AS TERRAIN VAGUE?

THE MATERIAL AND SEMANTIC EROSION OF
A REPRESENTATIVE "BELGIAN" SPACE[1]

Dieter De Clercq

The terrain vague as an analytical instrument

The Mont des Arts is a constituent of the collective memory of the Belgian state. After all, the slope between the Lower Town and the Upper Town in Brussels derives its character and identity from the exceptionally high concentration of national cultural institutions and monumental buildings that were constructed in the shadow of the Palais Royale. In addition, more recent programmes and functions (mainly infrastructure and offices) have nestled close to these palaces, libraries, archives and museums and have contributed to the representative character of this space.

However, at the time of further construction of the Mont des Arts – with a view to the 1958 World Fair – the symbols that were to embody the Belgian nation had already lost momentum. This politico-ideological shift is primarily characterised by the empty space on the Mont des Arts, that developed around the north-south underground rail link and that was never completely filled. The representative value of this central location has been further eroded by the simultaneous processes of globalisation (with Brussels as the capital of the European Union) and on-going federalisation (the increased autonomy of Flanders and Wallonia). There are signs of this, not only in the partial or total neglect of the architectural heritage, but also in the shift of the Mont des Arts from a central place to a peripheral transit area, together with the corresponding new uses and meanings of the public space.

In the light of the material and semantic erosion of this "Belgian" space, perhaps a good description of the actual condition of the Mont des Arts is offered by the term *terrain vague* (vacant lot). The Catalonian architectural theoretician Ignasi de Solà-Morales describes a *terrain vague* by summing up its different aspects and manifestations: "Areas abandoned by industry, by the railways, by the ports; areas abandoned as a consequence of violence, the withdrawal of residential or commercial activity, the deterioration of the built fabric; residual spaces on the banks of the rivers, rubbish dumps, quarries; areas under-utilized because they are cut off by motorways, areas on the fringes of housing developments that are closed in on themselves, with access tightly restricted for putative reasons of safety and protection."[2]

These strange spaces usually fall outside the operational circuits or operative structures of the city, or they have become unproductive residual areas. Disused 19th century infrastructure and undefined interstitial spaces in the postwar periphery are the most obvious examples of this kind of urban void.[3] Ignasi de Solà-Morales uses the term *vague* to refer to places, territories or buildings that share the double condition of vacancy (emptiness) and indefiniteness (vagueness): "On the one hand, *vague* has the sense of vacant, void, devoid of activity, unproductive, in many cases obsolete; on the other, *vague* has the sense of imprecise, undefined, vague, without fixed limits, with no clear future in sight."[4] Referring to the French noun *vague* (wave) – the symbol of movement, instability or fluctuation – he also points out the urban potential of the void.

1. This essay is based on my analysis of the Mont des Arts within the framework of the research project "Architecture, dwelling, discourse," carried out by OSA (Onderzoeksgroep Stedelijkheid en Architectuur) of the K.U.Leuven.

2. Ignasi de Solà-Morales, "Present and Futures. Architecture in Cities," in Ignasi de Solà-Morales, Xavier Costa (eds), *Present and Futures. Architecture in Cities* (Barcelona: UIA, 1996), p. 23.

3. For a discussion of the urban void see, e.g., Kristiaan Borret, "The 'Void' as a Productive Concept for Urban Public Space," in The Ghent Urban Studies Team, *The Urban Condition: Space, Community, and Self in the Contemporary Metropolis* (Rotterdam: 010 Publishers, 1999), pp. 236-251.

4. de Solà-Morales, ibidem.

A comparison of the Mont des Arts with the list of unproductive spaces de Solà-Morales displays as *terrains vagues* is somewhat far-fetched at first sight. The Mont des Arts is not vacant, but is characterised by an accumulation of infrastructure (whether operational or not) and of cultural institutions and offices. Nevertheless, the public space on the Mont des Arts does display a striking resemblance to the more canonical examples of residual or interstitial spaces. These are not formal affinities so much as the kind of interaction between the material infrastructure and the public space as shown in the present day use and experience of the urban space. This essay focuses primarily on the unexpected meeting between the splendid grandeur of the site and the disruptive character of the everyday (unplanned uses and revealing changes of meaning). It can thus be seen that the term *vague* – in its triple sense of vague, vacant and wave – is instrumental for an analysis of the public space of the Mont des Arts from a present-day point of view and within the wider framework of a changing public sphere.

The peripheral condition of the Mont des Arts

The proliferation of historical architectural styles and the accumulation of infrastructure on the Mont des Arts almost automatically oblige the observer to analyse the site from the perspective of historical transformation. Morpho-typological analysis is one of the most appropriate methods for mapping transformations of this kind. Applications of this method offer insight into the physical structure and "geological" layers of a place. They make clear that the successive spatial interventions on the Mont des Arts were almost all determined by strategic interventions to guarantee circulation and visibility (the visual axis on the Lower Town).

Since the independence of Belgium in 1830, the far-reaching destruction of the urban fabric and the accumulation of infrastructure have predominated over the reuse and reorganisation of the existing space. This *tabula rasa* in stages has weakened rather than strengthened the spatial unity of the Mont des Arts. The coherent structure was swept away and broken up at several times, resulting in countless spots and residual spaces without a clear function. Through the superposition of a few strategic spatial interventions – which largely ignore or even cancel one another out – the Mont des Arts has acquired the character of a peripheral, fragmented space in spite of the classical style of several of the buildings and squares. New networks, such as those of the inner city motorway and the underground train and metro links, have disrupted the formal layout of the Mont des Arts and created a number of undefined interstitial spaces. The formless character of these left-over spaces and the lack of spatial coherence rapidly produce an effect of disorientation on the average visitor. This is due not only to the contrast between representative spaces and informal residual ones, but also to the contrast between spaces above and below ground level. Many of the underground spaces not only contrast with the more representative space above ground level, but they also have an ambiguous status of their own: when seen from below they are above ground level, while when seen from above they are underground. A network of underground corridors has become surrounded by an intricate complex of spaces, with partly new programmes (car parks, conference rooms and archives), and partly residual products of the planned infrastructural elements (such as the space below the Ravenstein viaduct and the intermediate plat-form of the Gare Centrale).

Car park below the Rue Ravenstein,
Palais des Beaux-Arts, 1930s

The accumulation of spatial interventions on the Mont des Arts has led not only to fragmentation but also to the ongoing erosion of the existing urban tissue. Comparison of the figure ground plan of the 19th century neighbourhoods Terarken, Isabella and Putterie with today's brings out the drastic "dilution" of the fabric. For decades the whole area between Le Botanique and the cathedral looked like a dis-astrous *terrain vague* as the result of infrastructural interventions such as the construction of the Maquet Curve and the underground north-south rail link. The filling in of the gaps in the 1950s did not essen-tially change that situation very much. A few isolated buildings were added to the eastern side of the Boulevard de l'Impératrice – the "boulevard" above ground that covers the railway – with mainly Belgian programmes (Gare Centrale, Sabena and Telex buildings). These detached, inward-looking containers occupy an entire build-ing block. The morphological degradation of the block – traditionally characterised by its division into front and rear, a formal exterior and an informal interior – gave rise to an undefined residual space between the isolated containers. This (public) space is mainly occu-pied by parked cars and buses.

Rotunda, Gare Centrale

Rue du Cardinal Mercier

Place de la Justice

The Rue du Cardinal Mercier, located between the former Sabena and Telex buildings, is the most extreme example of this. Closed to through traffic at both ends, this street now functions exclusively as a kind of tourist coach terminal. The relatively closed character of the side walls of the adjacent modernist buildings – whose expressive façade looks down on the Lower Town – contributes to determining the peripheral character of this interstitial space. On the western side of the Boulevard de l'Impératrice – the so-called Carrefour de l'Europe – there was for a long time an even larger parking area, an urban void *avant-la-lettre*.[5] In the mid-1980s this empty space was turned into an underground car park and a more or less continuous row of hotels. What is supposed to be the Place d'Espagne is a dilapidated residual space where temporary infrastructure is erected for occasional performances and events. The peripheral character of the Place de la Justice is determined by the viaduct of the Boulevard de l'Impératrice, which spans the middle of what used to be a significant square. It is now abruptly broken up, provides access to various public and private car parks, and is filled with parked vehicles, graffiti, autonomous signs and a series of huge billboards – the only ones on the Mont des Arts.

The construction of the north-south railway link played an important role in replacing the unplanned medieval city – with its so-called slums – by a modern city, though equally unplanned. The infrastructure created a *tabula rasa*, but there were hardly any signs of a clear-cut vision for the reconstruction. As a result of the *ad hoc* filling in of the vacant areas, the Mont des Arts became a peripheral empty space in which older and more recent buildings appear as "islands." The above-mentioned interstitial spaces along the Boulevard de la Jonction – the rail route followed by the Boulevards de l'Empereur, de l'Impératrice, de Berlaimont and de Pacheco – are just a few examples that illustrate the peripheral condition of the public space of the Mont des Arts.

Some of the names of the boulevards, streets, and squares (such as the Boulevard de l'Impératrice, the Putterie or the Place de la Justice) still recall their original meaning or public function, but they have become empty signifiers. They do not play a clearly recognisable role for the city dwellers, they offer hardly any opportunities for public contact and they are not meeting places. They are used in a primarily functional way by a fairly diverse group of passers-by. The hopelessly fragmented, "empty" space between isolated objects is crossed by the tens of thousands of "foreigners" who are released from and swallowed up by the Gare Centrale every day. Other groups who really do frequent the Mont des Arts are relatively invisible (researchers, employees in cultural institutions) or are associated with this kind of casual station locality (homeless, tramps, skaters).

The Mont des Arts has primarily become a transit area that has gradually lost its former public function. The Place Royale is in essence the incarnation of this transformation of the public space on the Mont des Arts. Today the square is a roundabout for motorised traffic. The few articulations that do exist in the Place are almost exclusively aimed at the smooth circulation of that traffic. Commuters, tourists and museum visitors rush by this "non-place" – a term borrowed from the anthropologist Marc Augé, who defines "non-places" as those spaces that are necessary for transporting people (motorways, railways, airports, transfer areas), large distribution centres (shopping malls and arcades), entertainment parks, hotel chains, and the entire electronic network of cyberspace.[6] Augé sees these "non-places" as opposite to the "anthropological" place: the place that has acquired meaning through human activities, the spot where relations between people take place which are also visible in the space. Because of their lack of interaction and confrontation, the public spaces on the Mont des Arts also deserve the label of "non-places." Strangely enough the individual programmes (museums, archives, conference rooms, offices) do not in themselves offer any opportunities for the emergence of an intersubjective space to modulate or break open these "non-places."

The physical and mental vacancies
on the Mont des Arts

In recognising the indefinite, peripheral character of the public space on the Mont des Arts, we have distinguished a first meaning of the *terrain vague*. A second property that Ignasi de Solà-Morales attributes to the *terrain vague* is the emptiness or vacancy of the space in terms of both its physical (material) and mental aspect (concerning content). Thanks to the absence of activity, the loss of its original meaning or the change in its status, the vacant space often has a liberating poten-

5. See also Bruno De Meulder, "The restructuring of Belgian station environs: a present state of affairs," in *Facetten* no 4 (1999), p. 11.

6. Marc Augé, *Non-lieux. Introduction à une anthropologie de la surmodernité* (Paris: Seuil, 1992).

tial. For some city dwellers – such as photographers and artists, as well as youngsters, subcultures or marginal groups – these areas form "the privileged sites of identity, of encounters between present and past, at the same time as they offer themselves as the last uncontaminated redoubt in which to exercise the liberty of the individual or the small group."[7] Wastelands, parking areas, and undefined residual spaces often prove to be an ideal breeding ground for new practices and uses. The specificity of the urban *terrains vagues* is revealed in the unexpected or unplanned everyday – such as the use of the space as a place in which to meet, live, rest, consume or stage a performance. They constantly acquire changing meanings because users keep on reorganising and reinterpreting them.

The three main squares and parks on or on the borders of the Mont des Arts – the Parc Royale, the Place Royale and the Jardin de l'Albertine – are surrounded by uniform architecture with a symbolic content. The adjoining buildings mainly house national institutions of a political, financial or cultural nature. Taken as a whole, they represent an important part of the collective memory of the Belgian state. Container-like administrative buildings were erected along the Boulevard de l'Impératrice in the 1950s for what Francis Strauven already referred to in 1976 as "strange organs of a centralistically dreamed [Belgian] state:" the headquarters of national corporations (the Sabena airline, the RTT telecommunications corporation), the Banque Nationale, the Bibliothèque Royale, and the Gare Centrale.[8]

However, as the sum of the Belgian state's programmes the Mont des Arts remained a premature concept. On the one hand, the free space was not completely filled with national institutions, while on the other hand, the former headquarters and institutions increasingly degenerated to the status of subsidiary branches and empty boxes. The delegation of national powers to Flanders and Wallonia has brought about a drastic devaluation of Belgian symbols such as the royal family and the political and cultural institutions. Besides, most of the national corporations and banks have been privatised and/or are in the hands of foreign investors. With the globalisation and the unification of Europe, the ideological erosion of the Mont des Arts is being stepped up. The programmatic profile of the Mont des Arts thereby becomes more and more detached from the spatial

Goods entrance, Galerie Ravenstein

and historical centrality of the site. The declining national importance of the institutions present there and the loss of centrality affect
the representative value of the Mont des Arts.

Other public spaces on the Mont des Arts are also in a condition
of semantic ambiguity. This can be seen not only from the vacancy
and neglect of a part of the architectural heritage, the obscurity of
entrances and the absence of routing and signs, but also from the
occupation of the space by marginal groups and subcultures such as
the homeless, tramps, drug dealers, breakdancers, and skaters. The
"blurred" and mentally vacant space is reappropriated by these different groups in small fragments. Their relatively permanent presence as "residents" is in sharp contrast to the casual contact that
commuters, tourists, visitors to conferences or to the library and
museums make with the spot.

The skaters and breakdancers are driven out of the Gare Centrale
and the metro tunnels, but they nestle in their immediate surroundings: in the Galerie Ravenstein or the Place de l'Albertine.
These unplanned "meeting places" determine the atmosphere of
the place to a large extent. The breakdancers contribute to the disco
ambiance in the Galerie Ravenstein. Young skaters occupy the steps
of the Place de l'Albertine without participating in the cultural, administrative or economic activity that goes on in the surrounding
buildings. Unlike the temporary engagement of passers-by – that
does not require a stable or territorial appropriation of the space –
they leave sediment in the form of graffiti, or they make use of
objets trouvés (paving stones, traffic bollards, etc.). Moreover, they
appropriate a part of the (vacant) urban space, without emphati-
cally dominating it. Although different subcultures and marginal
groups meet – by chance or not – in or around the Jardin de
l'Albertine, this does not mean that their presence crystallises as a
critical urban practice or a (spatial) form of social protest. They
implicitly disrupt the representative character of the urban space by
a form of "active" recuperation or "consumption." Skaters, drug
dealers and tramps use the space that is defined elsewhere and by
other people. These practices of "expropriation" can be seen as tactics which, deliberately or not, disrupt the network of the calcu-
lated strategies followed by designers and power blocks (planners,
architects, institutions, authorities).[9]

7. de Solà-Morales, ibidem.

8. Francis Strauven, "Urban transformations of the inner city of Brussels
since the end of the 18th century," in
Wonen-TA/BK no. 15/16 (August 1976),
p. 11.

9. According to the French sociologist
Michel de Certeau, subversive practices
or tactics are characterised by inventive
activity or the creative appropriation of
predefined places. People who fall outside the authorities or the official bodies
do not have their "own" (proper) places
at their disposal, but only the appropriated space of the city. See Michel de
Certeau, *L'invention du quotidien*,
I. Arts de faire (Paris: Gallimard, 1990).

Jardin de l'Albertine

Galerie Ravenstein

Besides the degrees of mental freedom, more obvious, physical vacancies can be distinguished on the Mont des Arts in the numerous empty shops and offices. The surplus office space (Shell building, Generali building, Galerie Ravenstein) is due not only to the ideological shift outlined above, but also to the "peripheral" position of the Mont des Arts vis-à-vis the centre of gravity of office development in the eastern part of the city. The commercial apparatus that is almost entirely empty throughout the whole area can be seen as a silent witness to the lively commercial zone that the Montagne de la Cour used to be. The Montagne de la Cour was the meeting place for the well-to-do, where most of the luxury stores in Brussels were situated. However, the steep slope of this street had to make way for the curved route of the Coudenberg to ensure a smoother traffic link between the Upper and the Lower Town. The historical trade route between England and Germany, to which the Montagne de la Cour belonged, was further interrupted by the construction of the underground north-south rail link. The Mont des Arts emerged as a commercial vacuum between the up-market shops in the Upper Town (Avenue de la Toison d'Or, Avenue Louise) and the cheaper chain stores in the Lower Town. The numerous travel agents that are still located on the Mont des Arts are probably related to the Gare Centrale and the former Sabena headquarters next to it. The Mont des Arts also has a few music shops – a spin-off from the Palais des Beaux-Arts. However, the presence of different cultural institutions close to one another hardly generates any synergy. Nor have the numerous cultural institutions spawned an intricate network of restaurants, bars, shops and art galleries. Shops and catering establishments that are not directly connected with the station are closed or empty.

The hub of public life on the Mont des Arts is situated in the underground pedestrian corridors of the Gare Centrale. The station space itself has been transformed from a prestigious vestibule to a common transit area with many marginal functions and activities, such as (hidden) prostitution and cheap bars. The neighbouring Galerie Ravenstein, is now a seamless extension of the station and shares the same characteristics. The former bourgeois shopping arcade has gradually turned into a commuter corridor, with the accompanying tramps and homeless, flashing neon signs and drifting litter. The commuter flow gave rise to an economic micro-system of shops, snack bars and cafés. Commercial spaces that lie off the beaten track of passers-by – mainly on the upper floor of the rotunda – are empty or fall back on their interiors. Breakdancers and tramps take over this part of the public space or set up permanently there. The material emptiness of the arcade is accompanied by a shift in meaning (from shopping arcade to commuter corridor), creating new functions and forms of appropriation. Moreover, the physical emptiness of the nearby underground spaces (the intermediate platform of the Gare Centrale, the space beneath the Ravenstein viaduct) offers real opportunities for redevelopment.

Galerie Ravenstein

Recycling the terrain vague: a new wave?

A contemporary analysis of the public space on the Mont des Arts reveals not only the peripheral character but also the physical and mental vacancies (material emptiness and empty signifiers) of this residual urban space. By taking into account the different functions and programmes that are still active on this site, however, we become conscious of the latent strength of the Mont des Arts as an urban void. The third meaning of the French word *vague* – "wave" – refers precisely to the urban potential of these kinds of indefinite and vacant residual spaces. According to de Solà-Morales, the relation between the absence of use or activity and the sense of freedom and expectation is an essential aspect of the suggestive force of the urban *terrains vagues*. In this sense the Mont des Arts can be regarded as a true *terrain vague* in the heart of the city – as an inactive, interstitial space that can be (re)charged, transformed or recycled.

The potential of the urban *terrain vague* lies partly in the fact that it reflects the impact of the new conditioning factors (globalisation, networking, etc.). These factors are usually presented in a negative light, based on the idea that the city is no longer the centre of concentration, interaction and centrality. On the one hand, we can recognise in the city a centrifugal, exogenous force towards the periphery, in which new commercial activities, services, residential and administrative districts are situated. On the other hand, however, we also recognise a centripetal, endogenous force that is aimed at the historical city centre and the interstitial spaces or urban voids it contains. The potential of the Mont des Arts lies in the possible

Firemen's entrance, Gare Centrale

linking of the two processes, which could lead to interesting connections between the local and the global networks of economic,
social and cultural development. The physical and mental degree of
freedom associated with the shift that we can detect in the area
today can be deployed – together with the flows that are present –
to create a new dynamism on the Mont des Arts: *a new wave.*

The scattered urban fragments on the Mont des Arts can probably
be reactivated merely by targeted design interventions to create an
exciting synthesis. On the one hand, the qualitative and liberating
aspects of emptiness and absence can be retained and given content
through a programmatic development of the margins. On the other
hand, there is the option of bombarding the site with volume and
transforming the residual space into effective urban space. The project of the Hoogpoort Team (1983) and the recent project of Xaveer
De Geyter (1997-1998) for the Carrefour de l'Europe are perhaps the
most emblematic examples of these two, apparently antagonistic design strategies. Fullness and urban congestion are set against the
qualitative aspects of emptiness and absence of the *terrain vague*. Both
design strategies, however, draw on the metropolitan potential of the
site and the latent strength of hidden mechanical streamling of the
rail and metro system, which in turn generates significant flows.
However, this supposed potential of the Mont des Arts is not reinforced by its use in the present. That is why it is not enough to
design or cover over the urban void; new programmes have to be
developed, alternative scenarios have to be devised, and – perhaps
most important of all – a new meaning for the Mont des Arts has to
be discovered. The ideological shift of the site and the changing
nature of its users (the appearance of all kinds of subcultures on the
Mont des Arts) are just as much a part of the job of design today.

COUNTER-ARRANGEMENT

PRACTICES AND MEANINGS IN
THE PUBLIC SPACES OF THE MONT DES ARTS

Tom Avermaete

"A stronghold of culture," "a cold and inhospitable place," "a fantastic platform for the arts," "a great example of ill-considered Brusselization," "an ugly place:" these are just some of the many polyphonous descriptions of Brussels Mont des Arts.

Throughout the centuries, architects and urban developers have devised countless concepts and projects meant to give a clear identity to this place on the hill. The head-strong superposition and juxtaposition of infrastructure, buildings and plazas is the result of numerous intentional historical interventions. Yet, as with other urban places, the ultimate meaning of the Mont des Arts stems from the tension between what was planned and what is. The elements that generate this tension are clearly the buildings, monuments, and public spaces, but even more so the practices of the users: residents, visitors, passers-by. The way they identify the Mont des Arts, the actions they perform, and the daily paths they travel on the hill create meaning. Throughout routes, rhythms, and routines, this meaning is reiterated and continually reaffirmed.

The Mont des Arts differs from other urban places in that the large number of uses it generates and accumulates does not result in a clear-cut definition. The fact that the Mont des Arts is imbued with meaning through the practices of commuters, tourists, conference visitors, skaters, and breakdancers rather than through the everyday routines of the average Brussels resident seems to be of prime importance here. In the city's collective memory, the place has hardly any semantic charge. Inhabitants of the city have difficulty locating and pointing out the Mont des Arts. In their stories, the Mont des Arts is always an "other" space that seems to defy any descriptive perspective; a "contradictory" place that seems to challenge every symbolic network of references.[1]

1. This text is based on the research project "Architecture, dwelling, discourse," carried out by the OSA (Onderzoeksgroep Stedelijkheid en Architectuur) of the K.U. Leuven.

2. N., *Bruxelles. Le Guide Autrement*, (Paris, 1997).

Junction of "other" spaces

One of the reasons for the Mont des Arts' "other" or "contradictory" character can doubtless be found in its specific semantic strata. The Mont des Arts forms part of practices and spaces that simultaneously generate meaning on both urban and supra-urban scale levels.

The role that the Mont des Arts plays for the masses of tourists who visit Brussels every day is a clear example. Leafing through a number of Brussels' travel guides indicates that for the tourist the Mont des Arts is one of the most important elements in an imploded urban space of axes and dots. The place is subject to a logic characterised by "monuments," "panoramas," "sights," and "recommended routes." If the travel guide sees the city as a collection of fragments, then the Mont des Arts functions as a vague addition of the Palais Royal, the Jardin de l'Albertine, and the Musées Royaux, or even as the sum of the individual cultural institutions at the site. If the geographical categories of Upper Town and Lower Town are applied, then it disappears into the melting pot of the Upper Town's sights. When the Mont des Arts is occasionally listed as part of the Quartier Royal or the Quartier des Palais, then it is usually annexed to "the classical city with its palaces and museums."[2] As a spatial or conceptual entity, the Mont des Arts scarcely appears to exist in the universe of the tourist.

Rue Mont des Arts

However, as a platform that physically and perceptibly stretches out between the Lower and the Upper Town, the Mont des Arts has an instrumental role in regard to the various travel guides' dual

Parking entrance, Place de la Justice, 1959

ambition: on the one hand, the description of the material city and the history of Brussels, and on the other, the need to present an organised image of the city so that the most important sights can be visited within the predetermined time frame. Thus the panorama of "Brussels seen from the Mont des Arts" is one of the most frequently recurring images in tourist guides, and often functions as an introduction to the texts or a description of a walk.[3] On the urban scale level, the Mont des Arts is for the tourists an operational place, an urban space that allows for orientation both in as well as about the city. It is rather an instrument, a tool, than a carrier of meaning. Yet, at the same time, it is also the place through which thousands of tourists enter and leave the city every day.[4] During the daytime, the streets and left-over spaces next to the Sabena building and along the Jardin de l'Albertine become parking lots where tourist buses stop. Groups of tourists are dropped off for a quick tour of the old city, after which they continue at full trot to Bruges, Antwerp or Ghent. On a national scale, the Mont des Arts nestles amongst a network of sights and gets meaning as a gateway into or out of Brussels' inner city.

Not only for the tourists does the Mont des Arts unify meanings on a double scale. For significant numbers of urban visitors, it is a space that mediates between a regional and an urban scale. Indeed, the Mont des Arts has played a key role within the practices of Brussels' automobile drivers since the 1950s. At the time, when the demand and quest for parking spaces became one of the primordial concerns of urban life, the Mont des Arts turned out to be a *montes auri*: a perfect receptacle for fossilised mobility. Parking lots were designed, enlarged, and then redesigned. Streets were retraced, and footpaths were increasingly narrowed to create parking spaces for cars and tourist buses. However, the most important manoeuvre was the "opening" of the Mont des Arts in the late 1950s: in the hollow under the Jardin de l'Albertine and its adjacent buildings, car parks were built that transformed the site into a gigantic downtown supergarage with more than 1.000 short-term parking spaces.

As the main parking lot in one of the economic, administrative, and cultural centres of the country, the Mont des Arts today seems to impart a suburban notion of the public sphere. The mass of cars on, and especially in, the Mont des Arts should no longer be considered symbols of advancing modernity, but rather the prolongation of the intimate and autonomous sphere of suburbia into the historical city centre. Today the Mont des Arts acquires meaning within a logic of deferring the confrontation with the often imaginary uncanny characteristics of urban life. Only in the middle of the city, in the car parks of the Mont des Arts, is the intimacy of the car briefly exchanged for the notional "stress and chaos" of Brussels' public life – notional because nowadays, as a result of the increasing tendency towards "museification", public space in the historical city centre seems to have more to do with the "encapsulated" space of the car than it does with the rhythm of unplanned or confusing encounters, events, and confrontations. The interior of the Mont des Arts thus becomes a kind of "transition space," a place where the intimate (not to be confused with the private) is momentarily exchanged for superficial contact with the public – on the way to the Bibliothèque Royale, the Palais des Congrès, the headquarters of a bank or insurance company, or the shops downtown.

The place also bridges over the differences in atmosphere and scale for the 60.000 commuters who stream in and out of Brussels every day via the Mont des Arts' underground rail connections (train and metro).[5] For many civil servants, bureaucrats and clerks, the Mont des Arts is the space through which they daily reach the city of executive boards, banks, multinational corporations and lobby groups. For them, the place is primarily a passageway; part of a regional circulation network that connects the suburban home to the urban workplace.

3. See Charlotte Smets, Annelies Veys, *De Kunstberg. Een reflectie in toeristische gidsen* (unpublished paper, Leuven, 2000).

4. 2.2 million tourists visit Brussels every year (1998/2000 NIS).

5. The conurbation of Brussels accounts for the lion's share of the commuter activity in Belgium. Every day, 300.000 commuters from outside the conurbation come to work in the capital. Some 70% of the commuters choose to travel by car. See, for example: Axel Florijn, "Gemiddeld 37 minuten van huis naar werk. Pendelaars trotseren files" in *Het Nieuwsblad* (18 March 1998).

Commuters, Gare Centrale

However, the practices of commuters illustrate above all how daily routines and actions not only occur in the built environment, but how these actions also engrave themselves in the urban public spaces and, to a certain extent, actively shape the urban environment. The Galerie Ravenstein, connected to the Gare Centrale's corridor network via an underground entrance, is a salient example. Established in 1958 to promote Belgian design, over the decades it has slowly but surely conformed to the logic of the commuters. The shops that used to sell the best of modern Belgian design have now been converted into cheap sandwich bars, candy shops, and cafés that focus exclusively on the commuter, shutting their doors at night and during the weekends. The commuter's practice have transformed the Galerie Ravenstein, like other public spaces on the Mont des Arts, into a passageway between home and city, and in a certain sense into part of a network space. The Mont des Arts thus becomes one of the places where the transition between the regional and the urban scale, between the domestic world of the home and productive world of work, takes shape in a fixed sequence.

That this sequence has its own time frame, one that has hardly anything to do with the tempo of everyday life in the city, strikingly illustrates that not only the experience of space, but also the experience of time is exceptional on the Mont des Arts. The sequence of the train commuter is experienced as work time, i.e. time that must be used effectively and kept as brief as possible. As part of the timed journey between home and work, the Mont des Arts represents a pure race against the clock for the commuter. The banal character that the place assumes as a result of this, is underscored by the commuters via alienated statements such as "We're just passing through" or "We're only walking by," and by their classification of this sequence as useless or lost time, in contrast to the personal and meaningful time of domestic life.

Opposed to the commuter's compressed experience of time, there is the infinite time that one encounters visiting the Mont des Arts' museums, archives, and libraries. As exponents of a 19th century Western culture, these institutions embody one of the most important fantasies of modernity: the will to bring together all times and periods in one single place. They are created as places in which time constantly accumulates, and yet which can simultaneously withstand the ravages of time. They stand as infinite accumulations of time and material that never intend to disappear.

Inclusion and exclusion

The accumulation of time and material manifests itself on the Mont des Arts through a dual motion of inclusion and exclusion. As places that attempt to include a representative sample of the daily Belgian knowledge and culture production within their walls – the library, for example, collects every Belgian publication, ranging from popular magazines to scientific books – museums, archives, and the library withdraw these objects from the everyday. This dual motion irrefutably contributes to the contradictory nature of the Mont des Arts' public status. This manifests itself in the way that public institutions, such as the museums and the library are only open and accessible to those who hold a ticket. For other significant groups of citizens, these institutions are closed boxes which keep their none the less public information hidden and which fail to enter into any relationship with their urban public realm. This contradictory approach to the public sphere does not, by the way, seem to characterise the "public" institutions of the Mont des Arts exclusively, but also extends to its urban public spaces. As a site that consists for a large part of public spaces, the Mont des Arts is indeed a physically accessible space – the Jardin de l'Albertine and the Galerie Ravenstein, for example, are ideal crossings between the Upper and Lower Town – though on the symbolic level this turns out to be hardly the case. Inhabitants of Brussels do not engage in any emotional relationship with these public spaces: in the city's collective memory, the Mont des Arts is an off-limits island.

The best example of this kind of simultaneous accessibility and impenetrability is perhaps offered by the Palais des Congrès, which was constructed in 1958 when Brussels briefly became the centre of the world. The public role, within an international space, that the Mont des Arts momentarily played during that year's World's Fair – a good 600 conferences were held that year – still exists. Contemporary Brussels claims a prominent place on the global ranking of international conference cities, and even comes before London and New York in this regard.[6] With its total capacity of 7.000 participants, the Palais des Congrès is one of the most important hosts of

6. The 1995 annual report of the Unie der Internationale Verenigingen reveals that Brussels, in terms of international conferences, takes third place in the global rankings. In that year, 165 conferences were organised. The Belgian capital is only surpassed by Paris (211) and Vienna (175), and is ahead of Geneva (161), London (152) and New York (99).

Exhibition hall and restaurant, Palais des Congrès

major international conferences, organised by Microsoft or the Council of Europe's biomedicine group. The Mont des Arts thereby acquires a cardinal meaning within the "space of flows" of multinational corporations, organisations, and scientific associations. Just like London's Barbican Centre or New York's Jacob K. Javits Centre, it is a meeting place: a point of convergence in the ephemeral and borderless space in which contemporary corporations, organisations and, science operate. Within this border-crossing space, the Mont des Arts is a forum for meeting and discussion, a plateau for exchange of knowledge and information; a true public space, or so one would think.

Yet the character of a point of convergence within a contemporary corporate and scientific space is quite different from that of a true public space. The average conference visitor's "space of flows" consists of transatlantic flights, quick shuttle connections, enclosed hotel lobbies and air-conditioned meeting rooms. With its huge array of "in-house" facilities (private tourist office, restaurants, bar, and telecommunications centre), the Palais des Congrès is but one of these isolated and autonomously functioning spaces. The relationship between the cursory patterns of the conference world and the urban public spaces which are located outside the actual Palais is almost non-existent. Although large conferences of up to 7.000 participants regularly take place, neither the Palais des Congrès nor the conference visitors appear in any clear way in the public spaces of the Mont des Arts, apart from an occasional signpost or advertisement. The public sphere of the Palais des Congrès is an enclosed one, at once accessible and isolated. The conference is a meeting and an exchange involving only equal and like-minded participants. Urban dwellers, who do not meet or can not afford the price of entry, have no voice. The Palais des Congrès is arranged as an exclusive and excluding public space, where contact with the unexpected and unpredictable sides of the urban public realm is anxiously avoided.

Layering of practices: order and deviation
This simultaneous accessibility and isolation is only one of the many interrelated and contradictory aspects of the Mont des Arts. In its perimeter, the Mont des Arts also gathers practices and spaces that one does not easily find bunched together elsewhere in contemporary

urban space. Its specific geography certainly plays a role here. Indeed, it is almost impossible to determine with any certainty the distinction between underground and above ground on the Mont des Arts. Underground passageways, where one imagines oneself many metres beneath the surface, suddenly offer a perspective on the street level of the Boulevard de l'Impératrice. Whether the meeting rooms of the Palais des Congrès are located underground or above ground is completely dependent on whether one enters them via the Coudenberg or via the Jardin de l'Albertine.

This lack of clarity in the relationship between underground and above ground re-echos in the blurring of the distinctions between "low" and "high" culture, between clandestine and legal practices, between haves and have-nots. Upon leaving the metro corridors, for example, the beggars suddenly find themselves under the arcades of the Palais des Congrès and thus on top of Microsoft's annual meeting. A confrontation that would never take place in an international "gated congress resort," is everyday reality here. Upon leaving the conference centre, the white collars unintentionally come into contact with the reverse of their feted logic – the rattling McDonald's cup – or with the challenging tricks of skaters and breakdancers. Yet the fact that confrontations like these are considered unusual and thus undesired here as well is illustrated by a recent ban on skating on the Mont des Arts. The ephemeral and indifferent practice of the conference visitors do not seem to jibe well with the provocative performances of the skaters, who emphasise the "tactile" elements – the materials, textures, and sounds – of the Mont des Arts.

In the juxtaposition and layering of extremely varied, and often contradictory, activities and practices, one of the place's most important "characteristics" comes to the fore: the Mont des Arts simultaneously embodies order and deviance. The Musées Royaux des Beaux-Arts, the Bibliothèque Royale, the Cabinets des Estampes and the Archives Générales du Royaume are products of 19th century rational thinking. They are representations of the nation's rationale and order, of society's right-mindedness. Yet the Mont des Arts has also always been a place of deviance, a place where the dominant order is breached or inverted. In the 1960s, the Boulevard de l'Impératrice was already an important port of call for young toughs parading in their cars. This macho behaviour, adorned with the symbols of the new motorised culture, was not welcome on the street in front of the parental home; it had to take place "somewhere else" or "nowhere" – and thus on the Mont des Arts.[7]

Today, the Mont des Arts is populated by skaters and break-dancers. Since the end of the 1970s, when skating made its entry into Europe, the ashlar platform of the Jardin de l'Albertine has been an important meeting place for the national and international skating scene. On foreign websites,[8] the Mont des Arts is praised as one of the best sites in Europe "to be sessioned," and within Brussels it is certainly one of the favourite gathering places from which people begin their "free riding" into the city. At the beginning of the 1980s, the skaters were joined by the breakdancers.[9] The first official breakdance groups, composed of young immigrants with energetic names like Dynamic Three, Kamikaze Rock and Magical Band, began to form a part of the Mont des Arts public spaces; they appeared in the arcades of the Palais des Congrès, in plazas and on pavements, and in the smoothly tiled Galerie Ravenstein. With pieces of cardboard under their arms and ghetto blasters on their shoulders, they move from place to place. The speed of execution, the physical risks, the flowing succession of figures, and the pulsating rhythms are, for breakdancers and skaters, the appropriate instruments for attracting the attention of the passers-by. For them the Mont des Arts is an urban scene.

The performances of skaters and breakdancers are often disregarded as insignificant rhythms and routines, in which playing the game is all that matters. Yet in the Galerie Ravenstein or on the square in front of the Albertine, skating and breakdancing seem to counterbalance the numerous urban practices that consider the Mont des Arts a functional passageway. Skaters and breakdancers, after all, bring the physical and sensory experience of this place to the fore. With their tricks and movements, they add a physical and tactile component to an urban space in which the public sphere primarily unfolds within the closed and sterile spatial entities of the so-called "public" institutions. Yet this deviant behaviour is not unconditionally tolerated. Because the skaters sound out the limits of the Mont des Arts as urban environment by interpreting and using its architectural elements (stairways, railings, platforms, etc.) in new ways, their actions are frequently repressed. On the occasion of the Europe 2000 football

Jardin de l'Albertine

championship, for example, the city council completely forbid skating on the Mont des Arts, and cameras in the corridors of the metro were used to keep the skaters' aberrant behaviour in check.[10]

Counter-arrangement

The implantation on various scale levels, the specific and multiple temporality, the simultaneous accessibility and isolation, the multi-layered practices and the simultaneous presence of order and deviance all contribute to the designation of the Mont des Arts as an "other" or "contradictory" place. Michel Foucault describes such a place as: "… a sort of place that lies outside all places and yet is actually localisable"[11] and calls them *counter-arrangements*. According to Foucault, the oldest example of the *counter-arrangement* is the garden. The surrealist Réné Magritte seemed to agree when he interpreted the Mont des Arts as a garden in 1958, giving it the title "Mysterious Barricades" to his mural for the lobby of the Palais des Congrès.

In an essay on Magritte's oeuvre, Foucault writes that the surrealist's most important contribution was in shifting "modes of representing through resemblance to similitude." "Resemblance" Foucault suggests "presumes a primary reference that prescribes and classes copies on the basis of the rigor of the mimetic relation to itself. Resemblance serves and is dominated by representation. With similitude, on the other hand, the reference anchor is gone. Things are cast adrift, more or less like one another without any of them being able to claim the privileged status of "model" for the rest. Hierarchy gives way to a series of lateral relations."[12]

This is exactly where the value of the *counter-arrangement* can be found for contemporary city life: the fact that it unites a heterogeneous collection of normally incongruous practices and meanings, without this then resulting in a single unity or order. Instead, the relationship between the various practices and meanings is based on a process of coincidental co-ordination that continually leads to "other" combinations which evade every traditional frame of reference. As such the *counter-arrangement* represents an unprecedented degree of freedom that facilitates alternative ways of ordering the contemporary urban public sphere.

7. See the contribution by Bruno De Meulder on the Carrefour de l'Europe elsewhere in this volume.

8. URLs:
http://www.tumyeto.com/tydu/skatebrd/parks/foreign.html
http://inet.uni2.dk/~t01b02/skateparks/world.htm#be
http://homepages.go.com/~suislide/skateparks.html

9. See Alain Lapiower, *Total Respect. La génération Hip-Hop en Belgique* (Brussels: Evo, 1998).

10. See Michèle Vanderplaetsen, "Skaters in Brussel en Gent zijn boos. Wat weet de burgemeester van opgroeien in een stad," in *De Morgen* (Friday 2 June, 2000) p. 8.

11. Michel Foucault, "Of other spaces: utopias and heterotopias," in Neil Leach (ed.), *Rethinking Architecture. A reader in cultural theory* (London: Routledge, 1997, pp. 350-356), p. 352.

12. Michel Foucault, *This is not a Pipe,* (Berkeley: University of California Press, 1983), pp. 9-10.

CITY WITHOUT

Against a self-evident

PARIS IS NOT ROME. One of Gogol's short stories, Rome, is about a young Roman prince who goes to study in Paris and becomes entranced by the exciting city life that goes on there. "How he stood staring in astonishment, how impossible it was for him to collect his thoughts, when he walked through the streets with their throng of all kinds of people, their pattern of racing buses. He was struck at one moment by a café that dazzled with an unimaginable, princely splendour, and soon afterwards by the famous viaducts, where the muffled thunder of thousands of stamping footsteps, produced by a bustle of almost exclusively young people, which deafened him, and where the sparkling of the shops, indirectly illuminated by the glass ceiling, blinded him. Soon after he stopped in front of the posters that crowded in their millions in motley colours before his eyes to proclaim the 24 daily theatre performances and countless concerts." After the ecstasy comes the sobering up: Gogol shows the young man that the dizzying vitality of Paris is merely "a frivolous vaudeville." Having learnt his lesson, the prince returns to his native Italy, where the rediscovery of the landscape and the ancient monuments, the museums, archives and churches in "eternal Rome" restores in him a spirit of serene seriousness. There was a world of difference between this awareness of the peaceful solemnity of quiet and those nervous impressions with which he had so pointlessly filled his soul in Paris."[1]

Two types of urban life style are contrasted in Gogol's heavily moralising short story. Paris is presented as the capital of modernity, where the dynamic of 19th century capitalism is constantly alive, where life is multi-faceted, active and bustling. Rome is presented as the place of restraint and stasis, where the majestic splendour of history demands an elevated life-style. Paris the ephemeral, Rome the eternal.

While in reality Paris is just as much a historical treasure chamber and it is possible to imagine Roman life as frivolous, it is still worthwhile to consider our notions of city life in the light of Gogol's version. After all, the holding up of Rome as an example of urban life would meet with little approval from most of the well-known

1.   see Gogol "Rome," translated from the Dutch version in *Verzamelde Werken Deel 2* (Amsterdam: Van Oorschoot, 1984), pp. 235-283.

EXCITEMENT

KRISTIAAN BORRET

notion of "real city life"

urban planners of today. In so far as urbanity is still linked to the specific spatial context of the central city and is not regarded as a condition that can also be found elsewhere in the diffuse city, the dominant discourse of urbanism nowadays is much
closer to Gogol's characterisation of Paris as a city packed with modern life, though
without the negative moral connotations that he associates with it.

Generally speaking, we only consider a city to be a city if it has difference, quantity and speed, all interacting to produce a cocktail of conflict. This paradigm of the
modern metropolis as an overdose of stimuli was laid down in Georg Simmel's famous
essay *Die Grosstadt und das Geistesleben* (1903) and the fascination it elicits has been
seen countless times in modernist culture, such as in the collages of Paul Citroen or
in Alfred Döblin's novel *Berlin Alexanderplatz*. Beyond the oscillation between CIAM
functionalism and the successive reaction of neighbourhood renewal policy, the love
of the hectic dynamism of the big city has been explicitly articulated once again with
Rem Koolhaas' idea of urban congestion. At that end of the ideological spectrum of
urban planning, nervous metropolitanism is the way to measure to what extent a location displays the qualities of city life. The call to create maximal urbanism by devising
24-hour systems of programmes to guarantee round-the-clock liveliness is an obses-
sional product of this. But at the conservative end of the spectrum too the conviction
remains unshaken that the city must not be dull anywhere.

Although the movement for the reconstruction of the traditional European city,
which has been very influential in Brussels from the A.R.A.U., does not envisage daz-
zling modernity, it still enthuses about the conviviality of the bourgeois city in which
lively mixing plays an equally important role. What they have in mind is not the anony-
mous nervousness of Gogol's Paris, but the warmth and animation of the pre-industrial
city. However, the reconstruction movement cherishes the harmony of *Gemeinschaft*
and thus rejects the conflict-and-congestion programme of the modern metropolis.

The assumption that "real" city life is equivalent to liveliness has also directed the
criticism of the urban public space. For instance, during the neighborhood renewal
projects, the problem was formulated in terms of sociability: it was regretted that the

streets and squares of the city were no longer automatically a place for social contacts, but were fully determined by functional requirements. The urban society envisaged by this policy of renewal is one of small, sociable, tighty knit communities. In the 1980s criticism of the one-sidedness of building for the neighbourhood led to its replacement by more comprehensive urban renewal programmes that paid more attention to cultural and recreational facilities. To increase the vitality of the city, planners ended up in a reasoning that virtually profiles the city as a tourist product. By now the culture of traffic-free streets, shopping paradises and terraces which followed in the wake of urban revitalisation has reached saturation point in many cities.

The absorption of the city centre by private initiatives in the boom of city entertainment in turn becomes the pretext for a new generation of criticism. The new criticism is formulated in different, political terms and now tackles urban renewal itself. There are fears that the inner city will be nothing but an entertainment centre. After all, the conversion of the city centre into a permanent festival by the commercial and real estate sectors regularly leads to excesses and thereby endangers other aspects of ordinary city life. Commercial activities colonise the public domain of the streets and squares on all sides and attract all of city life to themselves, thereby draining it from other areas. At the same time vitality is often reduced to a form of diversified overabundance and spectacle that is in line with consumerism. In this way the emphasis on the liveliness of the urban public space comes to follow in the footsteps of further commercialisation and "festivalisation" of the city centre. One of the dangers of this reductive logic of vitality is that a space in the city is only called a "public space" if it is an important centre of the urban festivities, in other words if it attracts a crowd.

Meeting people, sociability and liveliness should not be the only framework in which to assess the urban public space. The discussion of public space is concentrated today not so much on the question of whether it is too boring, but of its public-political character.

Representation of a community, fundamental accessibility, freedom of speech, absence of exclusion and possibility of appropriation are qualities that are inherent in the special status of public space. The obsession with liveliness sometimes overshadows an ordinary but extremely fundamental criterium such as public property when we talk about the public character of the city.

So with the notion of city life connotations of fullness, quantity, mixture, diversity often slip into our minds unobserved. The notion of city life – and indirectly the notion of urban public space – is connected in an almost self-evident way with the idea that a city is not attractive if it is not lively. Of course, this is valid to a large extent. But once it becomes reduced to the assumption that what is not lively is not urban either, it degenerates into a fallacy.

That is why we could classify the Mont des Arts at a glance as a place where something is wrong. The Mont des Arts is not so lively because there are no cafés or shops in sight, the surrounding programmes lead a somewhat sleepy or hidden existence, and the interaction between the different publics and user groups is limited. But does that mean that the Mont des Arts is not an urban space? May we never consider a site that is central but quiet, extensive and monotonous as urban? Is it less authentic? Is it not exaggerated to expect "liveliness" at every place and on every scale in the city? Does a public space have to attract a lot of people and events before it can be considered urban? Why does it sound inadequate to call a place public because it houses public institutions that preserve and study the public heritage? Is an urban space problematic if it is primarily used by passers-by? Is urban life necessarily lively, or can it also be serious and restrained? Can we include in our notion of urbanity environments that are regarded as unattractive because they are not very spectacular? Can the Mont des Arts be urban without the need for excitement? Can we not admit a bit of Rome into our Parisian longings for Brussels?

BIBLIOTHÈQUE ROYALE DE BELGIQUE FOUNDED IN 1837. INFRASTRU

READING ROOMS WITH **1.000 SEATS**, SEVERAL MEETING ROOMS AND EXHIBITION HALLS, C.

+/- **4.000.000 WORKS**, ETCHINGS SECTION: **700.000 PIECES**, MEDAL DEPARTMENT: **2**

VERSITY STUDENTS AND RESEARCHERS, MAINLY BELGIAN **AROUND 100.000 VISITORS** A

RESTAURATION, RESEARCH AND COMMUNICATION **MUSÉES ROYAUX DES BEA**

DEPOSITORY: SEVERAL UNDERGROUND LEVELS, CONCERT AND CONFERENCE HALLS **(650 SEATS)**, REA

AND **406 SCULPTURES**, MODERN ART: **5.000 PIECES** (20% EXHIBITED), DEPARTMENT OF DR.

COMPOSED OF TOURISTS (52%) **AROUND 500.000 VISITORS** A YEAR, MAIN EXHIBITIONS **A**

TOURS, WORKSHOPS, COURSES, CONCERTS MISSION: PRESERVATION, RESTAURATION, RESEARCH, COMMU

STRUCTURE INAUGURATED IN THE 1970S. INFRASTRUCTURE: **APPROX. 55 LINEAR KM OF AR**

COLLECTIONS: PUBLIC RECORD, MAPS AND CHARTS, MANUSCRIPTS, ETCHINGS, **100.000 MICROFI**

ACTIVITIES: ON AVERAGE **4 EXHIBITIONS** A YEAR PUBLIC: COMPOSED OF RESEARCHERS AND UNIV

VISITORS PER YEAR. **MISSION:** CONSERVATION, HISTORIC RESEARCH AND COMMUNICATION **MUS**

LAND COMPLETED IN 2000 INFRASTRUCTURE: **11.000 M²** OF WHICH 3.600 M² OF EXHIBITION HALLS, L

PIECES (40 % 'SCHOLARLY' EUROPEAN INSTRUMENTS, 20 % OF 'POPULAR' EUROPEAN INSTRUMENT, 40 %

BITIONS, COMMUNICATION **PALAIS DES BEAUX-ARTS** INAUGURATED IN 1928. I

CONCERT HALL **(2.200 SEATS)**, THEATRE HALL **(165 PLACES)** COUNCIL ROOM **(80 PLACES)**, CHAMBER MUSIC H.

PUBLIC: **400.000 VISITORS** ANNUALLY, MAINLY RESIDENTS OF BRUSSELS MISSION: ARTS

PHILHARMONIQUE, THE SOCIÉTE DES EXPOSITIONS, ETC.). **CINÉMATHÈQUE ROYALE**

DISPERSED OVER SEVERAL LOCATIONS, AMONGST WHICH THE PUBLIC ORIENTED CENTRE IN THE PALAIS DES

AND A EXHIBITION SPACE (100 M²) COLLECTIONS: **41.000 FILM TITLES, 35.000 BOOKS**

PUBLIC: **90.000** TO **100.000 SPECTATORS** A YEAR, MAINLY CINEMA ENTHUSIASTS,

MENTATION AND RESEARCH, COMMUNICATION **PALAIS DES CONGRÈS** FOUNDED I.

ROOMS (RANGING FROM **10 TO 120 SEATS**), EXHIBITION HALLS, POLYVALENT SPACES, CAFETARIA, OFFICES

INGS ANNUALLY PUBLIC: **130.000** TO **180.000 PARTICIPANTS** A YEAR, OF WHICH

based on: F. Mairesse, *Etude descriptive des principaux établissements situés sur le Mont des Arts et ses alentours.* Rapport préparé pour la Fondation Roi Baudouin, Brusse

DEPOSITARY **33.000 M²**, **100 KM OF SHELVING** SPREAD OVER **17 FLOORS**, 15

H PANORAMIC VIEW <u>COLLECTIONS</u>: PRECIOUS RESERVE: **35.000 WORKS**, DEPARTMENT OF PRINTS:

PIECES, MAPS AND CHARTS SECTION: **150.000 PIECES** <u>PUBLIC</u>: LARGELY COMPOSED OF UNI-

.000 READERS <u>ACTIVITIES</u>: **10 EXHIBITIONS** ANNUALLY <u>MISSION</u>: CONSERVATION AND

S DE BELGIQUE FOUNDED 1801. <u>INFRASTRUCTURE</u>: EXHIBITION HALLS: **22.000 M²**

50 SEATS, MUSEUM SHOP <u>COLLECTIONS</u>: ANCIENT ART: **1.641 PAINTINGS** **(50%** EXHIBITED)

000 ITEMS, LIBRARY **275.000 VOLUMES**, **1.500 PERIODICALS** <u>PUBLIC</u>: MAINLY

50.000 VISITORS <u>ACTIVITIES</u>: YEARLY **4 TO 10 EXHIBITIONS**, CONFERENCES, GUIDED

RCHIVES GÉNÉRALES DU ROYAUME FOUNDED IN 1796. ACTUAL INFRA-

READING ROOMS **(100 SEATS)**, DOCUMENTATION CENTRE, LIBRARY, **2 EXHIBITION HALLS** **(300M²)**

L REGISTERS, PRIVATE ARCHIVES OF IMPORTANT BELGIAN COMPANIES, INSTITUTIONS AND PERSONALITIES

NTS, AS WELL AS GENEALOGISTS AND AMATEUR HISTORIANS, **3.500 READERS** AND **20.000**

INSTRUMENTS DE MUSIQUE FOUNDED IN 1877. RECONVERSION OF OLD ENG-

ING READING ROOM, CONCERT HALL, **2** CONFERENCE HALLS **(300 SEATS)**, CAFETARIA. <u>COLLECTION</u>: **6.500**

N INSTRUMENTS) OF WHICH **25%** ARE EXHIBITED, **20.000 BOOKS** <u>MISSION</u>: PRESERVATION, EXHI-

E: **APPROX. 30.000 M²**, EXHIBITION HALLS **(TOTAL 5.000 M²)**, CONFERENCE AND

TAURANT, OFFICES <u>COLLECTIONS</u>: NO <u>ACTIVITIES</u>: THEATRE, EXHIBITIONS, CONCERTS, PUBLIC SALES, ETC.

ACCOMMODATES **15 AFFILIATED ORGANISATIONS** (AMONGST WHICH THE SOCIÉTÉ

GIQUE AND THE **MUSÉE DU CINÉMA** CREATED IN 1938. <u>INFRASTRUCTURE</u>:

HICH CONTAINS **2 AUDITORIA** **(30 SEATS** FOR SILENT MOVIES AND **125 SEATS** FOR SOUND PICTURES)

STAURATION OF **250.000 METERS OF FILM** EACH YEAR, **1.800 SHOWINGS** A YEAR

BSCRIPTIONS A YEAR TO THE PROGRAMME <u>MISSION</u>: PRESERVATION AND RESTAURATION, DOCU-

<u>RUCTURE</u>: SPREAD OVER **3** BUILDINGS AND COMPRISING CONFERENCE HALLS **(1200 AND 270 SEATS)** AND 15

O <u>ACTIVITIES</u>: HOSTING **180 TO 200 NATIONAL AND INTERNATIONAL MEET**-

RS <u>MISSION</u>: PROVIDING CONFERENCE FACILITIES

aserre, *Rapport pour la Fondation Roi Baudouin*, Brussels, november, 1997, *Mont des Arts. From noble summit to artistic heights*, Brussel, Fondation Roi Baudouin, 2000.

HOW PUBLIC ARE THE TEMPLES OF CULTURE ON THE MONT DES ARTS?

Koen Van Synghel

Do the cultural institutions on the Mont des Arts make an active contribution to "normal" urban dynamism? Do they give public space extra functional value or do they behave more like fortresses toward the city? On reflection it seems that the public buildings on the Mont des Arts do not fulfil their public role particularly well.

This piece investigates the way in which the cultural institutions on the Mont des Arts relate collectively to the city, to its public space. It is not concerned with the internal functions of these institutions, but rather with the complex interplay of peripheral programmatic activities which enliven – or paralyse – the Mont des Arts. Even for an ordinary passer-by, the first impression is of a desolate void, the proverbial "metaphysical" void, dominated by introverted architecture. But the architecture, the depressing presence of Ghobert and Houyoux's post-fascist buildings for example, is not the only factor in the dysfunction of the Mont des Arts as part of the city's public space. There is a fundamental programmatic problem, namely the priority given to the archival function. Whereas today the Mont des Arts presents itself as a piece of fallow ground for urban interaction, what it means is that most of its institutions, such as the Archives Générales, the Bibliothèque Royale and the various museums manifest themselves in urban space as treasure chambers.

Bibliothèque Royale

One characteristic intrinsic of a treasure chamber is its defensive character: the treasure must be protected against the ravages of time, climatic conditions and theft. A treasure chamber therefore functions like a safe, a defensive storage place. Not surprisingly therefore the buildings on the Mont des Arts look more like some kind of prisons than open cultural establishments, so that people who live or work inside or outside these "symbolic prisons" are confronted by barriers and inaccessibility conceived in stone. There is nothing wrong with treasure chambers as such. Treasure chambers are fascinating. But while the narcissistic beauty of the Egyptian Pharaohs' pyramids may be an excellent thing in an empty desert landscape, it must be asked whether the treasure chambers of the Mont des Arts can rely on such a simple defence. Have they no social or urban role to fulfil? In other words, can these treasure chambers continue to function simply by virtue of their undoubtedly legitimate internal operations or, as public institutions, must they take part in defining the public space of the Mont des Arts?

There is much to be said for a place of absolute stillness, a place in the city for contemplation, free from destructive urban dynamism, like the eye of a hurricane. But the silence of the Mont des Arts seems to be much more a consequence and confirmation of the void created between the Lower and Upper Towns by the north-south link than a deliberate, tranquil piece of public space bridging the gap between the prosperous residential Upper Town and the Lower Town with its lower class – even volatile – neighbourhoods.

As necessarily defensive treasure chambers the buildings on the Mont des Arts make no contribution to the public scene. Rather they create major problems for openness and interaction with outside public space. The mainly archival role played by the institutions on the Mont des Arts impedes "natural" osmosis between inside and outside, between user and passer-by. It is strange to observe that the weak interaction between inside and outside is not really the fault of any architectural style or expression. For whether one considers Guimard's strictly neo-classical architecture on the Place Royale, or the rather more elegant classicism of the Place du Musée, or the severity of the Bibliothèque Royale and the Palais des Congrès, the Mont des Arts manifests itself as a kind of no man's land between the more vital Lower and Upper Towns. The main problem is the radical boundaries between inside and outside, radical in the sense for example of the high wall that the Bibliothèque Royale has put up along the Jardin de l'Albertine, but radical also in the way that entrances are closed off, and the surreptitious way in which rooms are opened up as museum space. The Bibliothèque Royale possesses exhibition facilities and also organises concerts, but the one-sided concentration on the function of preservation and conservation of the collection prevents its activities from contributing any dynamism to the Mont des Arts. Nonetheless the Bibliothèque Royale, with a total of 1.461 square metres of exhibition facilities (the Nassau Chapel, a great hall at No. 2 and the Salle de Houyoux at the Boulevard de l'Empéreur) plus the meeting rooms which are used as concert halls,

Jardin de l'Albertine

Place du Musée

plus the Musée de l'Imprimerie, the Musée du Livre, the Cabinets des Estampes et des Médailles and the Musée de la Littérature, has great potential for functions which could bring together the use of public space and the defensive conservation work of a library. On the pretext, justified or not, of staff shortage and a lack of means, such public functions achieve neither the atmosphere nor the dynamism required to make the intermediary spaces that are nonetheless provided in the Bibliothèque Royale work properly.

The Appartements de Charles de Lorraine, brought into use last year as a museum of the 18th century, represent an attempt to make a public building function authentically again. The problem however is that these apartments are the only ones still remaining from an ensemble of which only the façades on the Place du Musée have been retained. Consequently the Place du Musée behaves like an enigmatic picture, a lifeless landscape of relics of an eroded urban culture. While the Appartements de Charles de Lorraine attempt to preserve the memory of the original structure of the Palais de Charles de Lorraine, a completely new structure hides behind the other neo-classical façades of the Place du Musée, housing the auditorium and cafeteria of the Musée d'Art Ancien. While the cafeteria, as an informal entrance to the museum, could have "populated" the Place du Musée, today the square serves only as a service entrance for the reception and despatch of works of art. As a result the square gains little vitality, either from the Bibliothèque Royale, or from the Musée Royale, so that the illusory after-image of neo-classical architecture simply implodes into the shining oubliette which is the Musée d'Art Moderne. The absence of any public means that the planned ensemble of the Place du Musée and the Rue du Musée fails because of a surplus of public space.

The emptiness of the Place du Musée has in fact much to do with the lost status of this square. Originally a balustrade separated a part of the square from the semicircular entrance of the Palais de Charles de Lorraine. The Place du Musée was not even a square. Densely planted with trees, it acted as a kind of front garden for the palace. Restoring this situation would at once provide the museum with its own garden and a terrace, which in good weather could be used as a restaurant. When concerts are held in the Protestant church and spectators go out during the interval to get a breath of fresh air in the Place du Musée, one can appreciate how the activities of the cultural institutions on the Mont des Arts could make a positive contribution to the life of the city.

The dysfunction of the Bibliothèque Royale and the Musées Royaux as regards their interaction with the city cannot simply be dismissed as the result of historical mistakes or changing perceptions of the city. The spatial organization and museological arrangement of the collection in the recently opened Musée des Instruments bears witness to a complete denial of urban dynamism. It could be said that the effect of covering up the windows with hackneyed advertising posters has been to force Guimard's building, adjoining the Place Royale, to turn its back on the city. The requirements of conservation – protection against direct sunlight, what one might call the "treasure chamber syndrome" – can not justify the way this public building screens its operations from the outside world. The Musée des Instruments, with its children's studio, concert hall and library, has sufficient functions at its disposal to bridge the gap between it and the casual passer-by and the city at large. But tucking away the concert hall on one of the top floors, like a totally enclosed box, and inserting the library in the centre of the building where no light can reach it, bear witness to a misconception of the way a museum works, to its "urban mission" and furthermore to a misunderstanding of the history of the city; a historical misunderstanding which has to do with the fact that spatially the public sections of the Musée des Instruments can not function autonomously, in the way that for example the monastery church was formerly able to function independently of the monastery.

When it comes to misunderstandings and tampering with history, the Musée de Charles V (formerly the Palais de Charles V) could easily serve as a textbook example of a view of the deterioration of the city, the museum and ultimately the citizen. When the Place Royale was reconstructed last year as part of the renovation of the Tracé Royale, the subterranean ruins of the former ducal palace were opened up as a museum. In opposition to a contemporary view of the city and its history, the whole layout of the Place Royale is a feeble consecration of Guimard's classical layout and an ideological sanctification of a piece of outdated 19th century national history. True to Brussels tradition, the ruins, and thus the new museum, have disappeared underground, roofed over with a concrete slab paved with the inevitable cobblestones. Whereas these ruins could have opened up a secondary route from the Place Royale via the Palais des Beaux-Arts to the Lower Town, the historical site was put under a bell jar so that in some sense what should have been public space was privatised for interested tourists. Neither the city, the museum nor history are brought up here: all were sacrificed for the sake of simplistic satisfaction for tourists.

The impact of the Palais des Beaux-Arts and the Palais des Congrès on the Mont des Arts is of a totally different order. After all, for both institutions the main consideration is not the collection but the public. They have more in common than one might at first sight suspect. Functionally speaking, the Palais des Beaux-Arts and the Palais des Congrès play complementary roles. While in the strict sense of the word the Palais des Beaux-Arts is a "palace" or "home of the arts," the Palais des Congrès has facilities for conferences, offices, exhibitions and parking.

Over the years, as a result of the expansionary increase in the number of associations it houses, the Palais des Beaux-Arts has become strangled by a network of offices and other administrative functions. Not surprisingly, administrative functions have taken over space originally intended for exhibitions. Even the Musée du Cinéma is housed in rooms which were conceived by Victor Horta as exhibition halls. The entire operation of the Musée du Cinéma – that as a treasure chamber of the seventh art also sees its main task as archiving and conserving – has been put in hock for a crying lack of space and above all of suitable working space. And this while the Palais des Congrès and the Galerie Ravenstein still have free office space available. Structurally the Palais des Beaux-Arts and the Palais des Congrès are in fact connected with one another at the intersection of the Rue des Sols with the Rue Ravenstein which runs above it. Certainly therefore co-operation between the two complexes is not impeded by spatial barriers.

The Palais des Beaux-Arts can in fact be seen as Victor Horta's declaration of the function of the entire Mont des Arts, namely the bringing together of different disciplines, such as visual art, applied art, music, film, and theatre, in a single "home for the arts." However the enormous number of offices which have taken over space in the

Palais today foil one of Horta's crucial principles, namely that, like the Galerie Ravenstein, the building should function as a public forum and piece of the urban fabric. In contrast with the Palais des Beaux-Arts, the Palais des Congrès succeeds much less consistently in determining the character of the Mont des Arts. Despite its immense amount of space and the high rate of occupancy, the Palais des Congrès suffers from a lack of identity. The major part of its activities are underground, while the hybrid monumental architecture of the Palais de la Dynastie, of which it is also part, is misleading and certainly not the kind of architecture to suggest a conference centre. An extremely hybrid situation arises at the precise point where the Palais des Congrès cautiously emerges above ground, at the site of the cafeteria. A lack of clarity in the demarcation between public urban space and the privatised public space of the Palais des Congrès has made the terrace unusable. The interaction between the foyer of the Palais des Congrès and the Jardin de l'Albertine is every bit as problematic, largely because of the barrier created by the fountain located on the central axis.

One intriguing thing is that the need for space has encouraged the Palais des Congrès to make different use of the underground car park. Part of the space is used as an exhibition hall. During the Book Fair even larger parts are taken over as exhibition space. This is however very clumsily done: the rough, unfinished architectural language of the car park was neither sublimated nor exploited but instead subjected to ineffective attempts at camouflage.

Exhibition hall, Palais des Congrès

It will certainly take more than just a spatial master plan to get work started on any changes to the Mont des Arts; undoubtedly inter-active, interdisciplinary planning will be required. A possible moti-vation may be found in the problems common to most institutions, namely lack of space, problems of expansion and the need for mod-ernisation. For years now the Palais des Congrès has been dreaming of an extra hall capable of housing 2.000 people; the Bibliothèque Royale expects within three or four years to have used up all its available storage space; the museums are reserving ground on the Montagne de la Cour for extension and virtually all the institutions are struggling with the problem of digitising their collections.

However, apart from these spatial and practical problems, another – possibly more fundamental – problem shows itself. The Mont des Arts is mainly occupied by institutions linked with Belgium as a national state. But since the 1960s Belgium has been a state in disso-lution. The institutions on the Mont des Arts form part of the few remaining national institutions still under federal jurisdiction. But even here federalism is making its presence felt. For example, feder-alisation has influenced the partial removal of the national archives to Leuven and Louvain-la-Neuve. The Bibliothèque Royale is already experiencing competition from the recently opened and better equipped (certainly in terms of computer equipment) library of the Université Libre de Bruxelles. It is now considering plans to move its newspaper archives, which take up two storeys of storage space. Thus, the Mont des Arts has to deal with a state that is becoming increas-ingly federal and the implosion of national institutions. At the same time the attraction of the periphery (Leuven / Louvain-la-Neuve) is making itself felt by the way collections are being withdrawn.

The challenge presented by the Mont des Arts is to find a way to short-circuit the spatial problems between the different institutions and to turn them round into win-win situations. The battle for space on the Mont des Arts is now carried on by the institutions individ-ually, while neither the state nor the region has the authority, or can obtain it as the responsible party, to organise the development, in the general interest, of a comprehensive plan for the Mont des Arts. It should be borne in mind that during an investigation into the location of an "art and research centre" in Brussels, the nearby Gare Centrale was proposed by the collective DTN as a real, physical centre.

It is not this programmatic statement that is important, but the conviction that a building like the Gare Centrale plays a crucial role in the viability of the Mont des Arts. It is after all a fact that any intervention of significance in the Mont des Arts, such as a hall for 2.000 people or an extension to the exhibition facilities, would be quite out of proportion to the need to modernise the Gare Centrale. There are well-known nightmare scenarios for what would happen if a train ever caught fire in the Gare Centrale. The Mont des Arts would in any case benefit from better accessibility and an upgrading of the station, certainly if the Mont des Arts, besides its cultural role, could, who knows, one day become a place for people to live and work. The problems of the Mont des Arts can therefore certainly not be approached, let alone solved, merely from the point of view of the hill's art and culture. Is the question "Can art save the world?"[1] after all nothing more than a clever piece of rhetoric?

1. Slogan used in the poster campaign for "Antwerp '93, Cultural Capital of Europe."

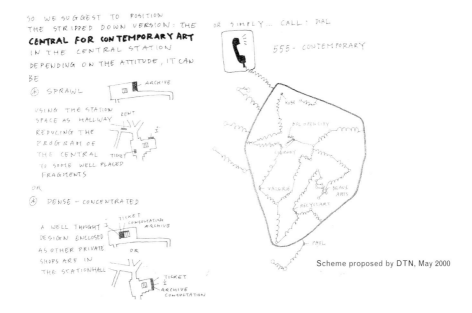

Scheme proposed by DTN, May 2000

THE VANISHI

Sophie C. De Schaepdrijver

Some places never change. Undisturbed by the turmoil of the world, they always remain the same. This kind of stasis (whether you regard it as a musty or a blessed state) is not the result of a deliberate choice, but of an honest failure to perceive any need for change.

The General Reading Room of the Bibliothèque Royale in Brussels is such a place. As a callow student I spent many somewhat absurd days there on compiling bibliographies. The cohort to which I belong has been saddled with a lifelong bibliographical fetishism as a result: after all those years, the sight of a tray of faded index cards still makes shivers of desire run through our bodies. A Freudian would no doubt label this emotional state as "anally retentive," but we consider ourselves as real experts.

So the Library – let us call it the Albertine to keep up appearances. More specifically, the general section, the big reading room, the card catalogue drawers, the shelves with national bio- and bibliographies, the counter where you wait for the books you have ordered. Practically none of all that has changed in the last 20 years. To order a book you still have the quaintly longwinded business of filling in a slip in triplicate (you have to indicate the dimensions – quarto, octavo... – of the work you want). The computer catalogue still covers only a part of the collection, so that you have to fall back on the venerable card catalogue drawers. My favourite is the thematic one: the impossibility of ever grasping the raison d'être of its classification makes research a celebration of seren-dipity. Only a pedant complains about the system. And after all those years you still see the same familiar faces: staff who entered the Albertina in the remote past of their years of service, their eyes focused on the coffee break and commuter train, who spend their days in complete aloofness from their surroundings, shifting the books back and forth like

ALBERTINE

unmarked packages. (I hasten to explain that this does not apply to the staff in this general reading room, for there are laudable exceptions.)

The half-hearted digitisation of the Albertine's books forces the reader to resort to traditional and pleasurable search methods – the physical visit to the library, the card catalogue drawers, the tangible book. But at least you can do that in the Albertine without attracting attention. The New York Public Library, on the other hand, seems to be gradually turning into a cybercafé. And that is a pity, because the NYPL is a wonderful temple of stately Beaux-Arts architecture in midtown Manhattan, erected thanks to the liberal gifts of famous plutocrats. Their credo was simplistic but touching: you can become anything in the USA. No one will ask to see your pedigree or diploma. Just go to the library. It is free, accessible, and has every book in the world. Read a Good Book and share the legacy of humanity!

Homeless people thirsting for literature are still allowed into the NYPL, but a lot has changed in the last few years. Part of the reading room is now earmarked for digital consultation: row after row of happy netsurfers behind their screens. We are assured that this is the future: pop into the NYPL and link up with the whole world! Of course, that is a nice idea, provided it is stripped of any hype. A library with 50 million books, periodicals, maps, musical scores, etc. is already linked to the whole world, there is no need for little toys, and certainly not when they block the view of what the place itself has in stock. After all, you can surf at home. You go to the Very Big Library precisely for what you can find there and nowhere else. Oh, the digital hype, source of so many futile efforts – and despite all the superficial differences, closely akin to bibliographical fetishism. It all diverts us from our true goal: go to the library. Read a book. Repeat the operation. And buy a book once in a while.

The full version of this text was published in *De Standaard*, 10-12 June 2000.

ART AND CULTURE ON THE MONT DES ARTS
A DESCENT AND AN ASCENT

Koen Brams and Dirk Pültau

Musée d'Art Ancien

As in most parts of urban space, work is also carried out on the site of the Mont des Arts. This essay focuses on one of the main activities on the Mont des Arts: the production of art and culture. We take this to mean all of the ideas, actions, statements or presentations that take place on the Mont des Arts, and which – in so far as they are at least accessible to the public – have an effect on the functioning of the public domain. Production thus includes the purchase of a book, the presentation of an author's oeuvre, the projection of the photographs of a royal wedding, the playing of a musical instrument, or the display of a royal bureau in a plexibox. We confine our remarks grosso modo to those activities connected with the field of the visual arts between 1995 and 1999. What does work in this field consist of and what results has it produced?

To get a clear picture of the answer to these questions, we draw two circles around the symbolic centre par excellence, the statue of Godefroi de Bouillon on top of the hill. The first circle contains those institutions that are literally on top of the Mont des Arts in the immediate vicinity of the Place Royale: the Musées Royaux des Beaux-Arts, the Musée des Instruments, the Palais des Beaux-Arts, the Musée du Cinéma, the Palais des Congrès, the Bibliothèque Royale, the Archives Générales du Royaume, and the Musée de la Dynastie. The second circle has less institutional weight; on the slopes of the Mont des Arts we find art galleries, cafés, restaurants, and the headquarters of a few important corporations such as Fortis.

The unification of the Mont des Arts

The two major institutions on the Mont des Arts connected with the visual arts are the Palais des Beaux-Arts, where the Société des Expositions (the Association for Exhibitions) is active, and the Musées Royaux des Beaux-Arts. While the Palais is a *Kunsthalle*-type building, the Musées Royaux constitute a fine arts museum. A similar situation can be found in Rotterdam – the Kunsthal and the neighbouring Museum Boijmans-Van Beuningen – or in the arrangement of the Kunsthalle and the Kunstsammlung around Grabbeplatz in Düsseldorf.

The combined collections of the Musées Royaux des Beaux-Arts cover the period from the 14th to the 20th century.[1] This is the most representative historical art collection in Belgium. The Musée d'Art Ancien includes not only an impressive collection of masters from the Southern Netherlands, but also, for example, a respectable collection of Northern Netherlands art from the 17th century, as well as German, French and Italian art. The later section begins majestically with David's revolutionary *Assassination of Marat* (1793). As far as modern art is concerned, however, the Musée d'Art Moderne lost the thread early on. Today it can only present a good overview of Belgian production, with the Magritte collection as its showpiece, the largest public collection of this artist in the world. The Musées Royaux des Beaux-Arts did not start collecting recent international art until 1990, when the embarrassing regional acquisitions policy was replaced by carefully selected, high-quality acquisitions, primarily from oeuvres which can be placed historically around the end of the 1960s. The *pièce de résistance* in this attempt to catch up is a collection of works by Marcel Broodthaers.

However, these acquisitions can hardly be called "contemporary." They do not indicate a form of participation in a debate on present-day artistic production, because they are purchased precisely because they are regarded as "already historical."

The Société des Expositions of the Palais des Beaux-Arts does not have a collection; it concentrates exclusively on organising exhibitions. The Société has a large exhibition area at its disposal, but because of the shortage of funds one-third of this area is rented to an auction house. In the remaining space the Société organises retrospective and thematic exhibitions (in the "main circuit") and presents recent art (in the Antichambres). Almost every exhibition held during the last five years has been on a 20th century subject. The last exhibition on the old masters was *I Fiamminghi a Roma 1508-1608, artists from the Netherlands and the Principality of Liège in Rome during the Renaissance* (1995).

During the last few years the Société des Expositions has made efforts to try out alternative exhibition models and to offer material for reflection. The projects of Ilya Kabakov and Hermann Pitz were invitations to reflect on the exhibition as a medium. Another initiative, *Loss of Memory, Responsibility and Collaboration*, was an extremely

1. See also our "Hedendaagse strekkingen in de Koninklijke: -8 - De collectie van de KMSKB," in *De Witte Raaf* no. 54 (March-April 1995), pp. 21-24.

Musée d'Art Ancien

problematical but well-considered attempt to present the work of a photographer and collaborator in an alternative way. However, the Société's programme is constantly disrupted by the activities of ex-ternal associations. For instance, the Société des Antiquaires rents out all of the available space every year to an art and antiques fair, the Europalia Foundation takes over the "main circuit" for two months every year, and the exhibition route is filled once every two years with an edition of the Prix de la Jeune Peinture Belge, a co-production by the foundation of that name and the Société. All these uniformly disastrous events make it virtually impossible for the Société des Expositions to develop a coherent exhibition policy, though the Société is partly to blame too. The presentation of the award winners of the Prix de la Jeune Peinture Belge is based on voluntary co-operation. Moreover, as we shall see, there are times when the Société even fills its main circuit in a rather frivolous way, and the programme for the Antichambres has been adrift for the last few years.

Before going into the policy of the two major arts institutes in more detail, let us first explore the rest of the Mont des Arts. Near the statue of Godefroi de Bouillon on the Place Royale we come across the BBL Cultural Centre, which belongs to a bank. It has organised exhibitions such as *Late Gothic Art from Bohemia, Moravia and Silesia 1400-1550*, or *In the Shadow of Babel. The Art of the Ancient Near East in Belgian Collections*. The BBL has also organised exhibitions of estab-lished modern artists and canonised art movements (Baselitz, Minimal Art, etc.) in its main building in the eastern district of the city. A few galleries with a contemporary exhibition policy appear to have fled from the Mont des Arts. The Galerie Albert Baronian in the Rue Villa Hermosa organised exhibitions by Hermann Pitz, Ricardo Brey, Patrick Corillon and others, but in the mid-1990s he moved to Kanaal 20, a complex of art spaces and galleries on the edge of the Brussels Pentagon. His former upstairs neighbour in the Rue Villa Hermosa, the Galerie Isy Brachot, stayed put but changed policy drastically. For a couple of years it was practically Brachot's avantgarde branch. It showed the archi-tect and artist Luc Deleu and the young artist Chohreh Feyzdjou, while canonised artists like Magritte, Beuys and Broodthaers were usually presented in Brachot's other space in the Avenue Louise. Today the gallery in the Rue Villa Hermosa functions almost exclusively to show the work of a single established Belgian artist: Panamarenko. Another gallery on the Coudenberg, *Les Maîtres de Formes Contemporains*, which specialised in multiples and editions by Sol LeWitt, David Tremlett and others, has closed down. Michèle Didier, the driving force behind *Les Maîtres*, is continuing her activity in another part of Brussels. Marie-Puck Broodthaers organised interesting exhibitions by artists like James Coleman, Rombouts & Droste and Joëlle Tuerlinckx in the *Galerie des Beaux-Arts* in the Rue Ravenstein, opposite the entrance to the Palais, but the gallery has had to make way for a sandwich bar and Broodthaers now organises exhibitions in a space in the Upper Town. Finally, the *Box* has disappeared, a display and arts space which was used by the Société des Expositions and for which young artists could make proposals.

Are there any active galleries left? We have to go down to the bottom of the Mont des Arts before we can find any galleries devoted to contemporary art, such as Galerie Velge & Noirhomme and Galerie Willy D'Huysser. There is only one striking newcomer in the second circle, the Espace Méridien in the Marché aux Herbes, the recent branch of Encore... Bruxelles, a foundation set up by Joël Benzakin and Michèle Lachowski, who used to be active in Kanaal 20. Encore... Bruxelles recently organised an exhibition by Daniel Buren.

Wherever we find ourselves as we ascend and descend the Mont des Arts, the conclusion is that this site offers a place for lively contemporary cultural production less than ever. The galleries that used to present young artists and invited major foreign artists have moved elsewhere in Brussels. The commercial activity connected with contemporary art has virtually come to a standstill. The second circle around the institutional heart of the Mont des Arts is barely distinguishable from the first. As a result, the Mont des Arts is more than ever a heavy socle for the classic, 19th century representative institutions. There are a few small art shops between the Palais and the Musées that sell kitsch versions of canonical art, but their relation to the institutions on the Mont des Arts is like that of the CD shops to concerts in the Palais des Beaux-Arts. It is as though nothing has a chance of surviving on this site, except as a relic or hobbyist's version of the sacrosanct cultural heritage.

The top of the Mont des Arts

In order to arrive at a more thoroughly based estimate of the nature and quality of the activities on the Mont des Arts, let us return to the top. What constants can be found in the programme of the two major art institutes?

Receptivity

The first point to emerge from the exhibition programmes of the institutes on the Mont des Arts is an extremely receptive attitude. This can be taken literally in the case of the Société des Expositions of the Palais des Beaux-Arts. In the past five years the Société has organised a couple of interesting productions of its own, such as the project *On the roof* by Ilya Kabakov in the main space, and a number of smaller presentations in the antichambres (Hermann Pitz, Victor Grippo, Chantal Akerman, Patrick Vanden Eynde, Franciska Lambrechts), but the Palais still functioned predominantly as a temporary stopping place for exhibitions that had been put together somewhere else, such as the solo presentations of the works of August Sander, Karl Blossfeldt, Jan Vercruysse and Andy Warhol and the thematic exhibition *Austria im Rosennetz*.

The Musées Royaux adopt a very passive attitude towards current models or conventions of exhibiting. The question of which specific approach is called for by a particular topic or an individual oeuvre is seldom raised. They automatically fall back on classic solutions, such as the monographic exhibition, preferably arranged chronologically. The receptive attitude can also be seen from the fact that the exhibition policy is simply dictated by the date of birth or death of well-known Belgian "modern artists." This led to the large-scale and dull retrospectives *Paul Delvaux* (1897-1994) in 1997, *René Magritte* (1898-1967) in 1998, and *James Ensor* (1860-1949) in 1999. The Palais also presented large-scale exhibitions of artists who called for an approach which took the qualities and weaknesses of the work on show more into account. The oeuvres of Alberto Burri and Roy Lichtenstein, for example, are based on a limited number of procedures. The passe-partout model of the "major retrospective" by which the Société allowed itself to be seduced in both cases automatically leads to endless repetition. The qualities of the oeuvres concerned were brought down to the same level, while a different form of presentation or the integration of works in a thematic exhibition could have brought out the qualities of these oeuvres clearly.

Historicism

When the Musées Royaux set up a separate section for modern masters around the middle of the 19th century, the distinction between "old" and "modern" was fixed by means of a date: 1801, the year of the foundation of the museum. Modern was what was produced after that date, old was what was produced before it. According to this principle, the Empire showpiece *Mars disarmed by Venus*, a late work by David, would belong in the modern section, while the *Assassination of Marat*, one of the three works that David dedicated to the martyrs of the Revolution, would have to be relegated to the "old masters" section. The year 1801 is no longer the benchmark for the museum, but the attitude towards history and the present has not grown much more dialectical. The most recent part of the collection is now displayed on the lowest level of the underground museum, level minus 8. The amorphous label "contemporary tendencies" has been devised for it, and these "tendencies" are presented as the last stage in a development spanning six centuries, a final "art historical period." Level minus 8 consists mainly of work by a generation of artists whose roots go back to the late 1960s and early 1970s – the most recent acquisitions included works by On Kawara, Carl Andre, Joseph Kosuth, and Robert Barry. As mentioned earlier, they are the result of a spectacular improvement in the acquisitions policy since the 1990s.

It is thus not what the museum purchases that is problematical, nor is there anything wrong with the fact that the purchases are confined to older work. The problem is in the arguments behind this option and how the art works are treated. Whether it is a "Bouts" or a "Broodthaers," the museum only handles art which it sees as no longer requiring any "handling." Everything fits into the rigid corset of a parade of historical art. Neither the old masters nor modern art prompt reflection today; the works are simply deposited in the vault of history. The museum justifies this historicising policy by referring to its role in the art world. It does not consider its duty to participate in the active formation of opinion, which is why it buys work that "has already proven its worth." The museum guards what has acquired its place in history. But what work has ever achieved that? Being "historical" is not an objective quality. History takes place in the dialectical field of tension between what we call "now" and "before," and that applies just as well to venerable art historical museums. The stuffy historicism of the Musées Royaux is the incarnation of the *cliché suprême* of a historical classic art museum. The dream is of an ahistorical gaze that looks upon art history as a static panorama. It is difficult not to recognise this sovereign immobility in other facets of the policy of the Musées Royaux, such as in the retrospective exhibitions of Delvaux, Magritte and Ensor. The security of a chronological scheme sidestepped any interpretative discourse. The commentary in these exhibitions consisted mainly of quotations from the artist; any other discursive intervention was studiously avoided. So apart from arranging the loans and copying his master's voice, the Musées Royaux did not do very much work at all.

Nationalism

The Musées Royaux have a solid Ensor collection, own the largest public collection of Magritte in the world, and are working single-mindedly on building up what is already an excellent Broodthaers collection. If we compare the collection policy with the last three monographic exhibitions, the question arises of whether the profile of the Musées Royaux should just be labelled Belgian. Are the Musées Royaux not simply trying to match a cliché of what it means to be Belgian? After all, it is not by chance that in particular the names mentioned above are cited again and again as the incarnation of the Belgian touch, based on so-called literary quality, middle-class irony, double-entendre, and so on. The intellectual poverty of the exhibitions made it easy to see them as part of a hero cult. In this sense, the Musées Royaux play their role of bourgeois temple of the arts on the acropolis of Belgian culture in a very servile way.

Elsewhere on the Mont des Arts this nationalistic reflex has its counterpart in the Europalia events that are organised in the Palais. Europalia showcases a different country each year. The support of the King and Queen guarantees an extremely conservative and representative approach. The Société des Expositions has also been caught in the nationalist trap. For instance, it cooperated with an exhibition on Dutch art because of the Dutch presidency of the European Union, and presented *Austria im Rosennetz*, an exhibition that accompanied the Austrian presidency artistically with the necessary mystifications concerning the national identity of the country in question. All of these opportunistic and ill-conceived events were reflections of the 19th century notions of nationality that are incarnated in an almost exemplary manner on the Mont des Arts.

Academic activity

What about the academic output of the institutions? The academic bulletin of the Musées Royaux (*Bulletin des Musées Royaux des Beaux-Arts de Belgique/Bulletin van de Koninklijke Musea voor Schone Kunsten van België*) is published once every two years, though with a time-lag that is characteristic of this institution: the latest bulletin, for the years 1992 and 1993, was only published in 1997, so that strictly speaking it is impossible to obtain a picture of what was being done between 1994 and 1999. The bulletin includes the list of acquisitions and of the exhibitions in which the institution participated or which it organised, as well as several essays – six in the latest issue. Sometimes there is a direct relation with the collection, but at other times that link is less obvious. There is no general theme, and no general discursive purpose. Typically, the bulletin has no introduction. It is a compilation of articles, producing the impression that its primary function is to legitimate the academic status of the institution.

It is unlikely that many of the catalogues and other publications produced by the Musées Royaux or the Palais to accompany the large-scale exhibitions will serve as works of reference. The exceptions are the publications of the Société des Expositions for *Fiamminghi a Roma* and for the exhibition on the Antwerp gallery *Wide White Space*, and the second volume of the catalogue of Dutch Old Masters published by the Musées Royaux.

Nor are the Musées Royaux the site of lively discussions of content or methodological debates. Apart from the occasional positive exception, the programme of lectures for adults is pedantic and conventional. The themes vary from Symbolism to Impressionism, just as we were taught at school. The Société des Expositions is one of the few organisers, even in Belgium, that does encourage debate now and then. An exhibition in the Palais is usually accompanied by a discursive programme – a lecture, a debate, a colloquium. For instance, *The Art of Collecting*, a presentation of Dutch art in connection with the Dutch presidence of the European Union, was accompanied by discussions of Flemish and Dutch collection and presentation policy.

The blockbuster

It is clear that the institutions on the Mont des Arts have paid more attention to their literal, financial input than to their substantial output during the last few years. There is even an inverse relation between the two. The institutions have not only discovered the blessing of the blockbuster, but they have also learned how to make deals. The Société des Expositions did a deal with the Paribas Bank (now Artesia) for *Art in the Bank, a selection from Rubens to Magritte*. The three retrospectives in the Musées Royaux received generous support from local corporations. The Genérale de Banque – which has been taken over by Fortis in the meantime – used the Magritte retrospective to celebrate its own anniversary in style. The only trend that the institutions share with the contemporary world of art is in the field of marketing policy.

La Belgique and its echo

The Mont des Arts is an acropolis of art and law. It is a location that the nation sets up to represent itself – literally with the Palais de la Nation (the Belgian Parliament), symbolically with the Musées Royaux and the various cultural institutions. In this sense it is hardly surprising that the art trade can barely stay alive here. The Belgian nation is in a profound state of decomposition. There is no longer any official place for Belgian sentiments. They are only allowed to appear in muted form as long as there is no suggestion of a political message: in the Stade Roi Baudouin, for example, or on the Mont des Arts, where famous Belgians are secretly celebrated as national heroes. The art dealers who were able to exploit the prestigious site of the Mont des Arts for decades were the first to realise that the Belgian label of quality is no longer good for trade. They moved out.

So the Mont des Arts has become the exclusive playground of national institutions. These institutions confirm what the Mont des Arts represents. The programme that fills the rooms echoes with the illusions of the Mont des Arts. There is nothing problematic about that, but what is problematic is the fact that the same institutions show no signs of consciously reflecting on what attaches significance to this site. They merely display a slavish subservience to the Mont des Arts. The Mont des Arts must not become a hive of artistic activity; the institutions that are active there need only be aware of their historical symbolism. If the Musée des Instruments planned a concert for its opening weekend on 10 and 11 June 2000 with the title *Festive Music at the time of the Brabant Revolution*, no one could accuse it of idle nationalism. The Mont des Arts resonates in this concert programme, but the difference is that this echo is heard here openly. It is a thematisation of the Mont des Arts.

The Musées Royaux also have a large number of works that copy the symbolic politics of the Mont des Arts – take the works of Louis Gallait and above all Gustave Wappers, especially his *Episode during the Belgian Revolt of 1830 in the Grand'Place, Brussels* (1835). This replication should be turned into something productive. It is precisely because the Musées Royaux and the Mont des Arts are so exemplary of everything connected with the classic cultural concept of the 19th century Belgian state that they can form the site where these concepts, ideas and representations are thematised. The symbolic weight of the Mont des Arts should be made the object of study and reflection. At the present time this intellectual legacy is only lethargically confirmed or concealed behind façades of academic seriousness.

There is only one institution on the Mont des Arts that cannot be accused of unconscious conformism or façadism: the Musée de la Dynastie. It is deliberately conformist, and hides nothing behind its façade because it is nothing more than a façade. The homage paid to the Belgian royal family by the Musée de la Dynastie is not surreptitious, but vivacious and freshly polished. It makes no secret of the fact that it is the open celebration of the Mont des Arts. This museum is therefore the most interesting place on the Mont des Arts. The other institutions can learn from it. The Mont des Arts must develop an unfortunate awareness of what this museum so naively and jauntily puts on a pedestal.

MUSEUM AND CITY:
ELEMENTS OF REFLECTION

THE MONT DES ARTS AS A RUIN IN THE REVANCHIST CITY

A MANIFESTO FOR BENIGN NEGLECT[1]

Erik Swyngedouw

Musings over the present condition and future potential of the Mont des Arts are inevitably framed against the backdrop of apparently similar practices and conditions elsewhere. I shall begin by considering how recent experiences with museum- or spectacle-based regeneration in London provides a powerful example of how the museum of the 21st century is made operational. This will be used as an entry to reflect critically on the contemporary urban condition and ease our way into setting out the beacons through which the case of Brussels and its Mont des Arts will be broached. Both the contradictions of the current late-capitalist form of spectacular urbanisation and the particular configurations of the Brussels case will be explored. I shall conclude that the actual development of urbanity in Brussels really takes place far beyond the confines of the Mont des Arts. The recent attention to this site is rather the result of the particular Belgian nature of the place, combined with a systematic lack of vision on the part of the local regional-national political, economic, and cultural elites. The political, cultural, and economic configurations of Brussels are more likely to lead to a development of the Mont des Arts as a museum of a national experiment, comparable to the Mall in Washington, DC, rather than to the spectacular developments that characterise most contemporary populist urban emblematic projects.

The city as museum: cultural strategies in a revanchist city

A few months ago, the Tate Modern opened its doors on London's South Bank and met with immediate critical and public acclaim. Long queues meandered along the landscaped gardens and visitors queued patiently in the drizzling rain to get a glimpse of what the new cosmopolitan cultural elite had staged and celebrates as the cultural icons of and beacons for our times. The Tate Modern is only a stone's-throw away from Greenwich's ill-fated Millennium Dome project. The latter is another bid to re-create the city in the assumed image of what is expected of a temple of culture at the turn of the millennium. It is planted as an extension of London's show-case Docklands Development, which was conceived to be the thriving hub of a globally networked and competitive city.

In many ways, these two millennial projects embody widely diverging and contradictory, yet uncannily related, visions and practices of contemporary urbanisation. The Dome aspires to herald and celebrate materially the enduring significance, politically and culturally speaking, of UK Inc. and is staged as a national experience. Even the choice of its location in Greenwich – the site of the world's meridian – symbolically attests to the national mission that the Dome's advocates imagined. It stands for an economic national project, supported by the state, designed by a national cultural icon and state appointee (Richard Rogers), co-financed by the national lottery, and portrayed as a showcase to advertise the promises of British technological know-how, its cultural achievements, and a vision for the urban future.

Of course, it is as much a shrine to corporate power and the fusion of national interest with a privatised liberal economy. British Telecom, British Airways, Marks & Spencer, Thames Water, and a host of other prominent companies, sponsor, officially supply or otherwise partner with what was conceived, planned, and commercialised as a national flagship project, first by a Conservative Government, but also embraced by Tony Blair as a symbol of the principles and practices of the "Third Way."[2] The market-driven and market-led shrine to corporate ethos and national culture, for which your average citizen would pay a considerable entry fee (at the end, grand urban development schemes are these days supposed to be profitable), became a grandiose disaster, a ruin before its date of expiry. The ruination of the Dome and the doomed urban vision that underpinned it signals the failure of spasmodic attempts to re-instil national identity and national pride within the harness of the new cultural and economic orders of the 21st century.

The Tate Modern, in sharp contrast, takes a decidedly different turn and celebrates an urbanism and cultural cosmopolitanism that has taken the ruins of modernity as its aesthetic and material foundation to re-enact a vision and practice of the city in which decay, museum, and 21st century urban experience blend together in a decidedly localised, yet uncannily decentralised and denationalised, global cosmopolitan experience.[3]

Housed in the former Bankside power station that was built as a shrine to national power and modernising progress in the mid-20th century, Tate Modern has now become a lynchpin of the cultural district of the South Bank that epitomises "Cool Britannia." This hub of faded national pride and landmark for London is now turned into a new urban experience, designed by Swiss architects Herzog & de Meuron, headed by Swedish curator Lars Nittve, and adjacent to one of the world's largest modernist centres of culture, i.e. the South Bank's unashamedly modernist 1950s redevelopment. Barely two months after its openings, it had already welcomed approximately a million visitors. Of course, here too, the private sponsors are prominently listed among the benefactors that the Tate foundation thanked, but entry is free. Inside, the new and the ruin are combined as Bill Viola or Damien Hirst mingle with Warhol, Picasso, or Monet.

The very sense of time as history, progress, the building up of ever new layers and of geographies of places as distinct historical-cultural entities is replaced by a celebration of the collage, the juxtaposition of works of art whose temporal and geographical frame of reference is transgressed and subtly disrupted. The displays produce an unhomely feeling of time apparently out of joint and space strangely out of place, but which create a unique sense of hybrid, multi-cultural location, identification and remembrance. Past, present and future, the here and distant, blend in ways that pervert received meanings of time and space, and transcend the celebration of ruination and decay that has been the very essence of the modern museum. Of course, it is easy to forget today that the area's revival has as much to do with the desire of the culture elites to reposition London in the global cultural and economic order as with the very successful struggle that local community groups and grassroots organisations (and notably the Coin Street Community Group) have waged since the 1960s to maintain affordable and decent housing for local people.[4] It is exactly the per-severance of community action that has preserved the area as a lived space and has suc-ceeded in producing an urbanity in which the lived, the everyday, and the porosities that define urbanity are maintained and nurtured.

However, regardless of the deep rift in the urban visions articulated by these two emblematic projects, they, of course, share the satanic geographies that choreograph the underbelly of contemporary globalized urbanism. Indeed, neither of them can escape the contradictions which rampage through the city as the political-economic parameters and discursive-ideological apparatuses that have infused everyday life over the past two decades and reshaped the urbanisation process in decisively new, but often deeply disturbing, direc-tions. The Bankside redevelopment reasserts the position of London on the cultural map of the world by paying homage to a denationalised hybrid cosmopolitan culture, rubbing shoul-ders with those who aspire to or celebrate similar multiple constructions of identity. At the same time, the inevitability of the reterritorialisations, upon which such revamped experi-ence is based, thrusts deep cuts in the social, political, economic, and cultural fabric of the city. Homelessness is spreading rapidly, social polarisation and exclusion have reached dizzying heights, immigrants die at the ports of entry. It is ironic, if not perverse, how cap-ital, as commodities and money, is freely floating around the globe, while immeasurable violence is inflicted on capital as labouring people – the neo-liberal utopia's reality. Urban land rents are sky-high and rapidly reconfigure the social geography of the city, while the colonisation of everyday life by the commodity has completed its full spectacular and phantas-magoric form. Despite the recent election of a London Mayor, the infamous "Red" Ken Livingston, the London public is conspicuously absent from the boardrooms and drawing tables where the alternative visions for 21st century London are dreamt-up and take shape. London may be a "cool" (read culturally hybridised, cosmopolitan, and globally and com-petitively well-positioned and connected) place, but it is a place designed, manicured, and financed by a particular global-local ("glocal") elite, and revelled in through the staging of cultural spectacles that try (although by no means always successfully) to subvert, under-mine, and marginalise the cultures of everyday urban life.

Cultural commodities such as museums, exhibits and spectacular plays shape an urban-ity that is colonised. The reconquest of the city by commodity and capital (after decades of wilful neglect and rampant deterritorialisation and emptying out) has produced a revan-chist city that has draped itself in the phantasmagoria of the spectacular commodity.[5] The latter announces, in its turn, no longer the ruination of a particular site, building, or social group, but the destruction of urban culture itself. As Gilloch remarks: "[j]ust as the experience of the commodity involves the commodification of experience, so the experience of the ruin is the ruination of experience."[6] In the millennial city, embedded in a neo-liberal utopian dream-cast, spectacle as the commodity-culture has become seemingly total. The ruination of the city is all there is apparently to see and experience. And this is the theme that we shall turn to next.

The museum as ruin/the city as ruin –
reversing the porosity of the interior/exterior

For Walter Benjamin, the ruin epitomises modernity and the modern city. The kaleidoscopic, mesmerising, fleeting, and forever recast materiality and porous experiences that constitute urbanity create the forever new. The commodity, with its emphasis on exchange- and exhibition-value, is of course, for Benjamin the material expression of modernity. The maelstrom of modernity in which "everything that is solid melts into air"[7] is nothing more than the eternal recreation of phantasmagoric images devoid of substance and meaning. The inevitable fate of the commodity-form within the cycle of production and consumption is to become old-fashioned, out-of-date, and obsolete. In its hollowed-out existence, the commodity turns into what it really is, a ruin. The spectacle as commodity represents a process of ruination, of decay and mortification. As David Harvey notes with respect to the commodification of the urban experience: "[m]any... cultural institutions – museums and heritage centres, arenas for spectacle, exhibitions and festivals – seem to have as their aim the cultivation of nostalgia, the production of sanitised collective memories, the nurturing of uncritical aesthetic experiences, and the absorption of future possibilities into a non-conflictual arena that is eternally present. The continuous spectacles of commodity culture, including the commodification of the spectacle itself, play their part in fomenting political indifference. It is either stupefied nirvana or a totally blasé attitude that is aimed at... [T]he multiple degenerate utopias that surround us do as much to signal the end of history as the collapse of the Berlin Wall ever did."[8] The contemporary city – this fantastic geographical celebration of progress, change, and innovation – has become the space of ruin. The commodified and spectacular museum-city as the heralded booster-strategy to revive urban cultural economies represents nothing else than the universalisation of sedimenting the tumultuous re-orderings of history into the ossified ruins of theatrically staged places. Time is frozen as place, a mere moment of space. When the museum-experience is turned into a pure gazing at the commodified spectacle and the city the generous, but conspiring, prostitute to stage it, real life of every-day urban experience is replaced by the reel life of the ever-the-same.

In the contemporary city-as-spectacle, the experience of the museum is radically transformed. The classically modern museum practices interiorising what was originally out-
side/experiential/lived, i.e. turning the public space of the strange encounter, the public
meeting, and the social process into the crystallised display of the frozen display-moment.
In the spectacularised city-museum, the porosity of inside-outside and public-private is
turned topsy-turvy as the porosities between inside-outside and public-private evaporate.
Whereas Benjamin could still picture and, on occasion, mock the bourgeois interior or the
shopping displays of the arcades as housing the obsolete, the ridiculous, the faded (yet
blindly, pompously, and arrogantly displaying the ruined artefact as desirable, permanent
and enduring – as utopia redeemed), the outside has now become itself part of the interi-
orised commodified spectacle.[9] While the porosity between inside and outside used to
reveal the sense of decay and mortification whenever the interiors were exteriorised again
in junk-yards and flee-markets – that is the moment when they enter the public again as
sublime phantasmagoric allegories – in the spectacularised city, the old is refashioned in
the context of the present. As with the city-as-museum, the exteriorised archaeological
remnants of bourgeois homes have quickly become part of the city-as-spectacle. In Brussels
the accelerating gentrification of the Rue Blaes and the Rue Haute in the Marolles or
around the Rue Dansaert testify to this in their own parochial mediocrity as much as the
more visionary and emblematic Tate Modern, Bilbao's Guggenheim or Seattle's Rock Museum
have been staged as integral parts of the city-as-museum, where the permeability of the
inside and the outside has now been rendered total. The city itself has become part of the
spectacularised commodity. It is exactly this process of interiorising the exterior within the
phantasmagoric web of the commodity that led Baudrillard to proclaim that the spectacle
is all there is to see, gaze at and contemplate; urban life turned into a staged archaeological
theme park experience.[10]

However, the assertion of modernity with a vengeance over the past two decades or so,
not least exactly because of the tumultuous re-ordering of the time-space co-ordinates of
everyday life and the perplexing reconfigurations of the choreographies and chronologies
of everyday practices in which the most familiar is staged at the other side of the globe,
while the most exotic appears around the corner, questions, if not subverts, the hegemony
of the city as spectacular museum. In addition, the ruin produces an uncanny feeling
– what Freud described as *unheimlich* – a feeling of being strangely out-of-place. Of course,
when the homely, the interior, blends seamlessly with the exterior; when the creative tension between interior/exterior fades away, exposing both as mere phantasmagoric forms,
emptied-out receptacles of literally disembodied spaces and experiences; when the erotic,
the sensuous, the life-as-play is violently seen and experienced as vacuous, home itself
becomes strangely unfamiliar, alienated and a grinding subdermal angst starts creeping in.
This is of course particularly strong whenever those processes that the spectacle relegated

to the invisible spaces of the urban margins or underground (skaters, illegal immigrants, sewage pipes, garbage, dirt, hooligans) surface,[11] become part of the gaze in unexpected ways and claim not their participation in the spectacle, but rather they demand staging the urban itself. It is exactly out of these close encounters with the unfamiliar and the *unheimlichkeit* of the "officialised" urban experience that the possibility (however problematic it might turn out to be) for imagining and practising a different form of urbanity resides; it is at these moments as well that the hegemonic discourse and practice of elite power configurations is threatened;[12] the moments when officially condoned violence and repression (whether in the form of permanent surveillance, CCTV (closed circuit TV) panoptical control, or sheer bodily violence) inevitably surface.

For Guy Debord, brooding on Benjamin's and Freud's insights, the continuous ruination of everyday practices and the disembodied uncanny urban experience that accompanies it in the spectacular city as the most advanced spatialisation of the commodity form, also harbours exactly the possibility of a celebration of modern life and of the production of a genuinely humanising geography of everyday urban life.[13] Subverting received meanings, displacing discourses and visions imposed by the city-as-museum, occupying, transforming, and actively creating new situations and spatial practices is exactly where the libidinous, exhilarating, and orgasmic possibilities of the urban experience reside. Strangely enough, therefore, the stale mortification of the museum-city reveals in its hidden underbelly exactly the potential for its transformation.

These excavations of the present configurations of the urban condition have profound implications, both for reading the Mont des Arts in the context of Brussels and, more importantly, for imagineering alternative elite's visions of the city (who other are we as essayists, architects, geographers, engineers, philosophers, readers, or museum-goers). This is the task to which we shall now turn.

The museum-city versus the Mont des Arts as ruined museum

The Mont des Arts is an ironic site. While many thousands roam every day through its underbelly in the uncanny spaces of the underground galleries and metro-train corridors, the surface space is emptied out, yet strangely re-appropriated by an unlikely mix of users, ranging from skaters to Japanese tourists and a lone academic. It is also ironic in the sense that the site became embellished and adorned, constructed and reconstructed in the image of an imperialist mini-power in search of its own emblematic spatialisation of nation-state formation, fusing together with a particular constellation of national political-economic powers. As such, a palimpsest archaeological urban landscape crystallised, celebrating what soon would turn out to be just a mere ruin of its own past imaginations.

Emblematic urban spaces are invariably vestiges of historical-geographical configurations of power. And the Mont des Arts is no exception to this rule. The Mont des Arts has become a ruinous geological layering of a national social space that has outlived its *raison-d'être*. As a museum-ruin, it is an allegorical space – national (the Bibliothèque Royale), royal (the Park, the Musée de la Dynastie), decidedly Belgian, faded representation of the fusion between bourgeoisie, grand national capital (the Société Générale), grand state power, and royal prerogative, but also enshrining and spatialising modernising desires (the Gare Centrale, Sabena building), celebrating national culture(s) (the Musées Royaux), yet strangely non-urban both in its experience and its function as transacting the inside of the suburban home with the interior spaces of urban-based work or leisure. As a museum-ruin of the 19th and 20th century, the site narrates in its dense stratification a particular (and, hence, decidedly contestable) discourse of, and embodies materially, the actual manifestation of the complex political-economic and cultural history of Belgium. The site is neither Flemish nor Walloon, neither Brussels nor European, but Belgian; it constitutes a u-topia in the literal sense of word, the embodiment of a place that is no more, except in the corridors of its ruins or in the minds of an outdated and outperformed elite with a less than glorious past, but without a future. What once constituted a relatively coherent power configuration (national capital – but closely knit to the urban bourgeoisie –, the state, and the king) that shaped – albeit not without its internal tensions and contradictions – the area to enshrine and represent the nation, has now become fragmented, kaleidoscopic, partly exploded, partly imploded, leaving behind a mere fleshed-out rump. The national capital groups that once determined the course of economic events in Belgium from their Brussels' headquarters have been denationalised (in the literal sense) and have become European, if not global financial institutions for whom Belgium, let alone Brussels, only matters to the extent it fits into and accommodates their corporate strategies. At the same time, international capitals – in fusion with regional elite groups – have become the new mandarins that now decide local economic fortune and are spatialised far away from Brussels's traditional geographic centre of gravity.

The national state has imploded after an agonising federalisation process that left the orphaned national cultural institutions on the Mont des Arts without political or cultural direction or identity; the royal institution is drifting, looking for a mission. The powers that shaped the Mont des Arts are now pulling in different directions, the site fragments in as many different islands and now widely diverging power strategies and fractured elite choreographies (see below). The feeble and failed attempts over the past decades to imagine and engineer a coherent reconstruction of the area already suggests an inability to forge a sufficiently coherent alliance to develop a hegemonic vision and push through an overall redevelopment of the area. The vacant site harbours a hollowed-out power centre.

It does not come as a surprise, in this context, that the Fondation Roi Baudouin, whose mission is clearly identified with and circumscribed by the royal national project, has turned to this site in an attempt to restore it as an urban museum of – and for – the nation.

It is equally quite telling that this reconstruction pursues a mere aesthetic embellishment and adornment that aims at restoring the symbolic meaning of the site, attracting a certain type of visitor, and at displacing, controlling, or otherwise policing those groups that threaten to appropriate the space and fill it with a different set of meanings and urban practices. Their approach is formalistic, but politically and culturally deeply significant, one that betrays an incapacity to generate an economic/political/cultural elite coalition that could generate a grand vision for the site. The strategic but futile attempt to persevere in holding on to the site as the embodiment of an outlived national shrine (a strategy that combines a fatal nostalgia, with a political mission and supported by what Gramsci would define as "traditional elites" or intellectuals)[14] will reenforce the Mont des Arts as a decidedly non-urban and, increasingly, anti-urban site; an area for mere contemplation and gazing, a museum-ruin to commemorate a museum-nation. Of course, any alternative hegemonic vision that would carry the support of the new global-local elites (see below) would very likely attempt to insert the site in the culture-driven competitive inter-urban global struggle for whom the spectacularised museum-city has to become the desired territorialised reality. The dilemma, therefore, resides in pursuing for the Mont des Arts a process of its preservation as a frozen, crystallised museum-space displaying and representing in its kaleidoscopic totality the particular 19th-20th century Belgian forms of modern state formation, or to a commodified/spectacularised museum-city space. Either of these would invariably turn the area into a decidedly non-urban experience, a ruinous city.

The latter option, which would pervert the Belgicist origin of the site, fails to bring together a sufficiently coherent local growth coalition, the former will leave the site as a romantically embellished Belgian museum. Arguably, the latter strategy, further emptying out the symbolic and material practices of the area, will no doubt continue to generate counter-strategies that will attempt to refill, reappropriate, and re-enact the area with urban practices more in tune with the rhythms and rhymes of the present urban process. Perhaps this may shape the imagination for the reintegration of the site as part of the everyday urban experience and might pervert the making or remaking of the site as either spectacular museum or expression of a non-existent nation.

In fact, the driving forces of Brussels's 21st century urbanisation process reside elsewhere. Nevertheless, the persistent absence of "hegemony of vision"[15] of and for the city remains a stubborn and disturbing condition. And this is what we shall turn to next.

A "glocal" city/space?
The Mont des Arts as epitome of Brussels's conundrum
The failure to turn the Mont des Arts – or, for that matter, any other site or project in Brussels – convincingly into an emblematic project that spatialises and grounds a hegemony of vision, supported by a broad coalition of urban elites, and shaping the public

spectacularised image of the city (the sort of process cities as diverse as London, Berlin, Barcelona, or Bilbao have so vigorously pursued) is of course directly related to the rapid spatial reconfiguration of the power geometries at play in the local arena. The now decades-old arguments and debates over the Mont des Arts and the succession of piece-meal interventions and alterations attest to the absence of a hegemonic vision that would be the key to a successful spectacularisation of the city. As we have argued above, this may turn out to be a blessing in disguise. Yet, it raises the spectre of an ossifying, petrifying urban space, vacated, emptied out and marginalised. Moreover, Brussels's recent history is exactly characterised by the manifest absence of any visionary project that generates sufficient political and economic muscle to be realised. Indeed, Brussels's conundrum resides in the apparent contradiction between its economic success in the face of accelerating de-territorialisation, social fragmentation, and polarisation on the one hand, and persistent inability to generate a coherent perspective for the 21st century on the other.

In what follows, this inability will be situated within the recent socio-spatial rescalings of the power choreographies of urban political, cultural, and economic elites and the ensuing (dis)articulation in framing the process of urban change. In short, the disarticulation between the power geometries of traditional political power configurations and coalitions in Brussels and Belgium on the one hand and, on the other, the newly emerging economic and cultural elites whose spatial reach is of a different scalar order, produces a complex layering of centrifugal, overlapping, disconnected, and incoherent constellations of power, incapable of generating common direction. An international, cosmopolitan, emergent elite largely shapes the economic dynamics and leading cultural practices, while local political and traditional cultural elites remain largely absent from the key arenas that underpin Brussels's future. The lack of a coherent growth coalition and of an accompanying hegemonic vision of the future translates in fragmentation, enduring conflicts within and between local political and economic elites, institutional exclusion and general malaise.[16]

At first sight, it is somewhat paradoxical that the Brussels region represents the third richest region in term of gross regional product in the European Union, just after Hamburg and the Ile-de-France. Both Flanders and Wallonia perform significantly worse.[17] Despite this vigorous economic performance, the internal socio-economic profile shows a much more disturbing and bleak underbelly. Recently, the average per capita income for Brussels has dived not only under that for Flanders but also under the average for an already poorly performing Wallonia. This indicates that a significant share of gross regional product leaks away to other regions. Of course, this is not particularly surprising, given the commuting flows between Brussels and the rest of the country and the geopolitical strategies that actively encourage this segmentation between Brussels as a space of production and Flanders and Wallonia as the eager recipients of the income flows. A restructuring of the service economy has begun to attach itself from the early 1990s onwards on to the intense wave of de-industrialisation of the 1970s and 1980s, which announced a still on-going period of rising unemployment, a seriously dysfunctional labour market, and a growing army of permanently excluded. In sum, we encounter in Brussels a rather paradoxical situation: capital accumulation turns around quite frenetically, but this economic performance is not accompanied by a correspondingly high socio-economic profile.

The accumulation process has an outspoken external or outward orientation, yet has very little embedding or anchoring in the local institutional, formal or informal, networks of power. Presently, over 38% of the Brussels population are of non-Belgian origin. This "disembedding" of the key economic actors from the institutional framework has far reaching consequences for the future of the city as a multi-cultural, heterogeneous, hybridised and dynamic place.

First of all, a significant part of the public service sector, which constitutes the pivot of the urban economy, is largely located in Brussels despite itself. The tens of thousands of jobs at the EU, Nato and other related activities, hosting an elite of transnational bureaucrats, are located in Brussels because of international geopolitical considerations, rather than for the intrinsic qualities of the city. In addition, the administration of the Flemish Community was located in Brussels for particular Flemish regionalist geopolitical reasons; yet the overwhelming majority of its leading civil servants flock back in the evenings to their peri-urban dormitories. The cultural and social elites that are associated with these institutions are largely absent from the arenas of power that define and shape the governance of the city.

Secondly, the private service sectors, and principally advanced business services, have rapidly globalised. The spectacular growth of financial services and their acolyte functions such as consultants and accountants, and the management of international capital flows are also largely concentrated in Brussels. Brussels has become part of a global network of cities through which gigantic flows of capital pass via the stock market, investment funds, and other more or less exotic financial instruments. The speculative carrousels of often international consortia of real estate developers frame Brussels as an easy and receptive target for profitable ventures. Yet, few of these key economic actors, which are culturally significant, locally present but globally active, are directly or indirectly involved in the networks of governance and management that give form and substance to the institutional structure of the city.

Furthermore, the historically important presence of a migrant community has resulted in the emergence of locally and economically now well-entrenched and enduring transnational networks and communities in terms of trade, production, personal relations, cultural exchanges, and the like. They constitute a thriving economic force, but remain excluded from the hubs of local power. This institutional marginalisation is, of course, also the case for the rapidly expanding niche-production and trade, such as in fashion, design, and other cultural activities. The multi-cultural practice of Brussels that takes shape in both "high" culture and popular "street" cultures (with boundaries that are rapidly blurring through a plethora of transgressive cultural practices) is internationalist in character. It is precisely this combination of creative fusion of difference, heterogeneity, and potential cosmopolitanism that can turn the city, at least potentially, into one of the exemplary sites for practising and celebrating a new post-Fordist and hybridised urbanism. Moreover, the spatialisations of these global-local economic and cultural processes and actors, that actually actively shape the urbanisation process, are both socially and spatially removed from the core spatialities of the traditional Belgian power configuration inscribed in and around the Mont des Arts.

The above economic spheres constitute the foundation of the economic development of Brussels and form the new "glocal" (global-local) elite. However, the rupture between this emergent and rapidly consolidating aspiring elite and the traditional political elite is almost total. This invariably and inevitably leads to fragmented and incoherent urban governance that is still rooted in outdated – but still eminently present – power relations and choreographies, and struggles between traditional elites. Moreover, the territorial fragmentation remains almost total. The almost semi-feudal power bastions of the municipal power fiefdoms and their local and parochial power networks, often based on deep-seated paternalistic and nepotist practices, lead to fragmentation, centrifugal struggle, to conditions of permanent semi-conflicts and to a perpetual displacement of problems. The parochialism of the local war lords inhibits, if not prevents, the formation of alliances between global progressive economic elites and an enlightened local political elite. On top of this, the institutional structure of the regional scales of governance are characterised by permanent tribal antagonisms along carefully cultivated linguistic ruptures that engender contradictions and conflicts which lead to persistent tensions, implosive forces, and a perpetual risk of disintegration and instability.

In Flanders particularly, but also to some extent in Wallonia, Brussels is framed as the "outsider-space," as a space on the margin. Indeed, the Flemish and Walloon political and economic elites – often aided by or marshalling a particular cultural discourse of regional identity and homogeneity – embody, actively cultivate, and perpetuate, albeit for entirely different historical reasons, an extremely ambiguous stance and often outright hostility vis-à-vis the issues that shape Brussels's future. This is most vividly expressed in the imagineering – that is the production of visions, images, and representations – of Brussels. Both the planning or policy documents of the various levels of government and the imaginings of the city by a significant part of traditional cultural, media, and political – but usually decidedly external – groups are founded upon an outspoken anti-urban imagination and discourse. The predominantly white, suburban, middle-class male and politically linked civil servants, architects, and the like, for whom the big city often invokes an image of poverty, disintegration, vandalism, criminality, immigrant-domination, script the city as a dystopian hotbed of all manner of perversions and insecurities.[18] Without romanticising the real problems, this endlessly repeated tune undermines what in many ways constitutes the essence of what urban life is all about. Indeed, the diversity, the playful heterogeneity, the socio-economic differentiation, the dense networks of the often informal networks of firms and companies that are simultaneously locally and globally active, the eclectic mixture of styles, languages, forms, desires, and preferences, give to Brussels a vitality (however much fraught with tension, conflict, and contradiction such a whirlpool might engender) that precisely defines the urban. This fundamentally distinguishes the city from the sanitised, homogenised, and standardised suburbs where – in Henri Lefebvre's words – nothing ever happened and nothing ever will.[19]

However, the cultural, social and economic carriers of this vitality and vibrancy are in no way embedded in institutional organisations or institutionalised elite networks. The latter remain dominated by internally conflicting, often incestuous, traditional elite formations that desperately attempt to cling to power positions and relations that have outlived their useful shelf life and are fossilised remnants of an almost transcended past. They embody the city-as-museum. In the maelstrom of these profoundly locally or regionally choreographed battles, the national cultural, political, and administrative rump of a past that has outlived its sell-by date, desperately clings to carving out some sort of niche that can either legitimise its continuing presence as a ruined perpetuation of a history that cannot be re-captured or, at best, salvage whatever national project that can be temporarily rescued from inevitable ruination.

Of course, Brussels has lived through rare moments when active and hegemonic growth coalitions provided and constructed a vision for the city, which – through often unholy alliances of unlike partners – succeeded in enabling important epochal transformations. For example, the urban restructuring which took place under Leopold II and the creation of a truly cosmopolitan – although deeply pre-colonial and bourgeois – city at the end of the 19th century, the hegemonic, nationally carried, growth coalition that fused around the Expo of 1958, or the speculative real-estate based construction and reconstruction wave that underlied the globalising visions of the tandem Vanden Boeynants/Charlie de Pauw in the 1960s and early 1970s marked such moments. Each of these left their inscriptions on the Mont des Arts. Of course, such hegemonic elite coalitions generate all manner of tension and conflict, and often lead to a deeply problematic rescripting and a reengineering of the urban fabric.

In sum, while the socio-economic restructuring of the last two decades or so led to the emergence of a new global-local elite that shapes the trajectory of urban economic change, urban governance remains locked in an amalgamated collection of traditional national-regional-local elites and their internal power conflicts. The internal conflicts between local

elites that do not govern, but stage and enact parochial, territorial, linguistic, and petty ideological feuds is a greater threat to the socio-economic and cultural development of Brussels
than enduring unemployment, the immigration issue or petty crime. Whether we like it or
not, it is the carriers of social power that shape the face and determine the future of the city;
the socially or otherwise excluded or marginalised just suffer from the consequences and
express this in manners we all know.

The Mont des Arts: Brussels S.A./N.V. or Brussels, Inc.?

The struggle around the Mont des Arts, or any other place for that matter, reminds us how
the play of power politics inevitably revolves around a spatial strategy; a struggle not just
in but for space. An emancipatory spatialisation, therefore, revolves around the reconquest
and production of spaces expressive of lived difference, of desire, of identity (however
fluid this may be), and of possible encounter. Ed Soja refers to these spaces as *Thirdspace*: the
lived, interstitial space that is worked out through perception and imagination; a space
simultaneously real and imagined, material and metaphorical, ordered and disordered.[20]
Ironically, relations of power and domination that infuse urban practices and which are
contested and fought against in innumerable ways help create the differentiated public
spaces that give cities such a sweeping vitality. At the same time, these forms of resistance
and subversion of dominant values (such as the skaters on the Mont des Arts or, for that
matter, the new forms of occupation of public space in immigrant communities) tend only
to perpetuate the conservative imagery of cities as places of chaos, disintegration, and
moral decay rather than as spaces where the prospect of hope, joy, and freedom resides.
Debord's situationist programme revolved squarely around recapturing the urban, especially as an embodiment of *jouissance* (pleasure); even though he already spotted the com-
ing of the anodyne theme park museum-city urbanism of the late capitalist "spectacular"
urban order, with its war of attrition against the public space.[21]

Throughout Brussels, in the interstices of its fragmented, disjointed, incoherent, kaleidoscopic, centrifugal places, a vibrant cosmopolitan, hybrid, multiple, and desiring set of
practices, activities, imaginings, and visions is brewing and fermenting; often in the midst
of pervasive processes of exclusion and disempowerment. They constitute the radical margins that are an integral part of new forms of 21st century urbanism, where new urban elites
are actively being formed. It is these practices that urgently require, if not demand, spatialisation – that is the creation of their own material and symbolic, but actual, urban landscapes. These spatialisations will require considerable powers of architectural and urbanistic
imagination and creativity. This also demands a further erosion of the traditional power
geometries and the insertion of new political-economic-cultural elites within the power
geometries of Brussels. There is an urgent task for forging new institutional and semi-
institutional networks of and for the new elites. This necessitates an urgent reconsideration

of the meaning of citizenship in terms of a multiplicity of identities that may relate to a variety of geographical scales (rather than in terms of nationality) and of citizenship rights, including the right to participate fully and actively in political and public life and, hence, in the production of the urban process. It also requires the elaboration of visionary urban programmes, not by white suburban middle-class men, but by the new "glocal," distinctly local, yet decidedly international, economic, cultural, and social elites.

The "glocal" city that Brussels already is, is currently embedded in a provincial and parochial institutional power structure and straightjacket. The Mont des Arts embodies this as no other site in Brussels. Hence, the attention paid to it, but also the acute sense of powerlessness associated with those who wish to reconstruct it in the image of the 21st century. The choice seems to be to turn the site into either a national museum of the 19th and 20th century, a memory to Brussels S.A.-N.V., or to reconstruct it, however unlikely it may be, as an emblematic project that resounds with the spectacularised and commodified urban order, dictated by a rampant global market Stalinism, and which would be part of moulding it in the image of Brussels, Inc., a museum-city. Neither of these options, however different they may seem to be, (like the Dome and the Tate Modern in London), raises an exciting or even remotely emancipatory urban vision.

The real urbanisation of Brussels, however, takes place in the politically still marginal interstitial spaces where strange encounters take place, where the new is experimented with before it can be spectacularised; spaces inhabited by people with multiple scaled identities that stretch from the most immediate and intimate to the global. These spaces are where the city of the 21st century as lived experience potentially resides and, perhaps, will be built. Wandering through Brussels, the possible and potential emergence, and on occasion nascent presence, of new geographies for the 21st century are hesitantly becoming more manifest. The Quartier Leopold or the Canal district, the Gare du Midi or the Rue de Brabant areas are just a few of the possible sites that scream out for urgent attention and for the production of imaginative emblematic new geographies that would foster and nurture what is already embryonically there. This, too, requires a grand vision, considerable creative power, a new enlightened power geometry, committed architects and urban designers (whether professional or just anyone trying to create a space, their space). Let's meet there. What have we got to lose but the boredom of the ruin of the city-as-museum?

How to capture and give form to the fleeting, the ephemeral, and the endangered? ... The experience of the urban environment provides the answer. It is, after all, in the Metropolis, that one become accustomed to, and esteems, the transient. [22]

1. I would like to thank Maria Kaika and Guy Baeten for generating some of the insights that are woven through the argument, and Lieven De Cauter for his supportive comments and critical advice. I alone of course remain responsible for twisting their suggestions in my own idiosyncratic manner.

2. The "Third Way" symbolises the political agenda and programme of Tony Blair's New Labour. Its most well-known ideologue is Antony Giddens, *The Third Way* (Cambridge: Polity Press, 1998).

3. For a detailed account of the Tate Modern's visionary conceptualisation, see Ivona Blazwick and Simon Wilson (eds.) (2000) *Tate Modern: The Handbook* University of California Press, Berkeley, and Rowan Moore, Raymond Ryan, Adrian Hardwick, and Gavin Stamp, *Building Tate Modern* (London: Tate Gallery Publishing, 2000).

4. See Guy Baeten (2001) *Urban Regeneration, Social Exclusion and Shifting Power Geometries on the South Bank* (Geographische Zeitschrift, London, forthcoming).

5. For a further discussion of "the revanchist city," see Neil Smith, *The New Urban Frontier – Gentrification and the Revanchist City* (London and New York: Routledge, 1996).

6. Graeme Gilloch, *Myth & Metropolis – Walter Benjamin and the City* (Cambridge: Polity Press, 1996), p. 138.

7. From Karl Marx, Friedrich Engels, *The Communist Manifesto* (1848).

8. David Harvey, *Spaces of Hope* (Edingburg: Edinburg University Press, 2000), p. 168.

9. With thanks to Lieven De Cauter for the suggestions.

10. See Michael Sorkin (ed.), *Variations on a Theme Park – The New American City and The End of Public Space* (New York: The Noonday Press, 1992) or Christine Boyer, *The City of Collective Memory* (Cambridge, Mass.: MIT Press, 1996).

11. Maria Kaika and E. Swyngedouw, "Fetishising the Modern City: The Phantasmagoria of Urban Technological Networks," *International Journal of Urban and Regional Research*, no 24 (2000), p. 120-138.

12. See Maria Kaika, *Metabolised Nature as the Domestic Uncanny* (forthcoming).

13. See Guy Debord, *La Société du Spectacle* (Paris: Buchet-Chastel, 1967). For reviews, see Ken Knabb (ed.), Situationist International Anthology, (Bureau of Public Secrets, Berkeley, CA, 191) or Simon Sadler, *The Situationist City* (Cambridge, Mass.: MIT Press, 1998).

14. Antonio Gramsci "On Intellectuals," in *Prison Notebooks* (London: Lawrence&Wishart, 1971). See also Edward Said, *Representations of the Intellectual* (London: Vintage, 1994).

15. See Sharon Zukin, "Cultural Strategies of Economic Development and the Hegemony of Vision," in Andy Merrifield and Erik Swyngedouw (eds.), *The Urbanization of Injustice, Lawrence and Wishart* (New York: London and University Press, 1996), p. 223-224.

16. For fuller accounts of this, see Erik Swyngedouw, "De Dans der Titanen en Dwergen: 'Glokalisatie', Stedelijke Ontwikkeling en Groeicoalities – Het Brusselse Enigma," *Revue Belge de Géographie*, Vol. 123, no 1-2 (1999), pp. 43-61; Guy Baeten and Erik Swyngedouw, *Dancing with Titans and Dwarfs: Elite Power, Global Forces, and the Political Economy of Glocal Development: Brussels' Conundrum* (European Planning Studies, forthcoming).

17. Europese Commissie (ed.), *Concurrentievermogen en Cohesie: Tendensen in de Regio's,* (Brussels, 1994).

18. Guy Baeten, *Clichés of Urban Doom. The Dystopian Politics of Metaphors for the Unequal City: a View from Brussels*, International Journal of Urban and Regional Research, Vol.25, no.1, (2001).

19. H. Lefebre, *Le Droit à la Ville* (Paris: Anthropos, 1972) and *La Production de l'Espace* (Paris: Anthropos, 1974).

20. Edward Soja, *Thirdspace – Journeys to Los Angeles and other Real-and-Imagined Places* (Oxford: Blackwell, 1996).

21. Andy Merrifield and Erik Swyngedouw (eds.), "Social Justice and the Urban Experience," in Soja, o.c., pp. 1-17.

22. Graeme Gilloch, o.c., p. 178.

THE MONT DES ARTS
BETWEEN MUSEUM AND CITY

Karina Van Herck and Hilde Heynen

The Mont des Art is not just the connection between the Upper and Lower Towns in Brussels. It is also a most peculiar and unusual place. For the Mont des Arts is also quite literally a mountain of the arts, where a never-ending accumulation takes place of objects and texts, of art and knowledge. This mountain preserves things for eternity, and presents them for the moment of today. It collects, conserves and stores a variety of things, which are carefully selected according to the criterion "this is Belgian." Most of the city inhabitants do not seem to care for this place. The cultural institutions which gather on this spot all bear the proud qualification "royal" instead of "municipal." They never referred to the city.

The different institutions collect things according to their different modes, but they are themselves objects of collection too. For the Mont des Arts collects and preserves buildings and architectural styles, as it stores spaces. It is a physical accumulation, a palimpsest, to which layer after layer is added in a continuous process of building and demolishing. An archaeological dissection of these layers would highlight the different histories in which the Mont des Arts took part: an urban history, in which it did not gain its place without a struggle, but also a history of the construction of a new state, or a history of the emergence and the loss of a once irrefutable belief in modernity and progress. In the name of the Belgian state, popular neighbourhoods were destroyed at this spot for the building of museums, archives and libraries, for the glory of progress.

The encyclopaedic museum

The ideological source of the Mont des Arts is situated in 18th century enlightenment, when rationalisation, systematisation and classification became the new key terms. From that moment onwards it was no longer God but man who ordered things – the *Encyclopédie ou dictionnaire raisonné des sciences, des arts et des métiers* (1751-1780) did not leave any doubt about that, claiming that "the era of religion has been substituted by the century of science." Man and his world were being investigated and classified according to rational and scientific methods. Man was severed for good from the *Ancien Regime* in which church and king were omnipotent rulers. The encyclopaedia – accessible to all thanks to new techniques of reproduction – was to become the instrument for collecting, ordering and distributing universal knowledge. The institution of the museum also emerged in this period. As a place exhibiting universal knowledge, it can be considered a built version of the encyclopaedia and an important agent in the construction of democracy. The story of the Louvre is characteristic of this evolution. In 1792, in the middle of the French revolution, the palace of the king was turned into the Musée Français. Tours were organised, cheap catalogues printed and on a regular basis the public was invited to visit the venue without charge. As a public place where history is presented as a linear evolution, the museum is one of the most important supports of the belief in progress, the distribution of knowledge and the nourishing of modern democratic thought.

With the emergence of the museum and scientific disciplines in the 18th century, the act of collecting is institutionalised and the nature of the relationship between man and collected objects changes. The act of collecting previously performed by the individual - described by Walter Benjamin as "a mode of practical remembering" - gathered objects which reflected personal experience. These objects provided a direct link with a living past and stimulated memory.[1] The objects in a museum on the other hand appear against a background of scientific knowledge. A distance is created between object and visitor, which enables critical contemplation but at the same time inevitably leads to a certain alienation. Within the museum the object changes into something else. Museum and mausoleum share more than just a phonetic resemblance, as Adorno observes.[2] Objects in a museum are withdrawn from their context, stripped of their "natural" significance and as a token of progress "buried" in the display of linear history. The museum provides all historical events with coherence and rationality by inserting them into a universal story: everything comes forth from what preceded it and the consequence of every event is presented some-what later, two or three rooms further along the trajectory. At the same time, this operation condemns what is preserved to the order of the past, denying it an intimate connection with a living reality. The museum thus displays a paradox: as a place of conservation it resists the notion of history as progress – because it protects objects against destruction by time – while at the same time it constructs the idea of history as progress by presenting objects as part of a chain.[3]

The enlightened subject can no longer see himself outside history. He mirrors himself in the past and anticipates the future. As a historical figure he no longer coincides with himself, or with his time. The result of this alienation is that throughout the history of exhibition, the issue of authenticity has gained more and more importance. This consider-ation however has not always been a crucial one. For example, the *Altes Museum* in Berlin in its initial years did not see any problem in covering the "holes" in its collection by exhibit-ing reproductions – a solution which today would not be acceptable. Clearly, the purpose of the museum was not in the first place to enjoy or contemplate objects of the past, but rather to instruct people by a systematic and educational survey.

Within this idea of the museum as comprehensive and encyclopaedic, it is obvious that the act of collecting is the core of the museum's activities. This inevitably leads to continuous growth. The never-ending accumulation of museums and institutions on the Mont des Arts is an example, as well as a distortion, of this concept. It was Leopold II who decided on the cultural destiny of this spot, but earlier in the 18th century, Charles de Lorraine had the old Palais de Nassau reconverted and extended into a neo-classical building complex suitable for the collection and exhibition of art and science. During the next centuries almost all scientific institutions which today are found dispersed throughout Brussels – like the Musée des Sciences Naturelles, the Université Libre, L'Ecole Centrale, and even the Jardin Botanique, were located in or next to this complex. With the erection of the Palais des Beaux-Arts by Alphonse Balat (1874-1880, today the Musée d'Art Ancien) the collections of historical art left the royal palace for the first time, mainly for reasons of space shortage. Thus the museum emerged as a public institution. A new type of building was born, typologically close to the palace, financed by the head of state and accessible to all. To support the new political regime, ceremonial public places – such as the Place des Bailles – were no longer erected in the heart of the city and in the shadow of the royal palace, but rather newly constructed public spaces which constituted a democratic realm.

Paul Otlet, from encyclopaedia to Mundaneum

The project of enlightenment which lies at the basis of the Mont des Arts, is also the source of inspiration for the radical proposal of Paul Otlet, a forgotten utopian thinker from the beginning of the 20th century, to erect his Palais Mondial or Mundaneum on the Mont des Arts. In Otlet's opinion the Mont des Art was to become the place on earth where all knowledge and all publications of mankind were to be collected, catalogued and made accessible. In line with the aspirations of August Comte, who envisioned a new and total synthesis of human knowledge, in 1895 Otlet founded the *Office International de la Bibliographie*, a universal library on cards, which collected data stemming from the most diverse periods and on the most diverse subjects.[4] In 1920 at the *Cinquantenaire* in Brussels he opened his Palais Mondial, a temple devoted to knowledge, education and fraternity among people. It housed not only his universal library, but also rooms for exhibitions. This Palais Mondial was an embryo of his great dream: the foundation of a world centre which would, on a permanent basis and supported by the most advanced technologies, carry out the aspirations of the Universal Exhibitions: to collect, present and synthesise the best and most diverse information from all over the world under the form of texts, objects, films, photographs etc. Otlet's project of a comprehensive and totally accessible archive constitutes in fact a modern equivalent of the library and the museum of Alexandria, the old Chinese encyclopaedias, the Western universities or the royal courts. With its universalising and all-encompassing ambition however it acquired a utopian dimension never equalled before or after.[5] Even today the Mundaneum, or the universal archives, proves its imaginary force. Continuously reformulated throughout the history of the museum, the idea of the mundaneum recently re-appeared in discussions on the future of the museum into the 21st century, imposing a rather utopian role on new technologies like the internet.[6]

Otlet's Mundaneum however was never realised. After the failure of several attempts in Brussels, it began to wander around the world, to end up on international territory with Le Corbusier's well known design project for Geneva (1928). Le Corbusier's project contains not only a Musée Mondial, that offers an overview of the position of the different nations within universal history and culture, but also temporary exhibition rooms for continents, nations and cities, meeting rooms for international associations, rooms for the *Office International de la Bibliographie*, universities and research centres, a botanical garden, sport stadiums and hotels, as well as infrastructural elements such as railway connections, highways, car parks and an airport. As a universal documentation and information centre, the Mundaneum has to be connected to the whole world, by physical means as well as through informational networks such as the internet.

Le Corbusier's design project for a Mundaneum clearly shows in its conception the influence of the Universal Exhibitions. The Musée Mondial can in fact be considered a permanent world exhibition where the concept of history that was prevalent in the 19th century remains valid. The spiralling and chronologically ordered trajectory in the Musée Mondial, which starts on top of the pyramid building with prehistory and finishes on the ground level with the present day, reveals an approach to time and history which is not fundamentally different from the one at stake in traditional encyclopedic museums. Situated at the end of the spiral, as the result of a condensed universal history, the present is constructed as the future past. With history as proof, man is elevated to heroism. For the goal of the Mundaneum, writes Otlet, is "to exhibit and to make known through text, object and word how mankind has raised itself from its humble origins to the splendors of its Genius, Heroism and Saints."[7]

The concept of the total archive embodies the human desire to comprehend and to contain in one place the image and the meaning of the world. Otlet envisioned the Mundaneum as "a representation of the world and what it contains."[8] The Mundaneum therefore cannot be reproduced; it is a unique museum. It is a representational machine, which presents the world as comprehensible and manageable. The hidden assumption is the very modern thought that the world consequently would be controllable.

Otlet applies a similar operation to the city in his conception of an urbaneum. This other representational machine gave rise to a design project by Victor Bourgeois, who PLATES PP. 142-143 imagined it as a large building with a panoramic view of Brussels and enough room to store all the cartographic, statistical and other information on the city. The visitor would thus be capable of overlooking the city while at the same time contemplating its structural properties by studying the collected documentation. The building moreover would act as a centre of discussion and exchange among the disciplines concerned with the city.[9] Just like the Mundaneum would collect and present all knowledge concerning the world, the urbaneum would document and centralise all knowledge concerning the city.

The Mont des Arts in a sense is related to these ideas (it is no coincidence that the Bibliothèque Royale was one of Otlet's favourite spots), but embodies them in a somewhat more limited way. Whereas in the Mundaneum reproductions, copies and facsimiles were supposed to provide a systematic documentation of all nations in the world, the institutions at the Mont des Arts prefer authentic Belgian objects. The library only collects publications printed in Belgium, the Archives Générales du Royaume collect Belgian documents and the Musée du Film stores all films ever distributed in Belgium. Whereas Otlet conceived of his Mundaneum as an instrument for the fraternisation of all people and explicitly stressed the international dimension of modernity, the institutions at the Mont des Arts first and fore-most advance the unity of the Belgian nation. Even when institutions such as the Palais des Congrès, that was built to house the international meetings during the Expo of 1958, or the Palais des Beaux-Arts, that had well-established connections with avant-garde movements such as *La Libre Esthétique* of Octave Maus, subscribe to an internationalist tradition, their main interest was to represent the idea of the Belgian nation internationally. Whereas in the Mundaneum, modernity was interconnected with the international in a self-evident way, at the Mont des Arts it is rather the modernity of the nation that is glorified.

The Mont des Arts is literally the fragmented product of the will to position Belgium on the map of the world. Universal Exhibitions (1910, 1935 and 1958) and celebrations of the independence of Belgium (1930) were the driving forces for the successive demolition of old neighbourhoods and the construction of new buildings and infrastructures on the site. What existed nevertheless was not erased as easily as was presumed in the endless series of consecutive building projects. Remnants unexpectedly remained, one had to build on top of relics or former streets, and older fragments had to be integrated in new con-structions. The result is that many witnesses of the past, such as the so-called Jewish steps, the Hotel Ravenstein, the Rue de l'Infante Isabelle and the Chapelle de Nassau, are present as relics. The Mont des Arts is thus an archaeological site par excellence; it is an archive of urban history, an archive of the city. The historical significance of the site exceeds the one of the collections. It is probably in this quality of the site as a historical palimpsest that its most relevant connection with the city resides – rather than in the official history of the nation which is enacted in its institutions.

Given its character as an urban palimpsest and its central location with a wide view of the Lower Town it is no surprise that for Paul Otlet the Mont des Arts was a favourable spot to house an urbaneum. This potential role however was never brought to fruition. In its present state, the Mont des Arts rather denies its urbanity and refuses to act as a represen-tational machine which could visualise the city in its intricacy and complexity. The Mont des Arts appears at present as a still place in the labyrinthine reality of the city, a place which only reveals fragments of urbanity: one finds here the embodiment of power and nationhood, but not the traces of everyday dwelling nor the confusion of hectic traffic. One is confronted with the old-fashioned solidity of the Bibliothèque Royale and the severe solemnity of the rise towards the Upper Town, but one lacks the flashing of cyber cafés or the maelstrom of a diversity of passers-by.

The Mont des Arts presents not only a limited, but also an outdated version of Otlet's, Le Corbusier's or Bourgeois' visionary projects. With its museums, its archives and its libraries that collect national art and science, with its Palais des Congrès which acts as a forum for international meetings, with its Sabena building connecting the Mont des Arts with the national airport and from there with the whole world, with its highway giving access to the heart of the city, with its Gare Centrale that is an important node in the Belgian railway network and with its Telex building that provided a node in a modern communication system, the Mont des Arts unmistakably subscribes to a 20th century concept of modernity which stressed exchange and communication as well as to a 19th century conception of national identity. It did not succeed however in maintaining this central role in different networks and in collective memory. In the last decades of the 20th century a shift occurred in concepts of centrality and in the functioning of networks, resulting in the increasing importance of suburban or ex-urban peripheral centres rather than inner cities, in the emergence of new communication networks – the internet – which superseded those based on older technologies and, last but not least, in the fading away of the idea of the nation. In this constellation, the Mont des Arts for now seems to have lost the struggle for supremacy.

From exhibiting to entertaining

As a place that denies its urbanity and does not have a central place in contemporary network systems, as a place where objects are preserved in the order of the past, the Mont des Arts nowadays barely connects to living reality. In a way it embodies the traditional notion of the museum as a kind of sacred space, as a place where a well-chosen collection of special things can provide a unique experience. As such, it defines itself as a space which is "outside" everyday life, outside the more mundane spaces of urban life. One could see it as a "heterotopian" space, where time and space evolve according to a special logic. Traditionally the museum is supposed to withdraw objects from daily life and from their destruction through time. It constitutes a threshold in the city, a *lieu de mémoire*. This documentary mission is still taken very seriously by the institutions that gather on the Mont des Arts. As a scientific bastion, therefore, it seems to be quite distant from contemporary developments in the museum world. Whereas the concept of the encyclopaedic or scientific museum is oriented towards the pure collection and preservation of art and knowledge, nowadays museums rather tend toward stressing the act of exhibiting itself. The constellation within which objects are displayed, the public itself as well as the building that frames all this are more and more considered the most crucial aspects of the whole museum business. This shift is paralleled by the tendency to no longer conceive of museums as high brow bastions which are withdrawn from daily life, but to see them as integrated urban elements which eventually take part in everyday life. Museums, it is said, have a social role to fulfil, a role that is linked with the place they take up within urban culture.

One could say that nowadays there are, roughly, two kinds of museums. There are those that attempt to integrate themselves in their community by establishing educational programmes, by developing different modes of information distribution and by a conscious policy of high accessibility. These museums consider it their mission to open themselves to the public at large and to enhance their penetrability as an institution. There are on the other hand also museums which rather stress their function of conservation, who focus on scientific research and make serious contributions to art history. They argue that it is still the prime mission of museums to act as places of memory and documentation. Whereas museums of the first kind attempt to communicate with as large a public as possible and to participate in public debates, museums of the second category focus rather on the object.

It is unmistakably the first category of museums, which is considered the most successful at the moment. Since the inauguration of the Centre Pompidou in Paris, the museum as a public pole of attraction supplants the museum as site of contemplation and study. Museums such as the Centre Pompidou act rather as cultural centres, participating in a culture of consumption, entertainment and mass communication. A large amount of extra programmes – workshops, temporary exhibits, libraries, bookshops, and restaurants – have supplemented the core functions of documentation and study. The museum is thus transformed into a container of activities, which forms a magnetic force within urban social life. Flexible, nonhierarchically ordered exhibition rooms, transparent façades, gigantic public spaces, a central atrium, splendid views of the city and easy accessibility strip the museum of its elitist character.

At first sight, one is tempted to welcome these attempts to attract a large audience and to integrate the museum in the daily life of the city. In a certain sense, this argument in favour of the urban and social role of the museum reformulates the older concept of the museum as a democratic institution, in that it was connected with the idea of the public and polis: museums initially were supposed to make the collections of the king accessible to the public and to thus contribute to the construction of the nation as a community of citizens. The museum was seen as an intermediary force between art, history, science and citizens. As an enlightened institution serving all parts of the population, the museum was supposed to stimulate a critical attitude and to enhance the construction of democracy. The didactic and educational aspirations that formed the basis of this model however have recently given way to an approach that favours the values of spectacle and entertainment, thereby blurring the critical distance between object and visitor and privileging immediate experience and quick consumption over study and contemplation.

The desire to communicate with a large public seems to imply the danger of superficiality. Museums are increasingly transformed into popular entertainment sites that are part of mass culture. Recently constructed museums like the Guggenheim in Bilbao, or earlier the Neue Staatsgalerie in Stuttgart are designed as urban sites, which take part in an intricate network of routes, squares and gardens. The museum is thus developing into a place where one strolls around throwing quick, distracted looks at the works of art, a place to see and to be seen, and a place to spend some spare time. It is an agreeable place to meet people, to browse among books, to shop for tasteful gifts. The consequence however is that in a constellation like this the museum threatens to overshoot its core mission of preserving memory. For as Andreas Huyssen observes, the success of the museum in quantitative terms – as a place for the masses to revel in memory – seems to be paralleled by a waning of historical consciousness, a loss of the sense of history. Capitalist culture, with its continuing frantic pace and its television politics of instant entertainment and quick oblivion, is indeed inherently amnesiac. In as far as the museums give in to the pressure of blockbuster shows and record numbers of visitors, they are accomplices in the process that leads to the paradoxical situation that memory and amnesia seem to operate in conjunction rather than opposition.[10]

The challenge

The institutions assembled on the Mont des Arts mostly conceive of their role within the old and familiar framework of enlightenment rhetoric, which entrusts them with the task of functioning as collection agencies for the best of art and science. By preserving, categorising and presenting this material they make it into public property. Thus they contribute to the construction of a democratic public realm. Nevertheless nobody can claim that these institutions act according to a very open, contemporary, public oriented strategy. Notwithstanding a few exceptional moments, the Bibliothèque Royale, the Palais des Beaux-Arts, the Musées Royaux and the Palais des Congrès operate as elite bodies where in a very serious way, and without too much publicity, art and science are being dealt with.

The ideas however that are prevalent on the international museum scene – the number of visitors, the quality and quantity of press coverage – do not seem to be of great importance to them (except for the museums perhaps that recently started organising blockbuster shows). Questions related to the social role of art works or concerts, questions related to the surplus value of printed matter over television or the internet, questions related to the value of multiculturalism do not seem to get more than limited attention. Although at this site a remarkable number of institutions are located next to one another, there seems to be scarcely any interaction among them, nor do they have any serious impact on the public space of the city. This situation of lethargy poses a problem, because it means that what the Mont des Arts potentially has to offer to the city and its citizens remains invisible and not easily accessible.

It might be, however, that this inertia also implies unexpected opportunities. Precisely because none of the Mont des Arts institutions has given in to fashionable tendencies or commercial pressure, the potentialities of the site have been preserved. Commercialisation, entertainment and cheap stunts have not (yet?) really taken over the Mont des Arts. The main question therefore seems to be: how to make sure that this museum site in the core of the historical city, this urban palimpsest with its multitude of hidden layers of significance, can play a more dynamic role within the urban constellation, without giving in to commercial pressures or claptrap? How to transform these museums and institutions in such a way that they re-connect with the public realm and the urban space, without giving up their time-honoured mission according to which they are to house the memory of (Belgian) Art and Science?

1. Rudi Laermans, "Ik verzamel, dus ik ben?. Kleine postume dialoog met Walter Benjamin," in *De Witte Raaf* no 58, (nov-dec 1995), p. 2.

2. Theodor W. Adorno, "Valéry Proust Museum," (1953) in Cornelis van de Ven (red.), *Museumarchitectuur* (Rotterdam: Uitgeverij 010, 1989), pp. 126-139.

3. Jorinde Seijdel, "Gemengde musea," in *Kunst&Museumjournaal* no 1, (1992).

4. Paul Otlet, *Traité de documentation. Le livre sur le livre* (Brussels, 1934).

5. For the Mundaneum, see for instance: W. Boesiger and O. Stonorov, *Le Corbusier et Pierre Jeanneret. Oeuvre Complète 1910-1929* (Zurich: Editions d'Architecture/Artemis, 1995), pp. 190-197. Karel Teige, "Mundaneum," in *Oase*, no 41 (1994), pp. 43-56. Lieven De Cauter, Lode De Clercq and Bruno De Meulder, "Van 'Exposition coloniale' naar 'Cité Mondiale'. Tervuren als koloniale site," in: Herman Asselberghs en Dieter Lesage (eds.), *Het musuem van de natie. Van kolonialisme tot globalisering* (Brussels: Yves Gevaert, 1999), pp. 45-71. Bruno De Meulder, *Reformisme thuis en overzee. Geschiedenis van de Belgische planning in een kolonie 1880-1960* (Leuven, 1994). Benoit Peeters, "Une Utopie Belge: Le mundaneum," in Antoine Pickels and Jaques Sojcher (eds.), *Belgique. Toujours Grande et Belle* (Brussels: Complexe,1998), pp. 142 –149.

6. We are referring here to the discussions held on the occasion of the enlargement of the MOMA in New York. The Museum of Modern Art (ed.), *Imagining the Future of The Museum of Modern Art*, Harry N. Abrams (New York, 1998).

7. Paul Otlet, "Palais Mondial" (1928), in W. Boesiger and O. Stonorov, o.c., p. 190-191.

8. ibidem.

9. Paul Otlet, "L'Urbaneum. Bruxelles, Cité Mondiale. Bruxelles, Grande Ville. Bruxelles, Capitale de la Belgique," in *La Cité. Architecture. Urbanisme. Art Public*, vol. IX, no. 10, 1931.

10. Andreas Huyssen, *Twilight Memories. Marking Time in a Culture of Amnesia* (London: Routledge, 1995), especially the chapter on "Escape from Amnesia: The Museum as Mass Medium," pp. 13-36.

LE CYCLE (OU CHAINE) FONDAMENTAL(E)
DE LA DOCUMENTATION

1 LE MONDE (LA REALITE)
2 LA PENSEE INDIVIDUELLE REPRODUIT
ARTIES (ELEMENTS) DU MONDE (CONNAISSANCE)
3 LA PAROLE INDIVIDUELLE REPRODUIT
ELEMENTS DU MONDE.
4 LA SCIENCE CONCENTRE SYSTEMATIQUE-
T LES CONNAISSANCES ET LES EXPE-
NCES INDIVIDUELLES.
5 LE LIVRE-DOCUMENT EXPRIME
SCIENCE.

6 L'ENSEIGNEMENT SE FONDE SUR
LES LIVRES-DOCUMENTS.
7 LA TECHNIQUE SE FONDE SUR
L'ENSEIGNEMENT ET SUR LE
LIVRE-DOCUMENT.
8 L'INDUSTRIE ET LES ACTIVITES
SE FONDE SUR LA TECHNIQUE ET
SUR LE LIVRE-DOCUMENT.
9 L'ORGANISATION (POLITIQUE ET AD-
MINISTRATION) SE FONDE SUR L'INDUS-
TRIE ET LA TECHNIQUE POUR DONNER
PLAN ET DIRECTION DU MONDE.

10 LE MONDE, FINALEMENT SE TROUVE MODIFIE.

| SOURCE:
PAUL OTLET
TRAITE DE DOCUMEN-
TATION (ILLUSTRATIONS)
N 25 | ENCYCLOPÆDIA UNIVERSALIS
MUNDANEUM
PARS [002] DOCUMENTATIO | MAT: 002
LIEU:
TEMPS:
PERS: | N° 8505 | |

THE MONT DES ARTS, BRUSSELS 2000
AND THE FONDATION ROI BAUDOUIN

Marie-Laure Roggemans

Within the Association of European Cities of Culture for the year 2000, Brussels chose the theme of "The City" and launched its project based on three essential premises and two options.[1]

The premises are:

1. That Brussels holds a geographical and symbolic position within the European Union as being at the meeting point of the cultures of the north and the south.
2. That Brussels is a multicultural city.
3. That Brussels is a capital many times over: capital of the federal state, of its two main communities as well as the capital of Europe.

The options are:

1. Brussels 2000 cannot be a "one-off." The 2000 events will be "introduced like an acupuncturist's needles in places that are carefully selected in the city and the minds of the inhabitants,"[2] in order to provoke renovation and a global change.
2. The interaction of cultures is enriching. Until now, Brussels has managed the coexistence of different cultures without any negative consequences, which is historically highly unusual.

In this context, the Fondation Roi Baudouin is co-ordinating two projects: that of the Mont des Arts in the city centre and that of the new partner associates[3] in the 19 boroughs that make up the Brussels region.

The main original feature of the Fondation Roi Baudouin's project on the Mont des Arts is to combine pragmatism and the achievement of concrete projects with a will to accomplish successfully a long term urban and cultural project.

The questions raised by
the redevelopment of the Mont des Arts

Many questions were raised by the survey of urban cultural facilities undertaken by *Cooparch* and *Sint-Lukas* for Brussels 2000. While the model of cultural democratisation remains valid, there are now new stakes at play which also require that cultural diversity be taken into account, "or if one prefers, of the cultural usage and practices that take place in the different social milieu."[4]

For a writer such as A. Huet, the approach to culture inspired by the model of the democratic ideal and popular education are such which took "all their strength and meaning from a time when society was seeking to constitute itself on the exclusive basis of homogenisation and inevitable progress." However, these positions "no longer allow for the understanding of the dialectic movement of homogenisation (social worlds which regroup people around a same cultural entity) and differentiation (social worlds which distinguish between people on the basis of the particular usage they make of the cultural entity) or of the creation of mass culture (grouping together around clothing or musical fashions, for example) or, again, of singularisation (the manner in which a person will differentiate himself from others beyond the following of a fashion), so characteristic of current cultural practices." Huet concludes that "it is this crisis of the relationship to culture which necessitates the questions about urban cultural facilities."

Huet takes up the following difficulties in particular:

- the difficulty for a society to realise that it is diverse: how can it deal with diversity alongside its tendency to reduce this diversity to a recognised culture?
- the weight of the reference to a recognised culture and the strong tendencies, in the name of cultural democratisation, to give it back to those who are deprived of it, either through diffusion ("the conquest of new audiences"), or through democratisation ("access to culture for all").
- The distinction that has been made between socio-cultural action and cultural action (often reinforced by the distinction between central urban cultural facilities and neighbourhood ones) and the ambivalence this carries between recognised culture and the culture of permanent education.
- The crisis in the symbolic expression of the cultural sphere. On the one hand, neither the concept of democratised culture, nor that of an elitist culture are still able to mobilise "beliefs, energies and struggles." There has been progress in the area of the democratisation of culture, but the question now is less about homogenisation of the cultural link than about cohesion ("the maintenance of a multiple unity"). At the same time, the culture of the elite is no longer dominant. On the other hand, the dichotomy between the culture of the elite and democratic culture is superimposed on that between the development of an international mass culture and localisation (socio-cultural policies implemented at the neighbourhood level).

The survey carried out by the Brussels 2000 team[5] shows that the cultural/socio-cultural differentiation between urban facilities and neighbourhood ones will lead to a loss of dynamism for existing facilities:

1. On the one hand, there is a need to recognise the "important" central facilities and their role on the scale of the "Big City" while fulfilling the requirement of involving other social and cultural worlds with the concern that their positioning allows the other facilities in the city to keep their place.
2. On the other hand, there is a need to take into account the other facilities (which generally have a historical link with the socio-cultural movement) as important relays for urban cultural action. These facilities therefore have a twin role to play: undertakings on a regional or urban scale and local undertakings defined by their location.

The four major lines of action for the
Fondation Roi Baudouin in the Mont des Arts area

Within the space of a few hectares, the Mont des Arts area holds some of the most important cultural institutions, buildings and historical sites in the country, and, as such, is faced with a number of major challenges. The first challenge is to open its cultural facilities to a wider and more diverse public. The second is to make neighbouring institutions and facilities function as a network and to encourage them to work more closely with additional and external partners. The third challenge is to ensure its international range.

As a guide for its activities on the Mont des Arts, the Fondation Roi Baudouin has put four strategic lines of action to the fore, in the short, medium and long term.

It is worth noting that in its role as a driving force, the Fondation Roi Baudouin works in close collaboration with the relevant public bodies at the levels of the federal state, the Brussels-Capital region and the city of Brussels. The consultation process it has set up has made possible a general mobilisation, a significant financial commitment from the relevant public bodies and co-financing by several private partners.

The first line of action

The Mont des Arts area has the highest concentration of big institutions and facilities not only in Brussels, but also in the country as a whole. In order to open wide its gates, greater visibility and access must be ensured.

With this in mind, the Fondation Roi Baudouin is supporting the following actions:
1. The setting up of local sign-posting
2. The setting up of a day and night scenography in the entrances and shop windows giving on to the Place Royale; the Musée d'Art Moderne has reopened its doors in the

Hotel Altenloh; the Musée des Instruments de Musique and the Musées Royaux des Beaux-Arts de Belgique are working on a common set for their front windows; the Musée d'Art Ancien will set up its new bookshop, art shop and café on the ground floor of the Gresham and Argenteau buildings on the corner of the Place Royale and the Rue de la Régence.

3. The setting up of a scenography for the visit to all the remains of Charles Quint's old palace, which include the basement of the old Aula Magna, the chapel built by Charles Quint, the old Rue Isabelle and the main part of the old Palais de Coudenberg, as well as remnants of the old Hôtel de Lalaing. This ensemble, which is linked to the Roi Baudouin Memorial and the Musée de la Dynastie, now stretches from the Rue de la Villa Hermosa to the Place du Palais.

4. The stimulation of the use of public car parks in the vicinity of the Place Royale.

The second line of action

To open up the area by helping to overcome the Upper/Lower Town separation and ensuring a greater mix of cultural, tertiary, residential and mobility functions in the area, taking account of the Sablon neighbourhood[6] and the presence of the Gare Centrale[7] as active elements in the opening up the area. The Fondation is making sure that all of the area's roads (including those that are currently "car drains") get the same quality of design as the Tracé Royal (royal route).

The third line of action

The architectural and urbanistic symbolism of a city is in the hearts of all and is also a marketing feature used effectively in other major European cities. This requires both a highlighting of the architectural and scenic heritage and an approach to public spaces that carries the image of a modern city. The cleaning up of the façades of the historic ensemble which includes the Bibliothèque Royale buildings and the Palais of Charles de Lorraine are under way. The same is true of the neighbourhood lighting scheme and the refurbishment of the Jardin de l'Albertine, both projects that are striving to introduce contemporary elements. Finally, planning permission for the recreation of the sculpture garden next to the museum is about to be granted.

The fourth line of action

Within the framework of its co-ordination of the different projects for the redevelopment of the Mont des Arts, the Fondation has always tried to involve the institutions located there. On the one hand, it has been holding round-table discussions with all the players involved every three months. On the other, it has tried to follow up this approach by organising five seminars at an international level, on the future of these great institutions and the challenges they face in the 21st century. These seminars are not aimed at the wider public, but at the officials of the institutions, the executives, the partners and the private players involved. They are destined to lay down the first stepping stones for possible interaction between the urban aims and the development of the neighbourhood on the one hand and, on the other, the museums in the area[8,] the Archives Générales du Royaume, the Palais des Beaux-Arts and the Palais des Congrès. The work done in these seminars will be sent on to a commission named "Mont des Arts et après," associated with the Fondation, which will have the time and means to formulate recommendations.

1. Report on the preparatory phase "Brussels, European city of culture of the Year 2000" (Brussels, 1997).
2. Robert Palmer: inaugural speech for Brussels 2000, February 2000.
3. As well as the activities carried out in the historic heart of the city, the Fondation Roi Baudoin was keen to empha- sise the public spaces in the 19 communes. Starting with an appeal for bids entitled "(Public) Art tamed" launched in 1998, the Fondation Roi Baudouin selected a number of public spaces in the 19 communes ("classical" public spaces, but also hospitals, public libraries, schools, public sector housing, cultural centres...) and called on artist- through an original means of dialogue - to redevelop them. 28 projects are being carried out.
4. A. Huet "De la démocratisation de la culture à la diversité créatrice," in *Lieux culturels*, *Les Annales de la recherche urbaine*, no 70 (March 1996).
5. See the report on the preparatory phase "Brussels, European city of culture in the year 2000" (Brussels, 1997).
6. In the case of the Sablon, a project is being studied for a link between the Jardin de l'Albertine and the Sablon via the Albertine patio.
7. In the case of the Gare Centrale, it is a question of ensuring that the SNCB (national railway company) project for easier access to the platforms has positive consequences for the linking of the Upper and Lower Towns.
8. Notably the Musées des Beaux-Arts, the Musée des Instruments, the Musée du Cinéma, the Palais de Charles de Lorraine, the Musée de la Dynastie, the Memorial Roi Baudouin and the museums housed in the Bibliothèque Royale.

Night scenography, Jardin de l'Albertine

VI

LABORATORY FOR
THE CITY OF TOMORROW

new conglomerate of institutions

Royal Membrane:
urban lobby between
Boulevard de l'Impératrice
and the station

1 ramp
1 ramp
1 ramp
1 ramp

1 rooflight

City Beach

1 gallery

1 ramp

metro

Horta Hall

new connections: doors, stairs and corridors

1 tunnel

1 stair
1 ramp
1 door
1 door

1 ramp

1 door

1 ramp

1 ramp

1 stair

1 door
1 stair

1 ramp
1 stair
1 ramp
1 door
1 ramp
1 door
1 door

1 door
1 door

1 stair

the Boulevard de l'Impératrice and the railway station will be a multifunctional urban lobby that gives acces to the subterranean entrances and routes of all institutes (like a membrane); the first jo

the Boulevard de l'Impératrice and the railway station will be a multifunctional urban lobby that gives acces to the subterranean entrances and routes of all institutes (like a membrane); the ROYAL MEMBRANE is added, the space between

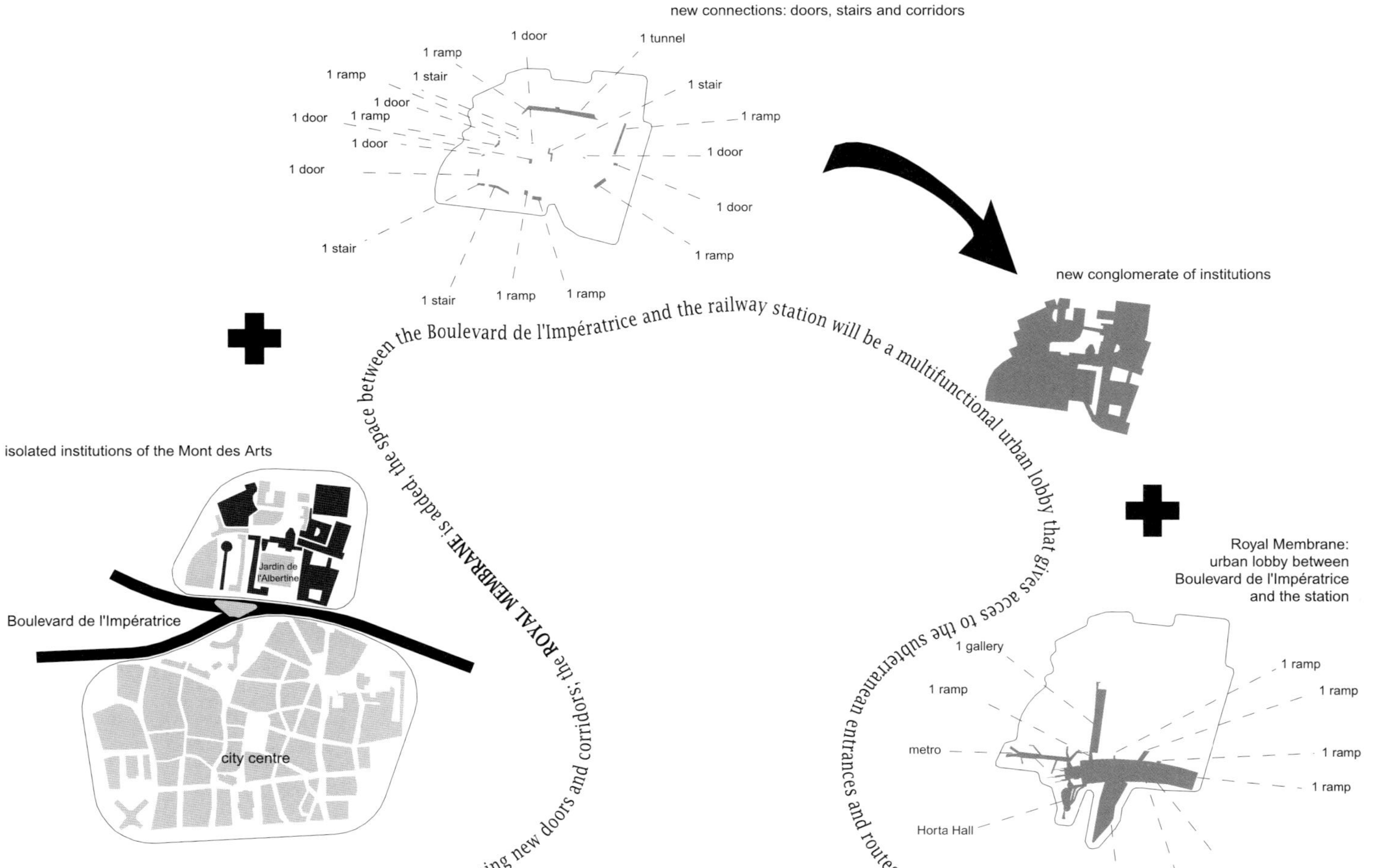

isolated cultural institutions can start to cooperate by opening new doors and corridors,

isolated institutions of the Mont des Arts

Jardin de
l'Albertine

city centre

Boulevard de l'Impératrice

Max.1 *Crimson*

The Mont des Arts: One Nation under Ground

...ke place, an international book fair, a conference on genetic engineering: the institutions temporarily take possession of (part of) the **ROYAL MEMBRANE**, their program (festivals, exhibitions, conferences) bleeds into the public realm: the **ROYAL MEMBRANE** connects the Mont des Arts to the city; a number of monuments to the royal family and decisive moments in Belgian history give the Royal Membrane its...

mayor theme exhibition:
Art Mountains and other Mountains

book fair with lectures,
Poetry International Belgium,
Semaine du livre (book week)

Oracle Europe,
three day conference
on war protocols

...point and visibility as a place and as a collection of cultural institutions, activities and manifestations; a complex of physical, organisational, visual and mental connections is the result with the **ROYAL MEMBRANE** at its core.

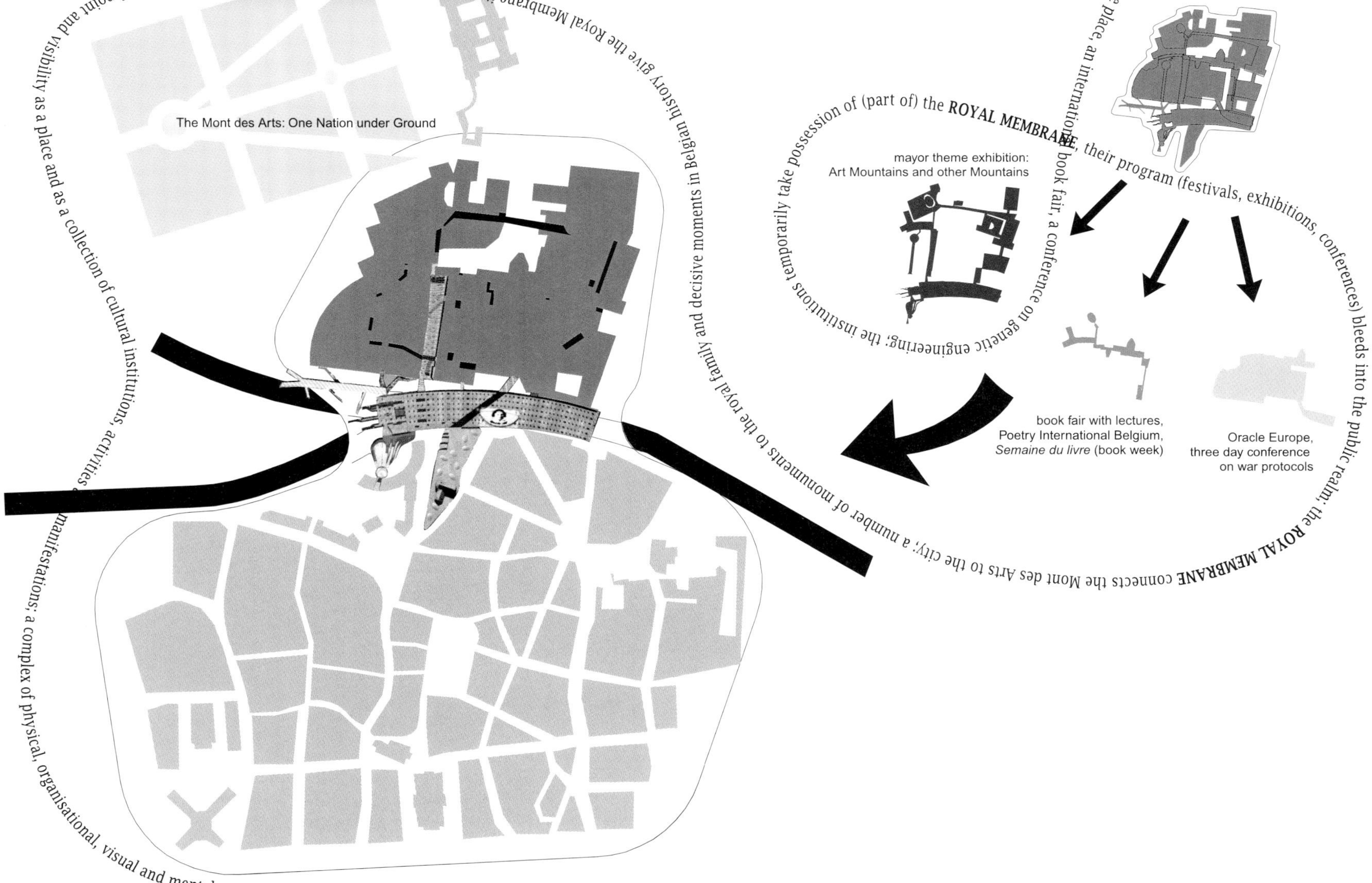

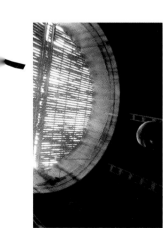

Leopold III equestrian statue, abdication of Leopold III: July 31, 1950

The Mont des Arts Brussels: One Nation under Ground

The Mont des Arts in the centre of Brussels consists of a number of high-culture institutions gathered around a monumental urbanistic ensemble of squares and stairs. Financially, politically and symbolically it is has been created by the royal family of Saxe-Coburg over a period of 100 years for their people: the Belgians.

The Mont des Arts, like a lot of other Belgian institutions, is being relentlessly criticized for its ugliness, emptiness, lack of identity and for its complete failure as a national monument or even as a public space. The Mont des Arts lacks luxurious connections to the city and its institutions are like crystal growths inside rock: hidden, isolated, autistic and precious.

The result is a collection of institutions that lead a secret life inside a flawed monument in full sight of the entire nation. Behind the stone walls and beneath the empty streets and squares people study books, practice symphonies, look at art, restore paintings, speak at conventions and listen to recitals.

At peak hour, tens of thousands of Belgians arrive in the city after a train ride from their suburbs and the villages of their parents in a subterranean station inside the Mont des Arts. From here they scurry through tunnels to their offices. At the end of the day they scurry back and are relieved when their train comes up out of the ground again to take them back home.

We do not want to make the Mont des Arts less empty. We do not want to make it into the kind of success associated with large-scale cultural and architectural interventions. We want to make it work on its own terms, but make it work better, much better.

By a limited number of discrete and inexpensive interventions we propose to short circuit the subterranean routes and spaces of the Bibliothèque Royale, the Palais des Beaux-Arts, the museum, the Palais des Congrès and the Gare Centrale and merge them into one sponge-like urban structure beneath the city. One opening punched in a concrete wall means that the convention centre might bleed into the corridors and auditoria of the Bibliothèque Royale. One pathway between the station and the Palais des Beaux-Arts might irrigate the Joseph Beuys exhibition with Flemish commuters, only four new doors are needed from the Ravenstein Gallery to the new Stuiver Gallery etc. Without any grand architectural gesture, the institutions will increase their surface, visitors, accessibility, funds and a new synergy will be created.

We want to preserve the mountainlike crust of emptiness, ugliness and impenetrable boredom. This is the protective layer that is needed to make cultural and urban institutions thrive. In contemporary Belgium, culture and economy come to fruition in the shadows, the cellars, tunnels, holes and pits. Not only cultural projects like reading, writing, talking, listening, playing and studying happen outside the city's gaze; the national memory itself seems to shy away from too much attention and daylight. There exists a secret consensus that the royal family is what keeps this country together. In Belgium underneath a thick crust of general apathy towards the royal family, lies a deep and serious feeling of need. Sometimes, as with the death of Baudouin, it breaks out and spills into the streets. The royal family is the secret connector, the invisible glue.

This is why to us the only way to rejuvenate the Mont des Arts as the symbolic centre of the relationship of the royal family with the Belgian nation is to put it underground. Beneath the Boulevard de l'Impératrice but on top of the underground railway tracks lies a secret space filled with concrete columns and strange crevices leading to the car park, the street or the train platforms. This space we have declared to be the counterspace, a mirror as it were, of the flawed monumentality of the Mont des Arts that lies in the open air. In this space we propose sad and beautiful subterranean monuments to the ambiguous memories the Belgians have of their royals, monuments to the cohesive power of collective shame and loss.

Just like its flawed counterpart on top, the Jardin de l'Albertine, this space organizes the different institutions of the Mont des Arts surrounding it. We propose to turn it into a subterranean and monumental urban lobby, that gives access to all the subterranean entrances and routes of the institutions and at the same time to the Gare Centrale and the old centre of the city, like a membrane: the Royal Membrane. The membrane is the monumental form that introduces the larger but more discrete project of punctures and connections through the stony walls and thick floorboards of the institutions around the Jardin de l'Albertine. The Royal Membrane and its monuments give this new web of physical, organisational, visual and mental connections the focal point and visibility the Mont des Arts lacks today.

Queen Astrid skylight, portrait in stained glass, † in car crash on August 29, 1935

"William Tell takes refuge in Küssnacht.'
"That was where the queen died,' whispered Louis.
"Where?'
"In Küssnacht.' (Küss, kiss. Nacht, night. Vlieghe.)
"I didn't see any queen,' said Vlieghe.
"Queen Astrid, dummy.' Louis laid the stress on the 'strid,' just like aunt Violet who kept a musty suitcase full of clippings and magazines about the life and death of the Swedish Swan who had come from the North to marry King Leopold and who had died of it.

From: Hugo Claus, The Sorrow of Belgium, Pantheon Books, New York 1990. p. 58-59

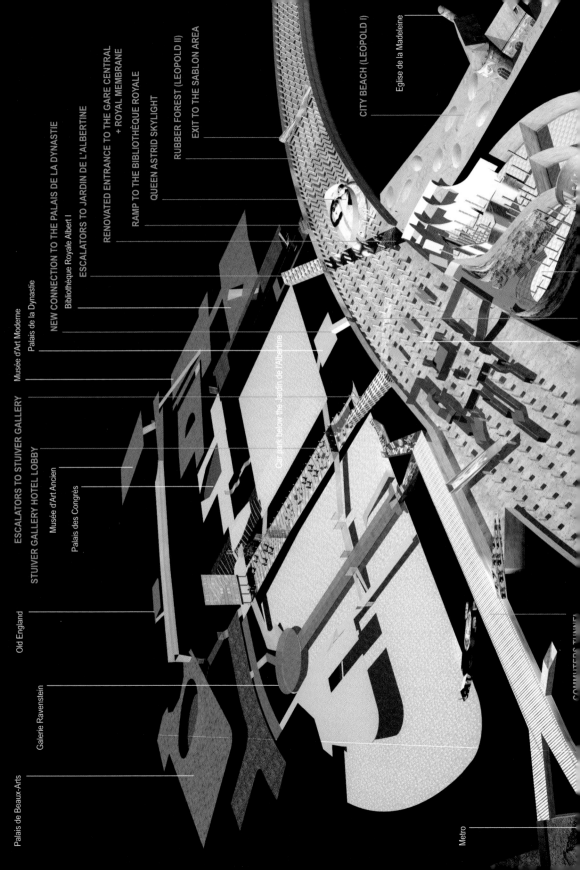

Palais de Beaux-Arts

Galerie Ravenstein

Old England

ESCALATORS TO STUIVER GALLERY

STUIVER GALLERY HOTEL LOBBY

Musée d'Art Ancien

Palais des Congrès

Musée d'Art Moderne

Palais de la Dynastie

NEW CONNECTION TO THE PALAIS DE LA DYNASTIE

Bibliothèque Royale Albert I

ESCALATORS TO JARDIN DE L'ALBERTINE

RENOVATED ENTRANCE TO THE GARE CENTRAL + ROYAL MEMBRANE

RAMP TO THE BIBLIOTHÈQUE ROYALE

QUEEN ASTRID SKYLIGHT

RUBBER FOREST (LEOPOLD II)

EXIT TO THE SABLON AREA

CITY BEACH (LEOPOLD I)

Eglise de la Madeleine

Car park below the Jardin de l'Albertine

Metro

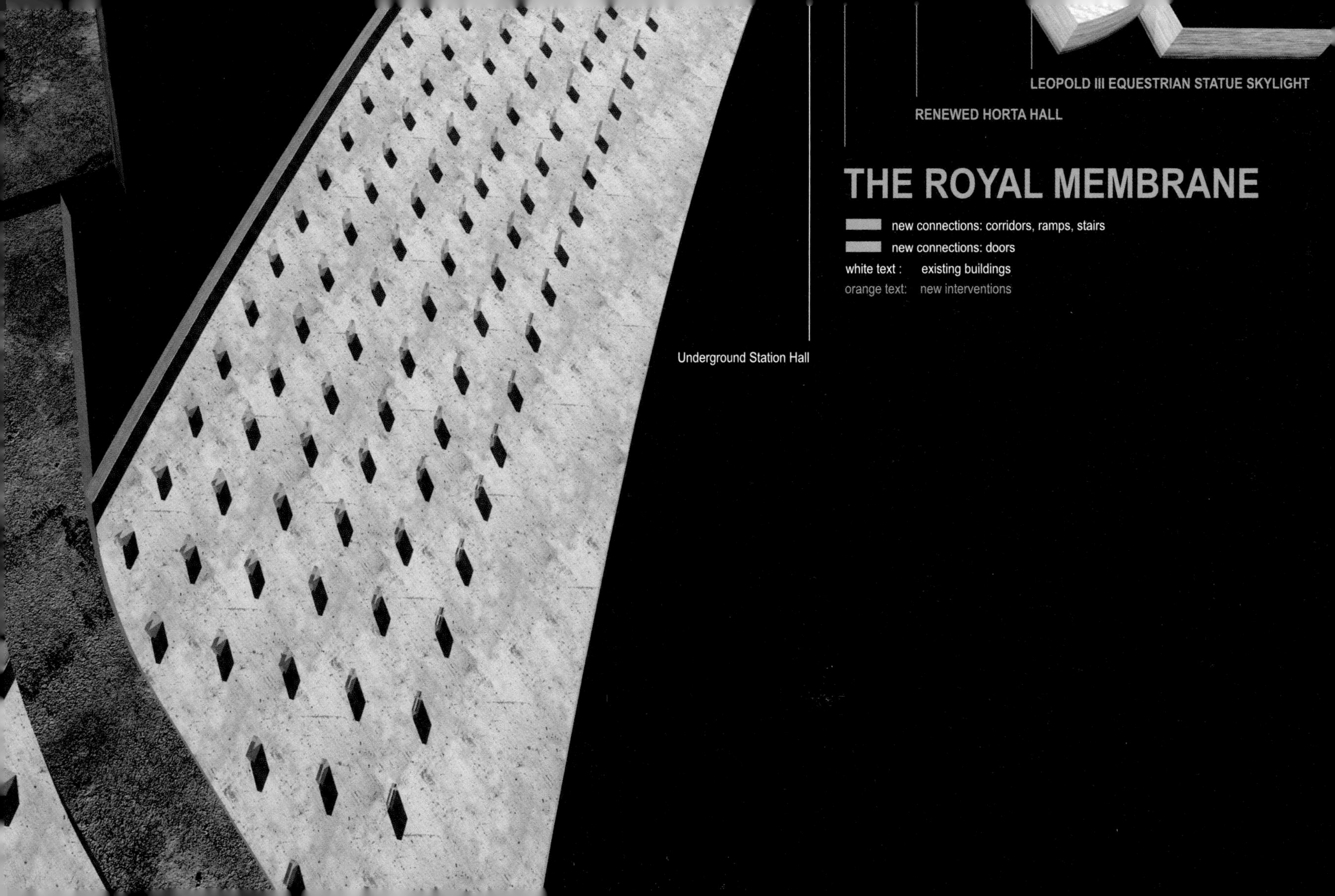

LEOPOLD III EQUESTRIAN STATUE SKYLIGHT

RENEWED HORTA HALL

THE ROYAL MEMBRANE

new connections: corridors, ramps, stairs

new connections: doors

white text :   existing buildings
orange text: new interventions

Underground Station Hall

CONTEXTUAL HINTERLAND

While the degraded condition of the Mont des Arts can be seen as interconnected with a much larger pattern of conditions and physical relationships in the Brussels region, it is the hypothesis of this approach that only a localised and defensive strategy can successfully recapture the centrality of the site to the life of the city. The contextual hinterland of operational relevance to the proposed transformation of the Mont des Arts is roughly the area of the old quarter "la Putterie," from the Place du Grand Sablon (A) at the south; to the Cathédrale de Saint Michel (B) at the north; the Place Royale (C) at the east; and the Grand' Place (D) at the west. Within this constellation is the Gare Centrale (E), the Place de l'Albertine (F), and the Place d'Espagne (G), but it is the Jardin de l'Albertine (H) which is reinforced as the epicentre of the area.

URBAN PATHOLOGY

The Jardin de l'Albertine is a void at the heart of the Putterie. Rather than connecting to its context, its four sides remain estranged: the monumental steps of the east and west edges; the mute portico of the Bibliothèque Royale to the south; the barrier at the Rue Mont des Arts on the north. This urban pathology is the real villain. Its dystopic presence must be reversed. Its transformation will catalyse the reconfiguration of the Putterie.

DE-MASKING THE MONT DES ARTS
Panorama Populaire
Design + Urbanism, New York

Partners-in-Charge: Richard Plunz, Viren Brahmbhatt
Project Team: Marc Ackerson, Biju Chirathalattu, Earl Jackson, William Kenworthey, Anna Pew, Melanie Taylor, Maja Vidak
Assistants: Akihiro Aoki, Liana Cassel, Shital Lakdawala, Gary Stoltz, Katherine Takahara, Tanja Villbrandt
Tim Macfarlane, Structural Design Consultant, Dewhurst Macfarlane and Partners, New York

MAIN AXIS
SECONDARY CONNECTIONS

NEW TRANSMUTATION
EXISTING

■ PHASING
▨ SECONDARY EFFECTS

PHASE 01

PHASE 03

PHASE 02

PHASE 04

AA

LAYERING

Important to this recentring is recognition of the several sublimated historical layers within the site. At specific moments the old (i.e. "pre-boulevard" and "pre-railroad") city remains under the bridging of the present-day streets and fabric. A lexicon of the spatial and temporal layering becomes a catalyst for the site strategy, with a sectional matrix of movement and light providing a new infrastructure that integrates and transforms the old.

DE-MASKING

The controlled excavation of the site allows it to be de-masked. The de-masking makes a series of public panoramas, transforming the hermetic domain of royalty to a new populist presence. The panoramas are understood sectionally; the Putterie is returned to the body politic through its diverse layers. The Mont des Arts is opened to the city as an emblem of the cultural diversity of the Belgian state.

TRANSMUTATIONS

Primary among the site objectives is the reinvention of physical connections between the Putterie and its context. Some conditions producing its isolation are recent; some have evolved over centuries. A historiography of the site is established through transmutation of the layers at those moments where reinforcement or sublimation of one or another morphological tendency is desired. For the vertical (sectional) city, the 30.0m and 41.7m levels are reinforced as the principal connective data between the Upper and Lower Town. For the horizontal (planar) city, the north-south and east-west axes are reinforced at their confluence in the Jardin de l'Albertine, with particular emphasis on the following operations:

Sublimation of the physical barrier at the southern boundary of the Mont des Arts, a condition that has dated from the original 11th century wall of the city. The fabric between the Bibliothèque Royale and the Musée d'Art Moderne is cut, allowing an opening from the Jardin de l'Albertine to the Rue de la Paille (I).

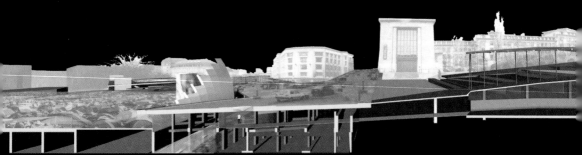

Reinforcement of north-south linkages and open space toward the area of the Place du Grand Sablon and the Palais de Justice through the new cut and across the Mont des Arts, connecting to the Rue Ravenstein/Coudenberg (J) and the Cathédrale de Saint Michel beyond. Thus, for the first time since the building of the first 11th century city walls, there will be continuous public passage.

Recentring of the east-west visual link and pedestrian circulation between the Place Royale and tower of the Église de Saint Jacques-sur-Coudenberg, and the Grand'Place and tower of the City Hall. Essential in this formulation is the visual remembrance of a particular piece of the old block, formerly existing within the Jardin de l'Albertine: the block of medieval origin (K), bounded by the former Rue de Montagne de la Cour and the former Rue des Trois Têtes. This block functioned historically to reinforce the east-west visual axis from the Place Royale to the Grand'Place that had been lost by the 20th century. The block reappears as the glass structure of the "Winter Garden." The axis toward the Place Royale is further reinforced by reconstruction of the east street wall of the Rue de Montagne de la Cour.

Reinforcement of the former Rue de la Madeleine within the Jardin de l'Albertine as a glass-covered "Galerie de la Madeleine" which extends the old axis of the Rue de la Madeleine to the Rue du Musée (L). This move is combined with the redesign of the entire Place de l'Albertine to integrate the Église de la Petite Madeleine (M) at the lower end with a new entry to the mezzanine of the Gare Centrale as well as the Palais des Congrès and Bibliothèque Royale. This new "street" realigns public passage with the Chapelle Saint-Georges (N) and the remaining fragments of the Chapelle de la Cour (O), presently embedded in the portico of the Bibliothèque Royale.

Sublimation of the neo-classical city, especially the principal façade of the Bibliothèque Royale with its estranged Jardin de l'Albertine; and of the Boulevard de l'Empereur (P), which, together with the sub-terranean cut of the railroad tracks, has formed a modern "wall" within the Putterie. The Bibliothèque façade becomes the ligament of the Mont des Arts through its integration with the new Galerie.

Reinforcement of the Boulevard de l'Empereur and the Boulevard de l'Impératrice (Q) as a progression of sectional linkages with the underground city; from the Place de l'Albertine, to the Passage Horta (R), to the Place d'Espagne.

Reinforcement of the gothic layer of the Place Royale, specifically the excavation of the Palais de Charles Quint (S).

FUNCTIONAL TRIGGERS

The proposal is predicated on infrastructural upgrading and corresponding functional "triggers" that will precipitate further spontaneous infill. The triggering functions are the following
(in order of priority):

Palais des Congrès (T): expanded to upgrade and augment the main exhibition space; accomplished principally through removal of the top floor of the parking garage under the Place de l'Albertine, to be replaced with a taller space for exhibition incorporated with a new public roofscape.

Cinémathèque Royale and Musée du Cinéma (U): expanded and reprogrammed to become a primary European research facility for cinematic theory and production, reflecting the status of its archival holdings; phase one expansion to the area of the original Horta garage and to adjacent new excavation in the second phase.

Winter Garden (V): programmed as the main public nexus amongst the Musées Royaux, the Bibliothèque Royale and the Archives Générales du Royaume, Palais des Congrès, Palais des Beaux Arts, and the Musée du Cinéma.

Galerie de la Madeleine (W): programmed as the principle east-west connection through the Putterie, incorporating a new linear "Museum of the City of Brussels," with visitors descending from the realm of "royalty" to "commerce" (and vice versa) along a path that traverses this historical divide. This progression is related to the re-roofing in glass of the archeological excavation of the Palais de Charles Quint in the Place Royale, exposing the ruins to the city above.

Place de l'Albertine (F): reconstructed for outdoor performances and festivals, to include the specta-board construction at the eastern edge.

Place d'Espagne (G): reconstructed and reprogrammed at the upper levels of the parking structure as a "black box" theatre and amphitheatre.

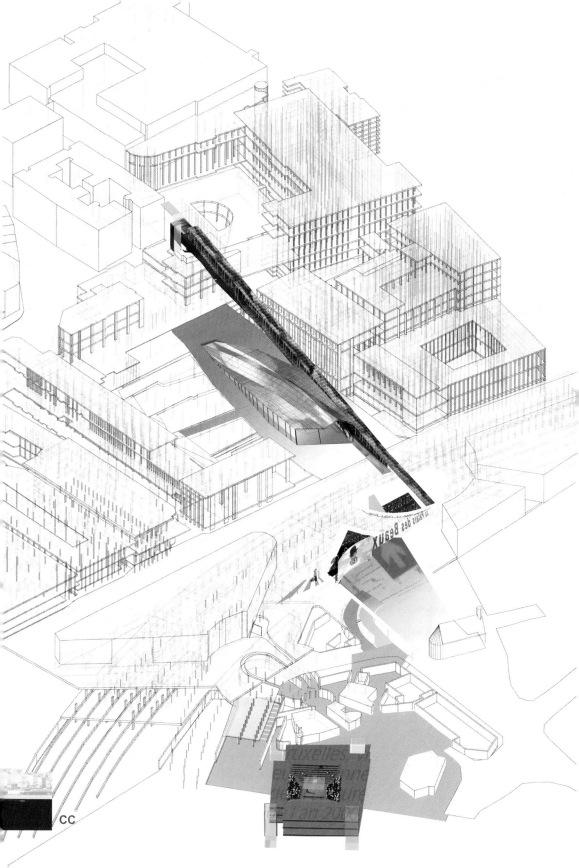

CC

SECONDARY EFFECTS

The first stage of infrastructural intervention will become the impetus for private reinvestment in the Putterie:

Stage 1: Reopening the site and integrating the Palais des Congrès with adjacent institutions will foster the rehabilitation of commercial space in Galerie Ravenstein-Gare Centrale as well as along the Rue Mont des Arts, complementing the activity of the reinvented Rue de Montagne de la Cour.

Stage 2: The Winter Garden and Galerie de la Madeleine, together with the redefined Place de l'Albertine, will attract the dense Grand Place tourism up toward the Place Royale, distributing it in all directions including the Place du Grand Sablon.

Stage 3: The improved aspect of public use in the site, together with typical urban amenities, will foster new rental activity in the building fabric to the north toward the Cathédrale de Saint Michel. The vibrancy of the Place du Grand Sablon will also serve to reinforce this north-south axis.

Stage 4: The Passage Horta westward from the Gare Centrale mezzanine will be reinvigorated with the development of the "Black Box Theatre" and the expansion of the Musée du Cinéma. The semi-vacant office space to the east will take on new meaning for digital enterprises.

CITY OF GLASS

The sectional city is experienced through revelations of the historic layers that are exposed through a series of glass structures. This "City of Glass" encourages readings of the subterranean city in the public space above. During the day, sunlight penetrates the lower urban world. At night, the opposite holds, with the subterranean world illuminating the public spaces. Three applications of structural glass are employed to achieve the strategy of urban transparency:

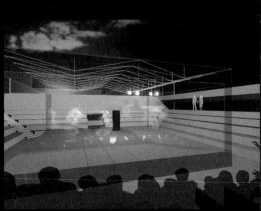

Winter Garden: The roof and wall cladding is a fully glazed frameless assembly using 25mm thick tempered and laminated panels 2m wide by up to 6m long supported on the long edges by triple-laminated glass purlins measuring 400mm deep by 45mm wide. The purlins will be supported at approximately 6m centres on tempered triple-laminated glass beams measuring 400mm deep by 60mm wide and spanning up to 4m in length as part of a cable-trussed assembly in which the glass beams will also act as the top compression chord. The trusses in turn will be supported by steel columns at the perimeter and by fully tempered triple-laminated spine beams measuring 100mm deep by 80mm wide, spanning up to 20m on to internal steel tubular columns. The lateral loads from the wind will be transformed through the diaphragm action of the glass roof plane to the top of the internal cantilever columns. To achieve this action the glass roof panels will be connected at all four corners to the roof trusses.

Galerie de la Madeleine: The glass roof covering of the cut is clad in frameless tempered and laminated glass panels spanning on to laminated tempered glass beams at 3m centres, designed and fabricated using technology developed for the Yurakucho glass canopy in Tokyo. The entire system employs laminated glass to endure post-breakage stability in the event of element failure.

Paving: Glass floor plates are laid in panels up to 2m by 2m fabricated from 19mm thick annealed glass sheets laminated with a minimum of two layers. The top surface of the panels is etched and sand-blasted to provide a trafficable surface. Application of this system is found over the excavation of the Palais de Charles Quint in the Place Royale; the paving of the Coudenberg over the expanded Musée du Cinéma; and in the paving of the Boulevard de l'Empereur at the Place de l'Albertine and the Boulevard de l'Impératrice at the Passage Horta.

Sleight of hand,
signal or manipulation?

Hilton Judin

This series of site photographs and plans in various stages of hand adjustment are intended as demonstrations of acts on the Mont des Arts. The hand signals are indicative of the actions desired but not yet done. These are in some ways not programmatic briefs in that they cannot be written (or programmed in code for that matter) but must be performed. They are meant to be used in place of a plebiscite which cannot be held, on even this most national of questions:

WHO ARE WE, IF WE ARE BELGIAN AND WHY ARE WE LEAST LIKELY TO BE FOUND HERE?

The problem might be one of articulating symbolic space in the absence of national incentives.

There are three movements that are being addressed in this description:
1. national identity, language and territory.
2. architecture consultation model.
3. test interventions of components are proposed as diversions to produce spatial commentary.

SPLIT

The simple confluence of region with community reinforces some of the divisions that run through a sense of enforced nationality in Belgium. Buildings, collections and legislation are accumulated here rather than discarded in the quest for a nation with a narrative.

Sides must always be taken.

National institutes are here on the Mont des Arts to accommodate, store and display the detritus as much as to define the nation.

WEDGE

An architectural intervention might as well ask if we can make these buildings and institutes more efficient. Can we make them better perform their duties and serve their function? In the case even of the district as a transportation node – moving people into and out of the city – greater speed with minimal cost are all that is required. In the case of the museums – the storage of more objects and their display to more and more people that visit them more often.

But these cultural components have also had to expand and contract, changing form and meaning, depending on current state and demand; conducting, exchanging and packaging national cultural production; symbolising and reproducing gross national concerns. Being both popular and serious. Sometimes resisting trends and at other times setting them. Reflection that is seldom subordinate to mass critical opposition.

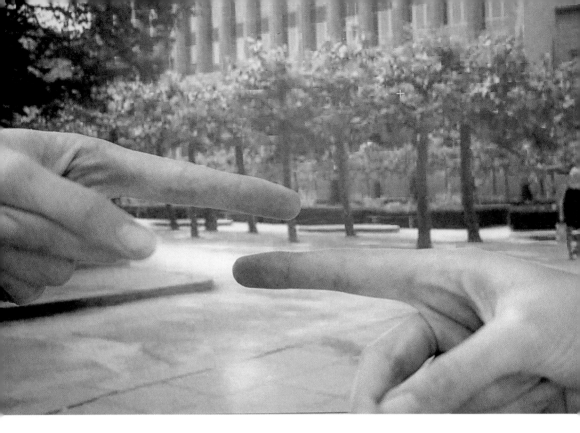

SHUFFLE

A question can be raised in this instance as to whether an architecture is also able to symbolise the absence or loss of the national rather than only its absolute presence.

Can architects command or define a space that is spiralling out of power?

Must this architecture continue to symbolise rather than actually enact the emptiness that is present?

How can these buildings function in their capacity as the last ditch containers of the national state? The symbolic representations of a passing monarchy?

Can architecture produce another story rather than the official sequential one laid out as that of this nation – Belgium? In other words, can others be brought into this space than those introduced by the surrounding institutions of power?

Must the space itself continue to disintegrate and empty in the manner it has before another can be fashioned or imagined? Or can it become some sort of space in-between, on its way somewhere? A space with more of itself to take in than what was left out, and could never be accommodated. **SPILL-OVER**

KINGS AND QUEENS

Who could be the constituency of the Mont des Arts when there is not simply the abstracted nation of the Belgians projected to fill it? When it cannot function as only a repository of this nation, without of course acknowledging the need felt to impose myriad tasks and cultural programmes within it. How can it come to embody more than the activities or performances traded periodically and belonging only to temporary sojourners. This symbolic space cannot simply be torn down in the act of replacing or renovating a district. Waiting for it to reclaim its popularity or significance as demand increases and the surroundings burgeon. Or nostalgia for the lost centre puts pressure on the political body to find this point again.

These days it is perhaps difficult to put oneself empathetically into a world in which the dynastic realm appeared for most men as the only imaginable "political" system. For in fundamental ways "serious" monarchy lies transverse to all modern conceptions of political life. Kingship organises everything around a high centre. Its legitimacy derives from divinity, not from populations, who, after all, are subjects, not citizens. In the modern conception, state sovereignty is fully, flatly, and evenly operative over each square centimetre of a legally demarcated territory. But in the older imagining, where states were defined by centres, borders were porous and indistinct, and sovereignties faded imperceptibly into one another. [1]

The centre or heart of the nation is demanded alongside the historical core and meaningful flow of a mythical past. Lack of conviction however resides in cultural institutions with official memories and inscriptions illegible in the present.

These vacant national spaces do not seem to really belong to anyone. No one takes responsibility for more than their immediate portion or frame of reference. Almost everyone passes through on the way elsewhere – as commuters, audiences, visitors, scholars – never imagining themselves citizens with right of passage. There is little value and no dramatic force behind any gesture carried out here. Who can remember the last time they took to the streets?

It is through this syntax of forgetting – or being obliged to forget – that the problematic identification of a national people becomes visible. The national subject is produced in that space where the daily plebiscite – the unitary number – circulates in the grand narrative of the will. However, the equivalence of will and plebiscite, the identity of part and whole, past and present, is cut across by the "obligation to forget," or forgetting to remember. This is again the moment of anteriority of the nation's sign that entirely changes our understanding of the pastness of the past, and the unified present of the will to nationhood. [1]

Flows of public in the Mont des Arts are partly sclerotic and partly stagnant. There are blockages that will not allow new connections to be made, and there are limited, although continuous, flows that drench the same terrain again and again.

How is a **PAUSE** to be introduced to allow people to begin to form some relation or concern for their surroundings, some responsibility or desire to do more than pass through this place? How to get them to hesitate before moving on, not recognising that this will take personal involvement – their participation – to change or work differently? How to bring about resistance to the natural flow of things through the space itself – so that things do not just happen as they always have; so that things do not just stay the same. So that things that are not working can be made anew. How to encourage dynamism and dissent where there was previously only a stagger and a glimpse?

What other forms of cultural identification are there in which these spaces can be claimed? A campaign in which participation is paramount – discussion not from a platform but in an arena.

How to alter direction when the destination seems the same as that of the day before. Where it is already pointed out for each person and instructed through signs.

Can we plan to disrupt the circulation and introduce alternative channels. To re-attach broken connections, adding adapters where necessary, splicing in converters and whatever new components are demanded.

CAN THERE BE A DEMONSTRATION IN PLACE OF A DESTINATION?

This even recent mythical magical past when we believed our centres held and we could depart from them in rapid succession (if only the connections happened on schedule). Corporate elements of attraction and repulsion are at work on the Mont des Arts. This place does not seem to belong to anyone by now.

Is there even a public out there? Must the void be filled?

Our tendency is to move outwards from here – as centrifugal figures -- and not towards this place in any deft motion. **COULD WE PUT HERE A SITE OFFICE FOR A NATION-BUILDING PRO-GRAMME?** If occupancy is opposed to vacancy, are we only looking at squatting (in the form of semi-permanent structures or platforms) or are we also looking at hidden layers (in the form of scaffolding or directives)?

BURY AND FOLD

We can imagine how we are to make this area a public concern. For a public can be generated as groups or participants with more than the passing interests of commuters or audiences. In some way, they must belong or own the area itself, as do the scholars and bureaucrats and officials for whom it has become a last bastion.

Bound as it is to a part of the city, the Mont des Arts had also to more than project but also actually supersede its national role. For although buildings here are still operating as signs of the state and monarchy, they must accommodate the cultural tasks of the national; behind facades of the previous centuries with their meanings no longer intact. The physical remnants – rather than the manifestation – of a nation once imagined by the state and its bureaucracies.

Problems we might recognise of division, multiple enclaves, and aggregated identities.

Redefine the function of the Mont des Arts and its relationship to Brussels and Belgium. Replace the mountain and the monumentality. Break down the scale of the palace and institute. Begin with its fragmented state and bring it together with people so that the buildings do not simply rub against one another but also meet. There is as much a task of removing as putting onto the site. Cutting away and paring down, exposing and prying loose. Taking away from a grand pile. From a bureaucracy in place as a defensive occupation, and a local legislation that makes change glacial and not liquid. Rather this place awash than in a state of suspended development.

"I DO NOT UNDERSTAND WHAT YOU ARE SAYING, SO TELL ME MORE OR EXPLAIN. COME CLOSER AS WE ONLY PASS EACH OTHER BY EVERY DAY. SOMETIMES WE SEE ONE ANOTHER ACROSS A STREET OR CROWD. WE HAVE YET TO MEET."

One of the tasks of the last century – moving people – required a concentration of activities with intricate connections between them. These intersections needed physical amenities more than transfers. Congestion developed rapidly, encouraging a move to the periphery to reduce such concentration. New technologies, demographics, commercial and consumption patterns reinforced this abandonment. Soon only certain transfers remained essential. Dispersion has been feasible through the movement of information as much as goods and people. While most production and storage has moved to the periphery, the cultural core has been left behind with most of these institutions out of the flow of things. Books, paintings, documents, and activities of the last century congealed; given as repetitive stored items to be put on display, rather than as elements to be generated and sampled and traded and utilised when necessary for contemporary cultural production.

"I HAD ALWAYS SEEN MYSELF AS A VISITOR, AN ONLOOKER, AND SO HAD LITTLE TO SAY. OF COURSE I DID NOT LIKE WHAT WAS HAPPENING, BUT HOW COULD I SPEAK OUT. WHO COULD I IMAGINE WOULD LISTEN? NOBODY EVEN PAID ATTENTION TO THE WAY WE WOULD ARRIVE OR DEPART FROM HERE. WHO COULD FEEL ANYTHING ABOUT THESE MATTERS. INVOLVEMENT WAS IMPOSSIBLE AS WE COULD NOT IMAGINE WE HAD IN COMMON ANY REASONS FOR BEING HERE."

Here people are rushing to work oblivious to their surroundings. This along with people wishing to view a painting, consult a document, or watch a music performance. Once low culture is separated from high, the task of putting them together is brought into play. We can commute and shop and pause to chat while esxperiencing a cultural event or taking part in a performance, if all this takes place in the underground passage system and not the museum. Our attention will always be difficult to grab for more than the moment it takes for anything to pass through our field of vision.

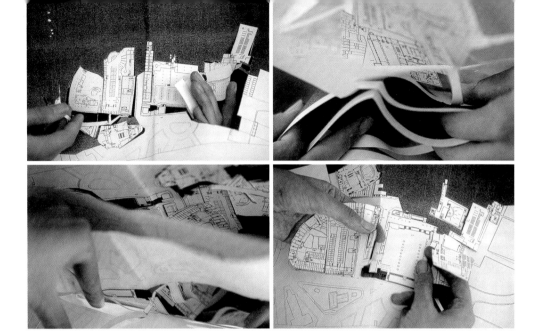

NEW CIRCUITS/BRACKET

Rather than to declare who we are by means of these institutes and edifices, by means of these events and arrangements. Rather than the vision of the last centuries of transportation hubs or states of the nation. Rather than the storage of objects and elements and sequences of who we might have been imagined or constructed or taught to be as good subjects. These vacant events with their urban manifestations are embedded just deep enough to be of little consequence.

What about indications? Hints, possible directions and corridors down which we might never have ventured? What about openings and interpretations of where we have yet to look, placing in question what is seen as underhand, doing away with legislation and imagining a tax-free cultural export zone? Some place and way of talking, demanding and having to argue for what we are actually doing here. Cultural circuits with transformers as models. Input as the sheer mass of people and objects accumulated not for storage and display but demonstration.

This must be a site of confrontation so that the battle for the heart of the nation can unfold. Tensions should not so easily be allowed to dissipate. If they are drained off and released after each point of contention, the accumulated argument is never there to be built. The centrifugal forces must be brought into play and exposed. If not gentrification, variations on the historical theme or enterprise zones, how about codes of conduct without behavioural modifications but fists nonetheless?

1. Benedict Anderson, *Imagined Communities*, (Verso, London, 1991).
2. Homi K. Bhabha, DissemiNation in *Nation and Narration* (Routledge, London, 1990).

OLD KNOWLEDGE, NOTHING NEW

BART VERSCHAFFEL

The structure and organisation of the area between the Gare Centrale and the Place Royale is spatially highly complex and difficult to interpret, but if we can go by the name, the totality of functions and activities is clear enough: the Mont des Arts. The place has a name, and the name indicates a programme. Nowadays it seems politically evident what art is for and to whom it belongs, it appears immediately obvious how the Mont des Arts should be organised. Art is there to be viewed, art must produce "experiences," and so the Mont des Arts needs visitors. This means that the disdainful, aloof character of the place and the façades has to be resolved, and the draughty open space needs better organisation and routing, to make the Mont des Arts attractive and inviting. Self-evident facts about art soon come to entail self-evident facts about the city and about the characteristics of the "genuine city:" it must be full of people and happenings everywhere and all the time – especially in the evening and at night – and rich in messages and meanings. The city means mixture, variety, difference. No immobility, no gravity, no obstacles, no things. A city should not look austere or lifeless. These evident truths and expectations turn the Mont des Arts into a problem: the link with the city has to be "resolved," small-scale services are required to make the area user-friendly and accessible, the functions must be directed outward, the activities must be diversified. In short: how can the Mont des Arts be turned into a place where all kinds of things go on, where people feel like being there and spending time there?

But the name is deceptive, and the expectation that the area is in need of being "activated" is inappropriate. For the Mont des Arts is not a district of the city like any other, nor is it a place where art or culture are **produced**. Rather, it is a place where knowledge is stored. It is in the first place a Mont du Savoir (Mountain of Knowledge). The Mont des Arts raises the question of the place to be assigned to Knowledge – the old knowledge that predates the internet – in the late modern city. It is not a question of following what is done elsewhere and turning the Mont des Arts and art into an attraction or a spectacle.

The Mont des Arts: the labyrinthine Musées Royaux with rooms and depots, paintings and sculptures, with more art than you can see in a day in the exhibition rooms alone; the Bibliothèque Royale with all the books of Belgium and more books than the whole of Flanders could read in a generation; the Archives Générales du Royaume with their secrets; the 7000 musical instruments in the new Musée des Instruments; the Musée du Cinéma that can show about one-thousandth of its collection each day; the hydra-headed Palais des Beaux-Arts where a lot goes on without being seen and sometimes very little goes on without being noticed. Somewhere in the middle of Belgium there is too much culture in one place. And it is not a question of the abundance of the (cultural) department store, nor of the cheery mass and diversity that has to be offered so that the unique consumers that we are can choose what matches our "personality," or what "interests us personally." It is not about the logic of consumption of the vast number of possibilities or of the range available. It is a question of ponderous and binding excess, of more than we can absorb and use. Every student knows it: there are too many books to read, too many pictures to be viewed properly, too much to know. Part of it has washed up on the Mont des Arts. While everything that is kept there is interesting and important, we would have to read and know practically all of it in order to be able to understand even some of it.

The Mont des Arts is not a cultural centre. It does not offer a pre-programmed and selected cultural package for consumption, put together for the interest and adjusted to the capacity for attention of the average "added value visitor." The Mont des Arts is the immense quantity of items that the intellectual and cultural history of the last millennium has accumulated here, in this country and in Brussels: rows of books that will never be read, films that stay in their boxes for decades, paintings that no one writes about. Knowledge has its own culture of experience, which included getting accustomed to this ponderousness and materiality, the surplus of history, the sorrow of the document, the opacity of all that we have forgotten, the awareness of our own incapacity and uselessness, the need to defend ourselves against that dumb, crushing presence of everything that we do not and never shall read or know.

The Mont des Arts is a Royal Mountain. Belgium still exists because Brussels is situated in Flanders, and so the country cannot be divided. You can start to divide the country, but that division has to stop somewhere. And in the centre of Brussels is one of those places, both symbol and fact, that are genuinely "indivisible," that at the same time represent indivisibility, and so willy-nilly become the difficult symbol of "unity." The Mont des Arts is not a part of Flanders or Wallonia; it belongs to Belgium, and that is why the Mont des Arts is a Royal Mountain. The Mont des Arts has very little to do with the city of Brussels. The city has its own cultural infrastructure and its own diffuse cultural and artistic life, which is barely concerned with that Old Culture, if at all.

When everything is taken into account, the best comparison with the Mont des Arts is the Vatican: a symbolic centre of the city and of the world, and at the same time an exclave, both a part and not a part of the city. The powerful and living proof of a past that is largely useless and contributes little to the present. A place where too much has happened, saturated in history, where it is impossible to start afresh. A place of accumulated old knowledge, of oblivion and of secrets, where people come and leave wearily in the evening. A place that is closed in the evening, and where nothing else happens then except all those books and pictures and things that endure remain silent. Is not the Mont des Arts like the Vatican? A place where even the visitors do not come for pleasure but to work or to find something out? Is not the Palais des Congrès like an underground St Peter's, the heart of the area, where hundreds of conference-goers come every day to speak and to listen? To start with, sentry posts could be set up down in the Rue Ravenstein and up on the Place Royale for Belgian Guards.

How could one ever love the Mont des Arts? No one loves the Mont des Arts. Surely it is not a question of making the Mont des Arts "attractive?" The Mont des Arts is not a tourist attraction. It does not need a crowd or people celebrating or enjoying themselves, but properly functioning institutions and proper working conditions for the couple of thousand people who come there every day – as employees or as visitors – because there is something they have to do there.

The Mont des Arts is absolutely not an urban void in need of a new programme or a new function. There **is** a clear-cut and important programme. The reality of the Mont des Arts carries more weight than its potential. That does not mean that nothing can or should be done there, but that there is no need to come up with something new for the area. The Mont des Arts is under-utilised at the moment: what is needed is to accept and reinforce the existing programme. Take the Musée du Cinéma, at present in the catacombs; it should be expanded to become a research institute of European quality. The exceptionally high concentration of academic and cultural institutions on a single site can be better used than is done at the moment. What is needed is a **general** management of the area: a management that at least coordinates the use of the buildings, and at most assumes the responsibility for the collected knowledge present there and optimises access to and use of that knowledge. The fact that the most important buildings are the property of the federal government, and that the academic institutions and the Palais des Congrès fall under the authority of a federal minister, creates both the possibility and the obligation to do exactly that.

The Mont des Arts: Focus of Culture

Conceived in 1934. Built in 1954 - 1965

AGENT PROVOCATEUR

Atelier Seraji

Project Team: Nasrine Seraji, Ralitza Boteva, Joseph Cho, Nicolas Fevrier, Roland Oberhofer, Jörg Stollmann, Jin Watanabe; Jacqueline Trichard, photographer; Cathérine David, curator

Museum of the 21st Century: Dispersal of Culture

A USER'S GUIDE

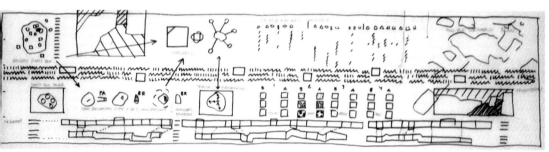

Exhibition Wall: June 2000

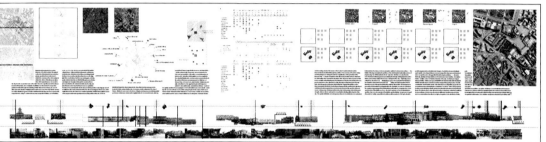

Exhibition wall: October 2000

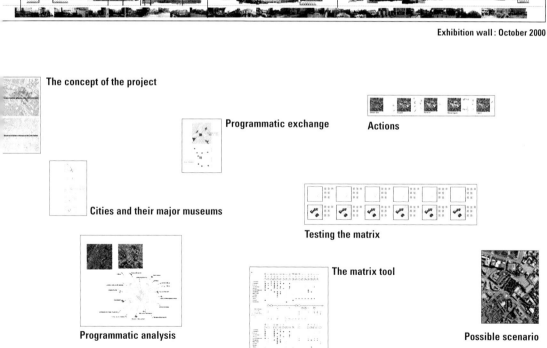

The concept of the project

Programmatic exchange

Actions

Cities and their major museums

Testing the matrix

Programmatic analysis

The matrix tool

Possible scenario

Highlighting the surface rhythm and surface repetition of the Mont des Arts

TO READ

The Mont des Arts:
A pretext for reflections on the Museum of the 21st Century

Any project on the site of the Mont des Arts presents two primary questions to be addressed:
1. What is the present and future of containers of culture? What is the museum of the 21st century?
2. What is the future of Brussels and the European city? Demolition? Reconstruction? Conservation? or refacing and reprogramming?

Brussels is neither Bilbao nor Almere. The site of the Mont des Arts is not vacant. It is not a void and it is not empty. The case of Bilbao has set a standard of reference for those politicians and decision makers who think of urbanism as a product – marketable just like any other merchandise. We are in a critical situation if we only think of the city as an object ready to be manipulated by any architectural form or to be treated like any product. The city is a concept not a form, and therefore a construct.

Brussels is not in any way comparable to Bilbao, nor to Paris, nor to any other city which has promoted itself through its cultural image. Culture is hidden in Brussels, as it is prevalent in the area of the Mont des Arts. The Mont des Arts is closed to the public, it is not accessible for a variety of reasons:
• The visitor is not attracted to anything. There is a prevalent sameness present.
• The public cannot perceive what is behind closed doors. There is a problem of sign and significance.

When something is invisible there is no need to add, rather, there is a need to highlight. We do not believe that there are missing pieces to the puzzle of the Mont des Arts; we think that the pieces are hidden and misplaced. Our project attempts to search for these pieces, be it in the site of the Mont des Arts or in the city, and place them in such a way that they become recognisable.

The idea of the museum in its classic sense (collection, archive and education) can not be fulfilled in sites such as the Mont des Arts. The site is seemingly another Louvre, but in reality it is not. The site strives for a central organisation, but this is impossible because of the programmatic heterogeneity and ownership policies of the site.

City as museum
Paris is the city of networks, the city of infrastructures, as opposed to London (its 19th century commercial rival) and Vienna (its 19th century cultural rival).

This is of course due to the vision of Napoleon being concerned with "practical" performance (harbours, canals, water supply); but he is concerned as much, with "representational" issues as Colin Rowe describes in *Collage City* referring to Las Cases and his reading of the 19th century city:
But the notion of city as museum, as a monument to the state and representative of its culture, as an index and as an instrument of education, which might seem to be implicit in neo-classical idealism also receives a microcosmic reflection in the notion of the house as museum; and we think here of Thomas Hope, Sir John Soane, Karl Friedrich Schinkel and, possibly, John Nash. For the Egyptian Temple which Napoleon wished to have built in Paris, and which would have "enriched" the capital, substitute the sarcophagus of Seti I with which Soane succeeded in "enriching" his own domestic basement and the analogy begins to take shape. Add Soane's Parlour of Padre Giovanni and his Shakespeare recess to Hope's Indian Room and Flaxman Cabinet and the traces of what Schinkel was to attempt in Berlin and Potsdam are abundantly present. Indeed we are surprised that the category "city as museum" with its sub-category "the museum street" (visible in places as far apart as Athens and Washington) has so far remained unidentified.

We think that the site should be a collage [1] as it has been, an will be in order to be attached to the specificity of Brussels. Thi collage needs to be seen and perceived architecturally, program matically and culturally.

The Mont des Arts exploded
The questions concerning the Mont des Arts will not be addresse if one improves the architecture of the site. Architecture throug building, contrary to what architects believe, is not important i situations like the Mont des Arts, though architectural "represen tation" could act as an *Agent provocateur*.

The Mont des Arts in Brussels was the idealistic attempt (1934 to generate a cultural centre as a place of identity. When con structed (1954-1965), the project of the Mont des Arts reads as reaction of both a nation and city to being characterised throug their fragmentation and decentralisation. At least once, the cu tural issues should be collected and presented under a unifyin term and its architectural representation. Even today, the deve opment that is foreseeable will lead to further concentration o culture on the Mont des Arts. Is this a longing for a unifying sym bol? Perhaps.

This concept of donating a part of Brussels entirely to cu tural institutions and the arts stands in an unfortunate trad tion. Throughout the 20th century, the city has promoted th construction of huge mono-functional structures, such as th European Parliament. Those were built at the expense of intac functioning urban neighbourhoods. It is time to reverse thi development. For us, thinking about the Mont des Arts mean thinking about cultural issues in a broader sense. It is necessar to reflect upon the cultural identity of Brussels not as a singl entity, but as an ensemble of autonomous fragments.

The question of the big museum
The city of Brussels has to find its cultural identity not throug concepts of cultural institutions from other European cities tha were developed in phases of strong centralised decision-makin (such as the Louvre or the Centre Pompidou in Paris and th Museumsinsel in Berlin), but through the position of the mu seum of the 21st century and this perhaps as a strategy toward the requalification of the potentials of the European city.

Even less should Brussels compare its situation to other citie that have promoted themselves through their cultural image b architectural objects such as the Guggenheim in Bilbao or th Museumsmeile in Frankfurt. These seductive architectural object function as tourist magnets, but they do not necessarily engag the city as a field of opportunities and trajectories in cultural ex change and production. The architectural and urban object stand in opposition to the notion of the city as as a total field.

A comparison of the scales of cities and their relationship o the museums to the fabric of their constituent city show that museum of similar size would be at least inadequate, if not disas trous. As the "museum" programme includes more and more aux iliary programmes, the object gets larger and larger. In Brussels, single object, whether architectural or urban, can no longer ac commodate this concentration of programmes. Culture must no be contained in a centralised object, but should be dispersed int the everyday life of the city.

Contemporary culture is already one of Brussels' strengths. has a diverse and lively scene that is activating different parts o the city. The spatial distribution of contemporary culture is de centralised as we understand it. Brussels has the opportunity t be an exemplary capital of contemporary culture only if it wer allowed to be read as a collage generated by its architectural an programmatic specificities.

1. A collage is both ironical and imprecise – an idea and an action.

DID YOU KNOW?

London
The Tate Modern

Monument as museum

Berlin
Museumsinsel

Museum district as urban object

Paris
Louvre / Centre Pompidou

Museum as State /
Culture as extension of public space,
an anomaly in the urban fabric

Bilbao
Guggenheim Museum

Architectural object as tourist magnet
and marketing image

Brussels
The Mont des Arts

Desire for centralisation of culture

5 km

1 km

THE INGREDIENTS

Central Brussels

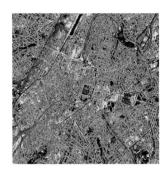

**The Object of
the Mont des Arts**

Object "Exploded"

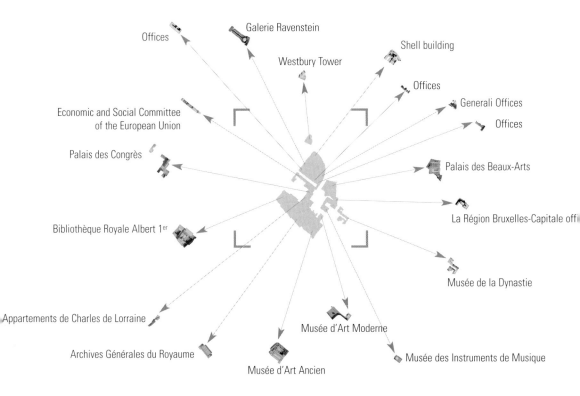

Offices

Galerie Ravenstein

Westbury Tower

Shell building

Offices

Generali Offices

Offices

Economic and Social Committee
of the European Union

Palais des Congrès

Palais des Beaux-Arts

Bibliothèque Royale Albert 1er

La Région Bruxelles-Capitale off

Musée de la Dynastie

Appartements de Charles de Lorraine

Musée d'Art Moderne

Archives Générales du Royaume

Musée des Instruments de Musique

Musée d'Art Ancien

IMPORT / EXPORT

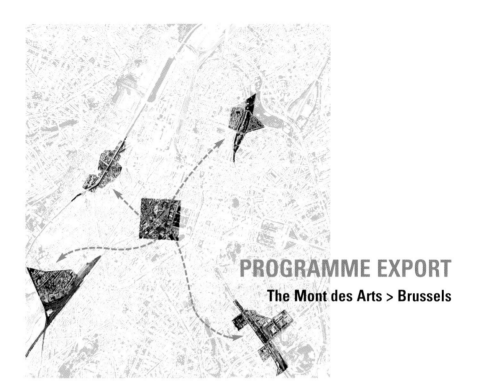

PROGRAMME EXPORT

The Mont des Arts > Brussels

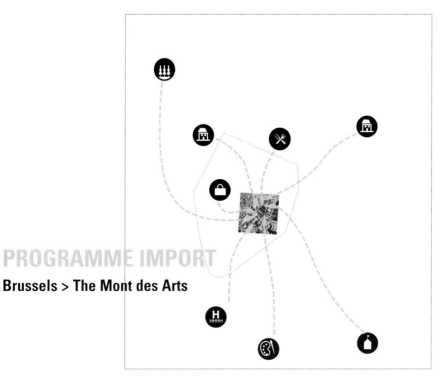

PROGRAMME IMPORT

Brussels > The Mont des Arts

PROGRAMMATIC MATRIX

2000

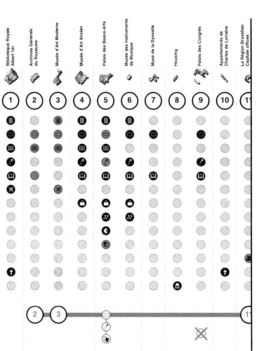

Index of Actions

→ Export to Brussels
← Import from Brussels
---- Programmatic Combination
✕ Erase
✂- Split

2001

Following our analysis, the problem of the Mont des Arts is primarily an issue of programming. The Mont des Arts has to be "exploded," first its concept, then its mono-functional cultural programmes, and finally its already existing physical manifestations, as far as they prevent the possibility of it becoming a live cultural part of the city.

Exploding means acting in two directions:
1. Bringing in programmes of everyday life that will attract the population of Brussels to this area.
2. Taking out cultural programmes that in themselves (or through their interaction with the site and other programmes) prevent the Mont des Arts from being integrated into the life of the city.

In order to understand the complex programming of the Mont des Arts, and be able to reorganise it, we developed the idea of the matrix as a tool.

The final "explosion" of the Mont des Arts is a question of process. In our project, the matrix operates ideally. In a process of negotiation with socio-political and economic "reality," many different solutions may be rendered. We try to simulate possible programmatic and architectural changes.

The matrix acts as an intelligent tool based on architectural decisions and urban strategies. It acts as a tool for the architect to represent an overview of a complex system.

The matrix needs a strong political and economic thrust in order for its potential to be fully realised.

POSSIBLE SCENARIO N°0834 (2001)

Cet obscur objet du désir

João Luís Carrilho da Graça, architect

ASSISTANTS:
Giulia de Appolonia, João Manuel Alves, Mónica Margarido, Filipe Homem, architects
João Rosário, computer grafics

THE "FLOATING RAFT"

THE INTRODUCTION OF A "WOODEN FLOATING FLOOR" OVER THE EXISTING PLACE DE L'ALBERTINE AT THE BIBLIOTHÈQUE ROYALE ALBERT I "LOGGIA" LEVEL HAS THE DOUBLE OBJECTIVE OF CREATING A SEMI-INTERIOR LARGE MULTIFUNCTIONAL SPACE FOR INFORMAL REPRESENTATION, RAVE PARTIES AND MEETINGS, AT THE 41.70 M LEVEL , AND OF REDESIGNING THE EXTERIOR SPACE OF THE SQUARE AT AN UPPER LEVEL WHICH ALLOWS DIRECT CONNECTION WITH THE BUILDINGS SURROUNDING IT. WE THINK THAT THE LACK OF CONTINUITY BETWEEN INTERIOR AND EXTERIOR LEVELS AROUND THE SQUARE IS ONE OF THE REASONS OF THE "WEAK FEEL" OF THIS

SPACE; THE CLIMATE IS ALSO A DETERMINING FACTOR AND THUS THE POSSIBILITY OF PASSING THROUGH A SHELTERED SPACE WHERE THINGS "HAPPEN," ESPECIALLY IN WINTER, SEEMS AN EFFECTIVE WAY OF REINVIGORATING THE SQUARE. WE ALSO REFLECTED ON THE FACT THAT THIS SPACE COULD HOUSE THE CENTRAL MANAGEMENT OF THE NEARBY BUILD-INGS (LIBRARY, CONGRESS CENTRE AND AUDITORIUM), BEING CO-ORDINATED BY A SUPERIOR INSTITUTION, AND ALSO WORK AS A POSSIBLE EXTENSION, ENTRANCE OR CONNECTIVE MEDIUM BETWEEN THEM.

WE TOOK THE RAFT AS A REFERENCE FOR TWO REASONS: FIRST OF ALL BECAUSE OF ITS IMPLICIT SENSE OF FLOATING WITHOUT DISTURBANCE AT LOWER LEVELS; AND ALSO BECAUSE OF THE NATURE OF THE MATERIAL ITSELF: WOOD, A SHORT-LIVED, ORGANIC MATERIAL, THAT ALLOWS EASY ASSEMBLAGE OF DIVERSE KINDS OF STRUCTURES WITH REGARD TO THE TYPE OF PERFORMANCE YOU NEED FROM THE SPACE.

AN INTEGRATION OF MASSIVE VEGETATION ESTABLISHES THE CONNECTION WITH THE RUE DES SOLS SIDE CREATING A SORT OF URBAN FOREST MEDIATING BETWEEN THE LARGE SCALE AND MONUMENTALITY OF THE LIBRARY AND OF THE NEW MULTIFUNCTIONAL SPACE, AND THE URBAN SCALE AT THE OTHER SIDE.

THE "ICEBERG"

THE FIRST SENSATION WE HAD VISITING THE MONT DES ARTS WAS THAT THE MOST IMPORTANT EVENTS WERE HAPPENING UNDERGROUND AND THAT THE PRESENCE OF PEOPLE WAS DIRECTLY LINKED TO THEM. THIS IS A CONSEQUENCE BOTH OF THE EXISTING INFRASTRUCTURES (LOCAL, NATIONAL AND INTER-NATIONAL RAILWAYS RUNNING UNDERGROUND) AND OF THE MAIN ACTIVITY OF THE AREA, "TRADITIONAL REPRESENTATION," WHICH IS LINKED TO A KIND OF ABSTRACTION FROM THE SURROUNDINGS, ACHIEVED SUCCESSFULLY IN THE UNDERGROUND AREA.

WE THINK IT IS MORE INTERESTING TO WORK WITH THIS EXISTING SITUATION RATHER THAN TRYING TO SUBVERT IT, BUT WE ALSO CONSIDER IT IS NECESSARY TO REVEAL IT BY MAKING THE UNDERGROUND VISIBLE IN THE CONTEXT OF THE SURROUNDING CITY.

IN CONSEQUENCE WE REVIEWED THE "NATURAL" ASSOCIATION OF CONCEPTS WHICH ESTABLISHES THE CRE-ATION OF A CERTAIN KIND OF ATMOSPHERE: IF PEOPLE STAY AND MOVE UNDERGROUND, WHY SHOULD UNDERGROUND NOT BECOME A PLACE WHERE PEOPLE CAN CONDUCT SLICES OF THEIR LIVES, ACCORDING TO THE UNIVERSAL CONCEPT OF THE CONDITIONS FOR HUMAN EXISTENCE.

WE CREATE THE "NEGATIVE" OF A BUILDING, A SPACE THAT IS DUG OUT INSTEAD OF BEING BUILT ON. THE STREET BECOMES PEDESTRIAN AND THE GROUND TURNS INTO GLASS, OVERLOOKING A BIG EXCAVATED SPACE BETWEEN THE TWO FACADES OF THE STREET, REACHING LEVEL 29.00. THIS 10.50 M HIGH SPACE IS A SORT OF CONSERVATORY WITH TREES PLANTED AT THE BASE, CROSSED BY FOOTBRIDGES, SOME EXISTING (LIKE HORTA'S UNDERGROUND ROTUNDA) AND SOME NEW, THAT CREATE CONNECTIONS BETWEEN ALL THE DIFFER-ENT UNDERGROUND LEVELS OF THE EXISTING BUILDINGS LINING THE BIG ATRIUM DEVOTED TO SHOPPING.

WE THUS INTEND TO TRANSFORM THE DARK UNDERGROUND TUNNELS AND A PART OF THE CAR PARK INTO A NATURALLY LIGHTED SHOPPING CENTRE PLANTED WITH TREES, BY MEANS OF AN "ANARCHITECTURAL" OPERATION. THIS PUBLIC SPACE INTERSECTS NATURALLY WITH THE UNDERGROUND RAILWAY TUNNELS, CREATING VIEWING POINTS OVER THE TRACKS.

BELOW THE PEDESTRIAN GLASS S

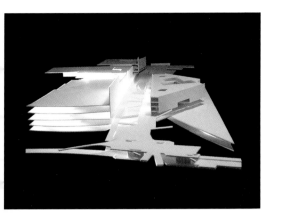

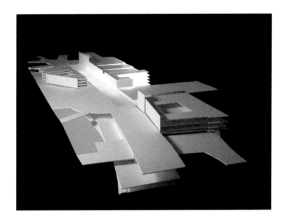

T H E   S U B T R A C T I O N   C   T E R I A

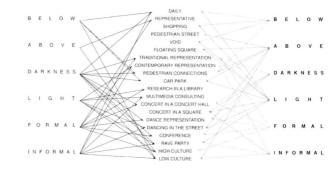

 FLOATING RAFT SQUARE  TRANSPORT INTERFACE SHOPPING HOUSING PARK

GENERATES A VOLUME OF **LIGHT** CF

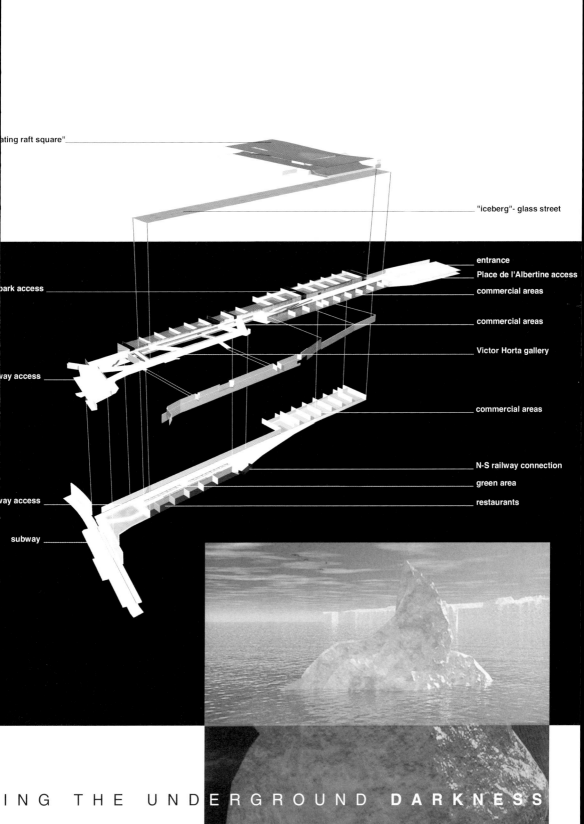

ating raft square"

"iceberg"- glass street

entrance
Place de l'Albertine access
commercial areas

park access

commercial areas

Victor Horta gallery

ay access

commercial areas

N-S railway connection
green area
restaurants

vay access

subway

ING THE UNDERGROUND **DARKNESS**

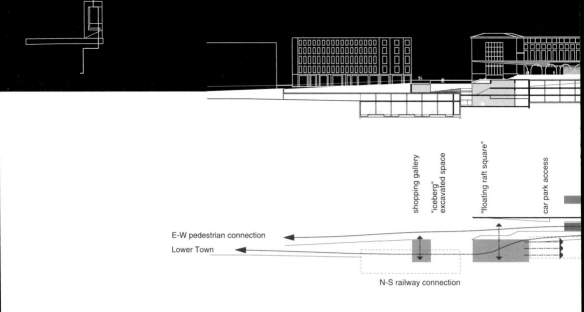

shopping gallery

"iceberg"
excavated space

"floating raft square"

car park access

E-W pedestrian connection

Lower Town

N-S railway connection

A B O V E THE EXISTING SQUARE AN **E**

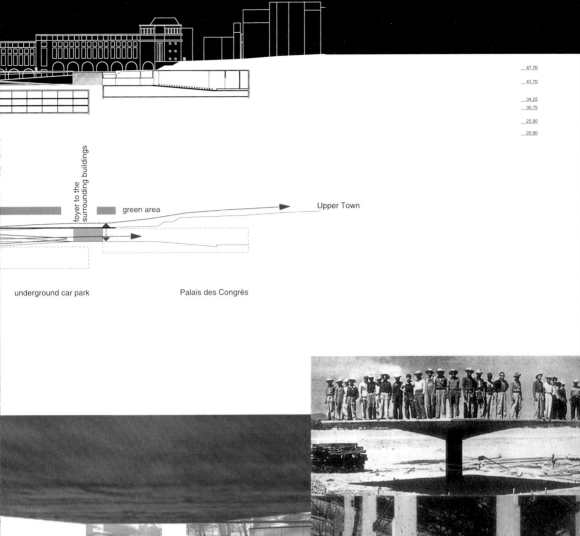

foyer to the surrounding buildings

green area

Upper Town

underground car park

Palais des Congrès

47.70
41.70
34.25
30.75
25.00
20.00

E R A L A N D   M U T A B L E   C O N S T R U C T I O N

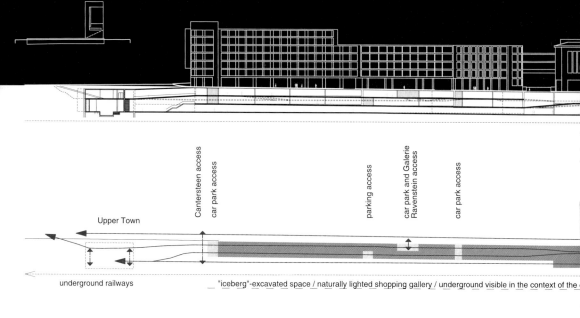

Upper Town

Cantersteen access

car park access

parking access

car park and Galerie
Ravenstein access

car park access

underground railways

"iceberg"-excavated space / naturally lighted shopping gallery / underground visible in the context of the

SUBWAY

CAPTURING AND RELEASING **FLUXES**

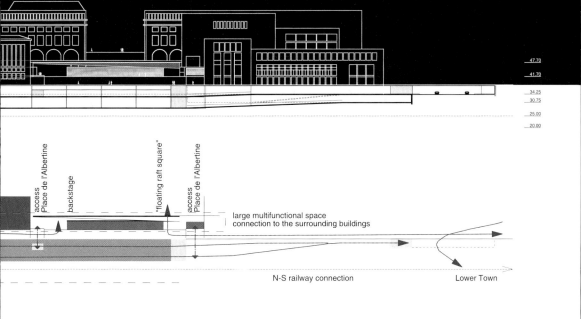

access Place de l'Albertine

backstage

"floating raft square"

access Place de l'Albertine

large multifunctional space
connection to the surrounding buildings

N-S railway connection

Lower Town

47.70
41.70
34.25
30.75
25.00
20.00

A HINGE BETWEEN NORTH AND SOUTH, EAST AND WEST FROM THE DEEPEST TUNNELS TO THE UPPER SQUARE

ONIZING SPACE WITH **MULTIPLICITY**

A PROPOSAL FOR

AND DYNAMIC

A SIGNIFICANT

CATHÉRINE DAVID

As conceived and discussed in collaboration
with Nasrine Seraji's team, the cultural
programme proposal for the (re)development of
the Mont des Arts should start from very
simple facts which have been brought out in
one way or another by all the participants
involved in the project. When one speaks about
the working process, it is also important to
point out the ambiguous position of the
cultural programmers who – as specific
exhibitions, artist(s), project(s), events or
festival programmes were not considered – were
supposed to operate on an abstract and
structural level implicating urban planning
and cultural policy decisions (or in this
specific case the complete lack of it) who
are in fact escaping from their responsibility
and consulting role.

CULTURAL COLLAGE

An overall cultural proposal for the Mont des Arts should
take into account the following elements:

The Mont des Arts has never been really at the centre of
the city, even less nowadays when a lot of activities and
construction have moved out of the centre towards the
eastern part of Brussels or even towards the outskirts.
Brussels is a small-scale European city with no real centre
and a configuration in the form of a collage of different
villages – but with nevertheless a strong symbolic
significance on an international level, that goes hand in
hand with the creation of big visible signs – there is no
point in re-enforcing or insisting on the
concentration/centrality of cultural events and
institutions which would unnecessarily counteract the
intense, plural and sometimes conflictive dynamics of
contemporary cultural life and scene in Brussels.
The Mont des Arts is the result of a failed mixture of
various historical or recent examples of concentrations of
museums/cultural institutions or cultural interdisciplinary
attempts like the Museuminsel in Berlin, the Trocadero on
the Colline de Chaillot in Paris (including the Musée de la
Marine, the Musée de l'Homme, the Théâtre National
Populaire, the Musée des Monuments Français, and the future
Cité de l'Architecture), the Centre d'Art et de Culture
Georges Pompidou in Paris, the Museumsufer in Frankfurt,
the future Museums quarter in Vienna.
In the same way the ancient art collections of the Musées
Royaux des Beaux-Arts are not comparable with those of 18th
and 19th century models of universalist museums, as for
instance the Louvre in Paris, the Victoria & Albert Museum
in London or the Metropolitan Museum in New York. The
modern art department of the Musées Royaux does not possess
a strong and canonical modernist collection as do the MOMA
in New York, the Tate Gallery in London or the Musée
National d'Art Moderne in Paris.

The Mont des Arts, in its structures and contents is the
visible expression of a very academic and mummified
"bourgeois" culture; of cultural practices and a structure
of consumerism that no longer corresponds to the cultural
expectations and attitudes of contemporary audiences. The
plural used here is important in a city including so many
different cultural groups as does Brussels.

Not only is the site as a whole undefined, highly
fragmented, amorphic, autistic, and centrifugal, most of
the buildings and institutions likewise offer a confusing
and unclear collage/juxtaposition of spaces and functions
not really readable from the outside nor even from the
inside. The most extreme example of this is without any
doubt the Palais des Beaux-Arts.

Contemporary culture, if not completely absent – one can
only mention the contemporary art programme in the
antichambres of the Palais des Beaux-Arts (PBA), some
contemporary music concerts in the PBA and the contemporary
film programme at the Musée du Cinéma – is, at the least,
completely invisible in the Mont des Arts area, which
reinforces the "dead" aspect given by the accumulation of
massive eclectic or academic architecture on the site.
Although one cannot say that the museum area is deserted
when exhibitions organised by the Musées Royaux des Beaux-
Arts attract 300.000 visitors or more, the real movement at
the site is in fact concentrated on the axis the Gare
Centrale – Galerie Ravenstein, that is intensively used by
commuters and people working in the area during the week.

Due to:
- a disfunctioning centralised/concentrated/specialised cultural definition of the site
- a non-specifically culture-oriented, partially lively use of the site (the Gare Centrale and the Galerie Ravenstein)
- the confused national/federal and somehow conflictual cultural policies and agendas
- the multiple uses and functions of the buildings
- a long tradition of non-co-operation between the different institutions/buildings

There is no point in trying to centralise and articulate a real interdisciplinary and organic cultural programme on the Mont des Arts and installing a Beaubourg or Bilbao kind of monument in existing or new buildings.

It seems more realistic and practical to transform the actual confusion of spaces and functions into a significant and dynamic collage.

The aim is to take advantage of this/these transformation(s) and projects for improving the art/cultural situation on the Mont des Arts/Brussels by improving certain contents/quality and serious infrastructural defects: developing the modern and contemporary art collection, improving the exhibition policy by organising more ambitious monographic ancient, modern and contemporary art exhibitions and by adding interdisciplinary and international programmes, developing forums for cultural and critical debates, redesigning and/or adding necessary multifunctional infrastructures like spaces for projections, lectures and performances.

Concerning the museums, apart from the new Musée des Instruments de Musique and the Musée du Cinéma, which are clearly identified, at least in terms of function, it is important to identify in a better way the ancient, modern and contemporary art collections and cultural activities. The amazing diversity and quality of the programme offered daily by the Musée du Louvre cultural department at the Museum Auditorium proves that a museum of ancient art is able to participate very actively in contemporary debates and to mobilise very different audiences, ranging from the tourist to the amateur, from the visitor to the "habitué/regular visitor."

At the Mont des Arts, the Musée d'Art Ancien could develop and improve the originality and quality of its exhibitions; the same could be said for the Musée d'Art Moderne that does not really deserve the "contemporary art" label. This part of its activity could be transferred to the Palais des Beaux-Arts, under the following conditions, of course:
a redistribution of permanent spaces for the exhibitions
a minimum of architectural alterations in order to open a multifunctional space necessary for contemporary art programming.

Each in its own way, these institutions could contribute to necessary critical and polemical cultural debate and forum activities which are very absent at the moment.

This redistribution and/or addition of spaces/boxes in the
Palais des Beaux-Arts would also allow the transfer to the
Mont des Arts of part of the experimental dance/theatre
performances; and to host decently at the Mont des Arts
contemporary events like *KunstenFESTIVALdesArts*. There is
also the possibility of recovering various spaces for
cultural activities in the many buildings that are empty or
partly empty at the moment or will be in the near future.
Temporary events or programmes organised by the Palais des
Beaux Arts, or independently organised, could take place in
the Galerie Ravenstein, which attracts very different
audiences and whose "sixties" atmosphere interestingly
escapes the usual "Gucci Prada Vuitton" or "Benetton Esprit
Gap" syndrome. In this gallery, experimental and studio
spaces could be positioned between the food and coffee shops
and other commuter necessities. These places could also adapt
their opening hours and organisation to this specific
context. The non-segregation between cultural and
service/commercial activities, including the opening of a
night bar and places for music could also contribute to the
animation of the area and to the possible mixture of various
audiences.

The redistribution of cultural programmes and activities in
the Mont des Arts's multiple institutions/boxes should follow
and emphasise the specificity, the qualities and the positive
potential of cultural life in Brussels in the following ways,
instead of hiding it:
- dispersion and mobility
- diversity and small scale
- the presence of many different cultural groups that should
be given visibility outside their specific (and cultural
ghetto) community spaces
- experimental and laboratory activities

Last but not least, part of the input for the reorganisation/activation of the Mont des Arts depends on a cultural policy operating from a broader and more ambitious perspective. It is a political and cultural decision to promote a living and experimental post-national culture in the political capital of Europe, rather than a mixture of Eurocratic pseudo elite/provincial-regional/ politically correct multicultural productions. Instead of superficial, official and artificial Europalia events or boring blockbusters, European joint efforts and collaborations (also on the budget level) in Brussels could contribute to the presentation of a living and polemical shop window for co-productions between European and non western cultural environments. This could be operated through a substantial programme of international studies and residencies. This would create a real European/international experimental cultural scene that the relatively small scale of Brussels in terms of metropolitan space allows.

In addition to the necessary cultural "highlights" (the Opera La Monnaie, the reorganised Musées Royaux, the Musée des Instruments de Musique and the Musée Royal de l'Afrique Centrale), Brussels could make an interesting contribution to European cultural originality and diversity. This would be possible through understanding and developing the specific urban, social and cultural dynamics, which result in a contrasting and productive contemporary culture, even if it comes with some unavoidable disorder and conflict.

THE MONT DES ARTS AS

ADVANTAGES OF AN UNSUCCESSFUL APPELLATION

When we first visited the Mont des Arts everybody seemed slightly disorientated. It was hard to know where one was, and even harder to locate the entrances of the many buildings. The most common and intuitive response to this representational architecture was to ignore it. Even the architects in our group did not really consider it and looked elsewhere; the underground areas of the Mont des Arts raised much more interest than the buildings themselves. It seemed obvious that the classical architecture of this museum area had lost the power to address anyone; it had no chance to send its message or to establish a successful interpellation. This Althusserian concept is based on the idea that ideologies have a material existence and call individuals, turning them into subjects. When someone's name is called by an authority figure, he turns around and at this moment he (only men are mentioned) is constituted as a subject. While Althusser only imagined successful and rather explicit interpellations, I would argue that they also occur in a more implicit and hidden way. It belongs to the nature of an interpellation in that it misses its receiver and fails to meet him.

The Mont des Arts, seen as what Althusser termed an "ideological state apparatus," embodies and reproduces a certain notion of culture; one can work on the assumption that it tries to establish an authoritative relationship towards subjects. What notion of culture is represented here? It certainly has nothing to do with the current enlarged notion where every field, be it politics or sport, is considered a part of culture. In contrast to this tendency towards culturalisation, the Mont des Arts stands for culture in a more restricted and traditional sense: culture presents itself as a primarily national accomplishment that has to be valued, collected and preserved. Likewise, art history is considered as a succession of styles and there are no questions about how the canon is constituted and what it excludes. In fact it is astonishing how natural the national bias seems: the museum collections, the library and the monographic exhibitions mainly focus on national accomplishments. The admittedly problematic concept of global culture has not yet appeared. The Mont des Arts is thus a total anachronism. It comes as no surprise that pop culture or fashion are not part of this notion of culture. Exhibitions of contemporary art lead a rather marginal existence with occasional exhibitions at the Palais des Beaux-Arts.

THEORETICAL SPECTACLE

Isabelle Graw

Watching the people who typically pass through the Mont des Arts – mostly tourists or commuters – it seems to me that they are not even slightly concerned with the notion of culture represented here. They all turn their heads in the other direction. Instead of acknowledging the building by contemplating it, people tend to follow their own trance-like path. One study has shown that tourists quite demonstratively turn their backs on the Mont des Arts and look at their coaches instead. Similarly, I also had a kind of absent-mindedness while walking around. Not looking, looking away, being absorbed in one's own thoughts: these seem to be the most common types of perception.

A walk around the Mont des Arts is too uncomfortable to be comparable with the experience of a 19th century *flâneur* (stroller). While a stroller uses city life and especially its boulevards as an inspiration, the Mont des Arts mainly invites rejection. In fact one does not want to be addressed in this way anymore, this monumental architecture will not impress, and therefore one tends to look elsewhere. In my case I was not actively disturbed by it but I did not want to engage with it. Not surprisingly this site has no public life and always looks deserted. The Mont des Arts does not attract people unless they have something specific to do – like the skateboarders who use the Jardin de l'Albertine or the conference-goers who disappear into the Palais des Congrès.

The monumental architecture of the Mont des Arts is paradoxical: on the one hand it is impossible to overlook it and on the other one cannot relate to it. The more overtly oppressive a situation, the more likely you withdraw from it. But compared to new architecture like the Sony Center in Berlin or contemporary urban landscapes such as Las Vegas, the Mont des Arts is less imposing. There are no signs, let alone billboards. The Mont des Arts is a message-free zone. Should one celebrate this condition? I doubt it. If it is true that it is in the nature of an interpellation to fail partially, then Althusser's ideological state apparatus works in a slightly more complicated way. First, it can incorporate the idea of rejection and second, individuals have a larger frame of action than Althusser imagined. They can for instance simply ignore the appellation.

The Mont des Arts can be seen as a model of repressive tolerance. It tolerates that one resists its interpellation. There have been other ideological state apparatuses that have worked in a similar way,

353

for example educational models of the 1970s. Students were encouraged to be critical of their teachers. Likewise there are critical ways to deal with the appellations of museum display. According to Irit Rogoff one has the possibility to look away. On another level, being accosted as man or woman does not necessarily impose a fixed identity. It is possible to question these seemingly natural classifications.

But what type of freedom arises when turning away from the Mont des Arts? One gains a mental space of one's own that does not change the material conditions. In other words, to attribute a potential resistance to this gesture seems slightly exaggerated and is a bit of a projection. Nobody who walks past the Mont des Arts consciously refuses to be interpellated this way, there is just no response. It's a situation that does not correspond to one's reality. Ignoring a situation creates a limited freedom similar to switching off a television programme or refusing to vote. It is hard to draw a clear line between sheer disinterest and conscious refusal. In principle one should not pin too much hope on social gestures; nevertheless certain social gestures seem more likely, adequate or inappropriate than others. It is for example hard to imagine anyone enthusiastically embracing the Mont des Arts. Why would anybody want to establish a nostalgic relationship with an architecture that refers to feudal conditions? The world it stands for is irretrievably lost. This museum area has lost part, if not all, of its cultural authority. Perhaps the reason lies in the conception here of the museum as storage medium: it collects and preserves a past which is considered as given and unchangeable. This conservative notion of the museum's function - which is based on a conservative notion of history - is very hard to legitimise today. The Mont des Arts is a demonstration of the non-justifiability of culture in general. Culture cannot be legitimised in the last instance.

But let me ask a few questions that undermine the assumptions made above. Why would a museum that hosts traditional monographic exhibitions like the James Ensor show in November 1999, or a library with a print collection possess less cultural authority than a museum that incorporates pop culture, controversial contemporary art and champagne receptions for sponsors? Could not the Mont des Arts be praised as a last bastion against the assumption that the differences between high and low culture and between private and public funding have collapsed? Instead of "musealising" virtually everything, from fashion shows to concerts, the Mont des Arts is based around the traditional arts while acknowledging their different frames: concerts happen in the concert hall with a specific audience, and art exhibitions are restricted to the museum. The Mont des Arts could be seen to take into account the differentiation of each cultural field. Could not this be the starting point for connecting it to more contemporary artistic production and debate? Instead of simply opening up the museum to new trends, the precise overlap between different disciplines could be examined, for instance involving collaborations between international choreographers and visual artists.

NO AUDIENCE ON STAGE – SPECULATIONS ON THE JARDIN DE L'ALBERTINE

If there is a centre to the Mont des Arts it is the Jardin de l'Albertine, which is a kind of outdoor stage. This square illustrates the inherent tendency of human behavior to become theatre. When performing on this stage one realizes that something is missing: the audience. What does it mean to be on stage without an audience? Is it possible to imagine everyday performances without spectators? Jacques Derrida has suggested that a speech act which engenders action does not necessarily need a receiver. According to Derrida, so-called performative utterances do not rely on the presence of a receiver, who might as well be absent. This goes against the usual definition of performance that implies participation or interaction.

Derrida's proposition is especially interesting in the context of art performances from the 1960s that actually do work like speech acts: they incorporate instructions for an action. Performances by artists like Vito Acconci, Yoko Ono or Franz Erhard Walter often consist of instructions that ask you to perform certain actions. The reception of these works has always emphasised their dependency on interaction. But quite often the requested interaction did not occur. Furthermore, when one comes across these art works today they exist as documentation (photographs or video) and the participation they seek becomes totally abstract. One could argue that the possibility of having no audience is inherent to all performances. Every child knows that it does not need a real audience for its performances. When a child play acts it works with a fantasy audience, and this does not weaken the performance, on the contrary.

This is also true for the skateboarders who use the Jardin de l'Albertine (which provides ideal skateboarding conditions). They perform on this stage whether there is an audience or not. Skateboarding is partly a means of self-expression, and according to Stanley Cavell, remaining expressive is a matter of a willingness for theatre, for display.[1] Skateboarding can be described as theatrical. It resembles choreography with ritualised movements such as jumping off the board that seem exaggerated to the outside observer. These seemingly manneristic and artificial movements are not directed at anybody in particular. They belong to the theatrical repertoire of the skateboarder. A lone skateboarder acts this way whether the performance is seen or not. Maybe the Mont des Arts is a testing ground for what I would call a theatrical turn. People tend to play themselves whether they are observed or not. The idea of life on stage is internalised to an extent that the borderline between authentic and performed behaviour is blurred.

The Mont des Arts is also theatrical in terms of its monumentality. One feels belittled and annihilated by its proportions. People become insignificant, irrelevant and replaceable. The Mont des Arts anticipates the failure of the idea of identity. Here 19th century architecture provides for an experience usually associated with the postmodern. Effects usually attributed to global capitalism can also be detected: faced with the monumentality of the Mont des Arts one becomes an atomised, monadic individual whose interactions are virtual and whose material existence is highly mediated. This architecture makes it impossible to distinguish between real and staged events. Everything that happens here automatically turns into theatre.

NOTES ON SCHLINGENSIEF – A SCENARIO

The Mont des Arts is an early manifestation of what Debord later called the *Society of the Spectacle*. Today, in the 21st century, Debord's vision has totally fulfilled itself. All human experience is connected to commodities and their ownership or consumption. Faced with a totalised spectacle there is no position available outside. It is impossible to be immune to its appellations.

What would happen if the German *culturepreneur* Christoph Schlingensief came to Brussels and set up his container on the Jardin de l'Albertine? Would the above modes of appellation, audience participation and spectacle be altered? Schlingensief operates with urgent, insistent messages that accost their audience quite successfully. Possibilities of misunderstandings and failed communication are things he always welcomes. As Schlingensief designs his activities within the realm of the media it is quite impossible to ignore his propositions.[2] They are highly mediatised events. Schlingensief is a favourite guest on talk shows. As his projects are based around provocation, reactions to them are guaranteed and occur quite regularly. Schlingensief works with a non-idealistic model of participation that does not over-estimate its potential. People who take part in a Schlingensief project are faced with an established format and limited choices.

A brief introduction to Schlingensief: he is a German film maker and theatre director who has the reputation of being an *enfant terrible*. His actions are considered provocative and straddle the line between theatre and politics. Last year he founded a political party called *Chance 2000* which staged

political rituals and presented its candidates in a circus format. It was impossible to know whether the aims of this party were serious or whether it was all meant as a comment on the empty spectacle of politics. Schlingensief's actions are always unsettling. One action consisted of asking all the unemployed people in Germany to take a swim in the Wolfgangsee to see if the water would overflow. The Wolfgangsee is where Helmut Kohl takes his holidays. Schlingensief was interested in producing a disquieting image of unemployment. The image was more important than the actual outcome: not enough unemployed people came but the beautiful picture of the Wolfgangsee flooding Kohl's garden remained.

In 1997 Schlingensief had a chaotic TV show, *Talk 2000*, where the guests were the moderators and the conventional rules of the genre were undermined. Schlingensief works from the premise that every successful appellation is filtered through the media. The political is irreversibly fused with the televisual. His strategies are models of exaggeration, overaffirmation and taboo-breaking. He embraces social symptoms like celebrity, greed or racism and takes them on with no holds barred. Instead of an analysis of capitalism he is interested in developing strong images. Asked to perform for the board of the Deutsche Bank, he proposed that 1.000.000 D.M. be collected from them and thrown from the Reichstag. The idea was not accepted.

Schlingensief consistently blurs the line separating theatre and reality. But in the last instance his projects fall into the category of theatre. Recently Schlingensief has been considered as a visual artist, a designation I find problematic. He has participated in group shows like *Children of Berlin* in New York. This rather hasty designation of him as an artist shows how desperate the art world is for a shimmering, charismatic figure who successfully addresses the mainstream. If one must invite Schlingensief to be in an art exhibition one should be aware of the specificity of his way of working compared to the visual art context.

With these precautions in mind, I would propose that Brussels 2000 takes over Schlingensief's most recent project *I love Austria*. Its name would have to be *I love Brussels* and the project should be carried out in Flemish and French. All other modifications would be left to Schlingensief, and he should decide whether to tackle the theme of racism again (in Belgium) or work with other symptoms of this country's political unconsciousness.

Schlingensief was invited to do something in the context of the *Wiener Festwochen*. He put a portacabin in front of the Opera House in Vienna, a site that is as equally loaded as the Mont des Arts as a tourist trap which stands for high art and national culture. A portacabin contrasts with the stone

monumentality of an opera house, suggesting the cheap and provisional. What one associates with portacabins are construction sites. More recently portacabins have been used as clearly temporary and cheap homes for those seeking political asylum. In German-speaking countries the portacabin also evokes the real life TV drama *Big Brother*. This very successful programme on RTL was set in one. A group of people lived together completely cut off from the outside world, observed by cameras day and night. In its set-up it resembled a sociological experiment on group dynamics. But it also incorporated a further piece of social research: every week the inhabitants of the portacabin *and* the TV audience were asked to vote on who to throw out. The one left inside after this elimination game (Peter Sloterdijk) would get the money.

Schlingensief took the eliminatory logic of *Big Brother* and put it into the Austrian context, where the outspokenly racist FPÖ is part of the goverment. He announced that he would put a group of asylum seekers (waiting for their cases to be heard) in the portacabin. It was never quite clear whether he had engaged actors or whether real asylum seekers were playing themselves. The Austrian people could follow events inside the portacabin on an internet TV channel. They could vote for who to throw out by phone. The winner would be whoever managed to marry an Austrian. On top of the portacabin there was a sign saying *Ausländer raus* (Foreigners out).

The reactions were immediate and foreseeable. Heated debates and protests occurred on the site and in the newspapers. The right-wing populist *Kronenzeitung* mobilised anger about the project. Whilst conservative reaction targeted Schlingensief's dirtying of Austria's image, left-wing criticism focused more on the dangers of the over-affirmation strategy, as well as Schlingensief's own starring role. These different type of protests materialised in front of the portacabin: conservative Austrians shouted *Foreigners out* to Schlingensief himself and anti-racist organisations from Vienna demolished the sign. This latter initiative was of course welcomed by Schlingensief. There is no doubt about the success of this model - an appellation based on misunderstanding and failed communication. But Schlingensief also works with a differentiated notion of audience. Instead of insisting on a totalisation, his projects produce different audiences and effectuate their differentiation.

In Vienna you could watch how different ideological segments of society were mobilised and responded. Likewise, Schlingensief works with the virtual public sphere of the internet as well as the literal public sphere. He demonstrates the interrelations between different public spheres: if you want to create a public debate you have to know that the internet produces a literal public and vice versa.

Schlingensief knows the rules of the game and he does not prevent the media from being fixated on him. His projects rely on him being the celebrity even though he works within a team. He invited Austrian celebrities to the portacabin, knowing that their presence would create automatic media attention. For Roland Barthes the spectacle only makes sense if it touches the material life of consumers. Schlingensief's spectacle fulfils this criterion.

It has been suggested that all social interaction has become theatrical, and Schlingensief's projects assume it. The German philosopher Hans Thies Lehman has proposed that the individual formerly known as citizen should now be considered an actor. Schlingensief gives a vivid description of this state of affairs. People can play themselves. A performance of this type would become part of the history of the place, its shadow looming over the Mont des Arts. Schlingensief's portacabin works with the existing situation, and while not offering perfect knowledge, offers a clear vision of how to change it.

1. Stanley Cavell in an interview with Juliana Rebentisch, to be published in Texte zur Kunst in September 2000.
2. The artist Fareed Armaly implied that the media had overridden the importance of earlier spatial interventions in the Mont des Arts in a show called Brea-kd-own in the Palais des Beaux Arts, Brussels 1992

Brussels as it might been

Riken Yamamoto & Field Sho

Credit/authorship...Riken Yamamo
Beda Faessl
Motoki Yasuha
Mari Tochizav
Shunji Yamanaka (L.E.C
Thibault Van Honack

Brussels as it is

The main difficulties and problems around the Mont des Arts area are deeply related to the whole of Bruss
Therefore a single limited architectural intervention cannot really be the solution for this interwoven problem s
ation. We have to take a more general look at all the traffic and infrastructural elements. Especially visible bes
the constant presence of cars is the whole access difficulty of Mont des Arts and the bad connection betwe
Lower and Upper Town.

We interpret the whole old centre part of Brussels, filled with museums, historical buildings and places, as a liv
national monument area. However, there is an urgent need for a change in the regime of streets as the arteries
the city centre.

ussels as it might have been

e idea is to work with the street space by changing the current traffic regime. We propose a mix of small safe
biles that can be used on exactly the same streets as pedestrians at a very slow speed.

e centre of Brussels can thus become a role model for coexistence of several pollution-free means of trans-
tation, along with pedestrians. The street space can again become more of a multi-use area of mobility and
, the largest public space and built-up downtown area.

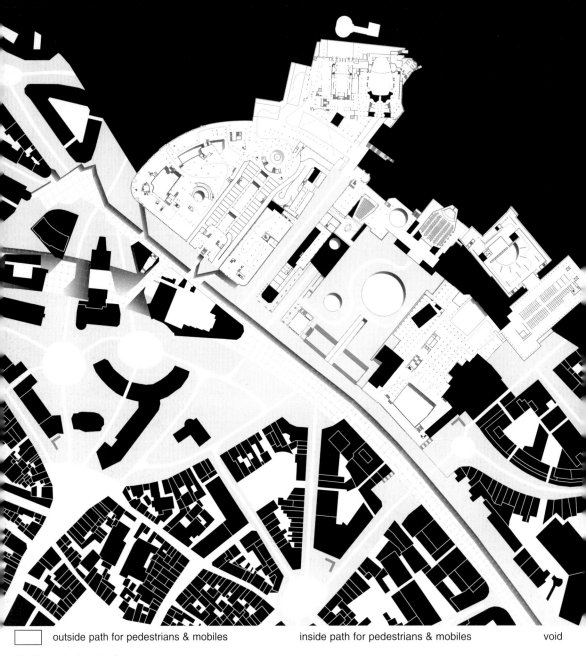

| outside path for pedestrians & mobiles | inside path for pedestrians & mobiles | void |

Paths of circulation

The paths of circulation can freely pass in the built-up area of the former streets. Some paths can even enter covered public areas of buildings. As the mobiles we think of can be compared to the size of electric wheel chairs, they could even access elevators or smaller rooms.

This means a radical change in thinking about traffic and streets. The street turns into a landscape area where pedestrians and mobiles mix with inline skaters, cyclists and skateboarders etc.

landscape area   ■ interior for pedestrians or foundations only   ■ storage station

e forgotten underground city

nslucent street surfaces give natural light to forgotten underground areas of the Mont des Arts. Huge holes with
ɔes penetrate it to give access to the path network. Street space thus extends into the public part of buildings
ɟ equally, the public content of these buildings, like exhibitions, can flow out into the streets. The public acces-
.e part of the Mont des Arts could indeed be dramatically extended.

ingle organization could manage all space resources, combined with outsourcing a part of the huge stock into
archive building elsewhere, and create a lot of added free space. Together with the already existing public
ıces and the path network, the Mont des Arts could become a very large multi-use activity area, the central
ɔkbone for all sorts of cultural events, ranging from EU-related themes, all staged in Brussels, as for example,
ıssels 2000.

The urban traffic system

Brussels will be organized into a centre zone with a transition t[...]
fic zone around it. The centre zone will be reserved for polluti[...]
free mobiles and vehicles at a maximum speed of 10 km/h. In [...]
transition zone, conventional gasoline driven cars will only [...]
allowed for parking and delivery at a maximum speed of 30 km[...]
A new electric mobile called "speed seat" is developed to drive[...]
these two zones. At transition points like huge parking areas, r[...]
way stations, subway entrances etc. there will be storage static[...]
set up for these speed seats with rental and supply units.

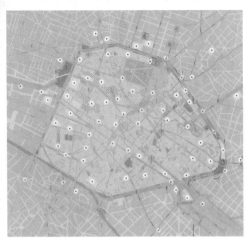

| | 10km/h area | | storage station |
| | 30km/h area | | car parking |

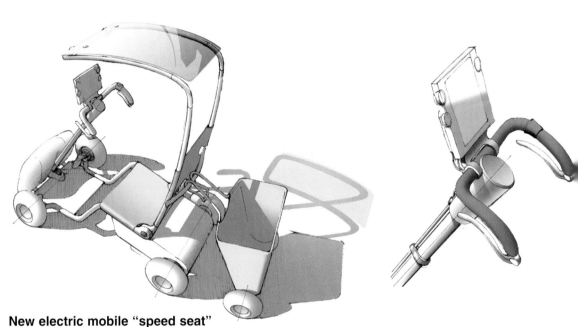

New electric mobile "speed seat"

technical Information	dimension l /w/ h	1500/ 800/ 1600 mm	standard features	navigation monitor with positioning system (detachab[...]
	height	650 mm		speed control syste[...]
	weight	45kg		auto driving syst[...]
	turning radius	1.5m		safety cush[...]
	top speed	30km/ h (60km/h)		automatic stacking syste[...]
	power supply	electric engine		full equipment for handicapped peo[...]
	removable battery	12V*38Ah	optional features	shopping c[...]
	mileage per charge	50km		child's s[...]
	brake system	rear drum brakes		taxi equipme[...]
				hard cabin ty[...]
				double mo[...]

double model

standard model

folding

stacking

front cover

shopping cart (option[...]

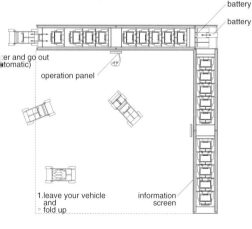

battery charger

battery

ter and go out
tomatic)

operation panel

1.leave your vehicle
and
° fold up

information
screen

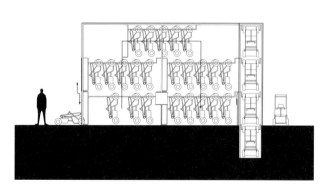

rage station for speed seats

rage station for speed seats will be set up with automatic stacking system. Like gasoline stands today, the sta-
s will function as public magnets with additional features like information screens, media connection points,
be even a small coffee bar or some daily food stores.

child's seat (optional)

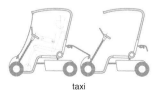

taxi

hard cabin model
(high-speed model)

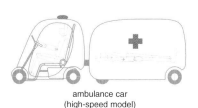

ambulance car
(high-speed model)

bruxellessnq as it might have been 2000

Pick up a "speed seat" at many locations in Brussels.

Paths of circulation pass freely in the area of the former streets.

Translucent street area with visual contact to the underground city.

storage station

Underground spaces are very large multi-use cultural activity areas.

Huge holes with slopes penetrate the forgotten underground areas of the Mont des Arts.

Speed seats can enter building public spaces, even a museum.

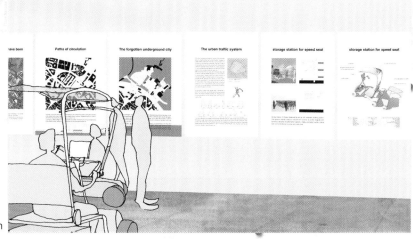

site for exhibition

FOOD FOR THOUGHT:
IDEAS FOR THE MONT DES ARTS

Paul Vermeulen

Since the city of Bilbao, so it seems, hauled itself out of a crisis via the Guggenheim, the appetite for large scale, prestigious and mediagenic cultural objects has grown noticeably. Even in Brussels, nobody's and everybody's capital city and a wasteland as far as city marketing is concerned, there are tentative proposals in the air. Bert Anciaux and Erik André, two ministers in one of the many regional governments located in Brussels, let it be known one fine day that they were entertaining two grand schemes, one a theatre, the other a museum for the contemporary arts. Anciaux has in fact been responsible for a number of new theatre projects and hardly a museum can be mentioned that has not been blighted by a shortage of finance, in spite of his grand ambitions. There is ample opportunity for cultural policy; enough to keep several ministers busy. But how enticing the new, the grand, and the spectacular is, how tempting is it to focus on one project, on a one-off investment, even if it is extravagant, on a clearly defined object that fits exactly into the picture (the fragmentation of the Guggenheim is of course mere pretence). Tempting for politicians but also for the general public.

If that is the case, then the prospects for the Mont des Arts are not good. A simple concept, for example "port closed down, post-industrial city boosted by cultural vortex" is not feasible. Everything is complex, everything is the very opposite of simplicity. Despite successive waves of demolition, a new leaf has not been turned over. Remains were always left behind, every new beginning had to be made from half finished work. The amalgam created in this way, a heterogeneity that is anything but picturesque and fragmentation to which no one will admit ownership, is unusable as a background for a new silhouette. Incidentally, culture cannot present itself as the unexpected newcomer sent by God; it is one of the oldest residents of this earth. Even a shy resident, who does not want to be prominent, hiding, for preference, as an arbitrary tenant in a corner of the elegant Place Royale, if not partially or totally in underground hiding places like the Palais des Beaux-Arts or the hole by the Musée d'Art Moderne. The most visible part, the Bibliothèque Royale, with a dignified porch turned away from visitors and approached by a steep climb, makes it abundantly clear that it would rather not have any visitors at all and even its neighbour, the Palais des Congrès, with its numerous mean entrances, tries to discourage visitors. This indifference to visitors is understandable in the sense that most of them move around underground, in the corridors to the trains, the metro or the car parks.

An impossible background, therefore, where the hero has hidden away and one waits in vain for the extras. Not a suitable location for a success story for the camera. It is not going to be a Bilbao, but is there no other comforting story that can be told? Ancient cultural bastions can be upgraded, brought up to date. Berlin built on its Kulturforum and its Museuminsel, Paris extended the Louvre, first underground and then with the Jeu de Paume and the gardens of the Tuileries, later by annexing the Musée d'Orsay along the Solferino bridge. Can the Mont des Arts not take its honourable place on this list? Possibly, but it must be realised that the Louvre, the Museuminsel and, even, to a certain extent, the still young Kulturforum, won their places in their cities long ago. Their upgrading did not threaten their relationship with the city. For the dismal Mont des Arts in Brussels, too large and too small, the situation is different. It cannot be avoided: whoever touches the cultural bastions on the Mont des Arts touches the city, and vice-versa.

This introduction, which repeats what is claimed more extensively elsewhere in this book, seems to me to be essential now that I am launching the discussion of the ideas submitted for the Mont des Arts, because the level of expectation must be properly focused. Those who expect a sequel to Lampugnani's museum parade – an exhibition which could be seen in various European cities and demonstrated the most remarkable museum designs of recent years – will be disappointed. Those who expect a series of cultural performances on a well-lit stage, creations by inimitable authors who wish to elicit our admiration, will remain wanting. There is no stage, no background and no foreground, possibly no city and even no museum. What the Mont des Arts needs now is a debate, and to feed this debate, ideas wide-ranging enough to embrace the vagueness of the assignment. What is required are true historians, technicians, visionaries, therapists, philosophers, scientists, cultural connoisseurs, cultural entrepreneurs, urban designers, and architects. Finally for ideas, knowledge is needed, and this is to be found in abundance at the beginning of this book.

The ideas have now been supplied. My intention therefore is not to attempt to recapture them in great detail but to reinterpret and rearrange them and to present them in such a way that a debate is started – although because of their wide-ranging nature, the one idea does not automatically exclude the other.

Do the authorities have any ideas with respect to the Mont des Arts? The Fondation Roi Baudouin has shown the patience of a saint in its endeavours. It has installed a Calder from the World's Fair 58, tended the garden, attempted to create a through route in the bastion of the Bibliothèque Royale in the direction of the Sablon and encouraged the inflexible cultural institutions to become good neighbours. However limited the goals, the efforts are worthwhile and they have brought the day that the Mont des Arts comes under a single management body ever closer. Less hopeful is what the city of Brussels intends to do, as demonstrated by the Urban Development Department. They want to demolish the tower blocks in the Pentagone, of which a number of small but attractive ones are close to the Mont des Arts, because they think that they do not fit into the historical city. In particular, there where the results of history are so heterogeneous! That these once modern creations are still regarded after several decades as undesirable foreigners reveals Brussels at its most small-minded. That which is threatened should be cherished. In this book, the empathy with which monographs devoted to the patrimony of the Mont des Arts are written is noticeable. The fact that one is captivated by this hotchpotch, and even can love it, begins to answer the question posed by Hilton Judin and also Isabelle Graw, namely that the numerous passers-by do not seem to be interested in this particular location.

The aggressive politics of standardisation in Brussels does not only focus on the heights, but also the depths, the underground layers constructed under buildings and streets throughout history. According to Alain Sarfati's plan for the foot of the Mont des Arts, trees should be planted in abundance. By giving the artificial ground level a "normal" appearance by designing lanes and public gardens, the underground city is further camouflaged. It is precisely these exuberant underground reserves which provide most of the ideas for the guests (architects and programmers) of Brussels 2000. Sarfati's plan is useful here as a foil to those of Riken Yamamoto & Field Shop. It contains an even greater amount of green space – it seems as though the Parc de Bruxelles runs right across the Mont des Arts, and the Lower and Upper Towns coalesce – but the spatial concept is very different from that of Sarfati. In the first place, the green space is repeatedly interspersed with what seem to be circular lakes, but are actually entrances to the underground where the artificiality of the ground level is revealed. Moreover, the green space does not serve to enhance the streets or emphasise the axes but rather to diminish them. Buildings are mere notches in the green space. Where Sarfati strives for a standardisation of the public open space, Yamamoto strives for homogenisation. His initial sketches showed linear incisions that lifted some axes out of a mikado, scattered by whimsical history. This was somewhat arbitrary, and instead he developed an approach that treats the area as a field, with green space on all sides and non-directional incisions where the lines seem to be no more than wrinkles. Yamamoto plays down lines to a great extent. In order to eliminate any semblance of priority, cars are banned and the "speed seat" appears, an amazing chair with wheels that is taken out of its rack and is used alongside cyclists and in-line skaters. For the "speed seat," the last barriers are abolished: the thresholds between interior and exterior. The weary tourist drives into the museum and out again towards the Grand'Place. Yamamoto's interpretation of the public open space culminates in Asian science fiction. In this vision of the city, the worrisome buildings fade away. Gadgets are the catalysts of the community. Just like a metropolis in the Far East, Brussels derives its identity from swarms of small vehicles, mobile prostheses, micro-architecture, attached to the body. The converse is that the whole city centre becomes a tourist theme park.

Design + Urbanism also tries to balance the flows of tourists between the Upper and Lower Towns and also makes incisions at ground level to provide the underground city with daylight and more visitors. But that is as far as the similarities go. They have taken the laborious unravelling abandoned by Yamamoto to heart. The key to that lies in the city's history, whereby with impressive knowledge of the area, they excavate the traces that have been buried or removed. This looks like archaeology but also like psycho-analysis. The Mont des Arts is reconciled with the city by confessing in public its disturbed relationship with the city: by declaring it the theme of the public space. Where the development of the Maquet Curve has more or less straightened out its relationship with its turbulent past, in the expressionless Jardin de l'Albertine the syndrome emerges on the surface. There the repressed traumas of the past must be brought to consciousness. Some of them can be healed without scars. The north-south route between the Sablon and the cathedral – which the Fondation Roi Baudouin also has its eye on – is almost painless whereby a barrier originating from the middle ages can finally be removed. The east-west wound, however, has been more ostentatiously bandaged up. Design + Urbanism's arcade and winter garden, drawn from ancient city maps, recreate as it were the Jardin de l'Albertine into an archaeological site. The pedestrian bridge ignores the heavy, meaningless buildings and focuses its attention on the delicate remains below. The only possible programme for this constellation is a museum of city history, for which it is itself a piece, a mock up, a full scale model. The urban design becomes a didactic device. The archaeological ambiguity towards the existing situation – sublimation according to Design + Urbanism – is emphasised by the abundant use of glass, whereby historical strata appear to be piled on top of each other to form a virtual space. Here no sentimental and ignorant pastiche such as at the Carrefour de l'Europe further on; the ground level becomes an interface on which history is projected with cool precision. The glass pedestrian bridge across the Jardin de l'Albertine cannot, nevertheless, accommodate all east-west traffic; the Palais des Beaux-Arts, for example, is inaccessible via this footbridge. That other, no less functional, passageways are not marked with signs at ground level, reduces its legitimacy to some extent.

In some proposals for the Mont des Arts, the notions of centrality and urbanity are questioned. Bart Verschaffel throws the cat among the pigeons and argues for resistance in the urban space, resistance that Yamamoto imagined had been dissolved. He defends the Mont des Arts as a source of documentation and study, a bastion of science against the hordes of shuffling culture consumers, a foreign body in the biotope of the spoilt tourist. If this seems to be appropriate for the library and the archives, it is problematical for the museums. The fact that across the world museums mutate into shopping malls justifies a certain degree of longing for tranquil places where one can, as a lone adventurer, contemplate a temple of art treasures. The recommendation to invest in adequate facilities for books, documents, art works and their invisible acolytes is undoubtedly worthy of consideration. But a museum with only professional visitors is not really conceivable. And, above all, the Mont des Arts does not have the pomp, the magnificence, and the power to become a vatican or a kremlin. Its unapproachableness and impenetrability do not arouse curiosity, envy, speculation, or longing. It is at its most inaccessible in terms of the imagination.

The mirror image of Verschaffel's proposal is that of Nasrine Seraji. She too is of the opinion that a mountain full of treasures and a living urban experience are irreconcilable. She chooses the latter and not, like Verschaffel, the former. She therefore blows up the Mont des Arts, in programmatic terms of course. The pieces are given the most differentiated content possible, so that its mono-functional character changes into a fragmented puzzle. One of her ideas to be immediately implemented – shared by João Luís Carrilho da Graça – is to convert the, in Brussels, much-maligned Westbury Tower into dwellings. Furthermore she wants – just like Yamamoto – to get rid of the national archives. There is something to be said for this too, because the secretive and bureaucratic atmosphere created by this building is not in harmony with the aims of its neighbours who are keepers of art treasures. But the most controversial element in Seraji's programmatic matrix is undoubtedly the proposal to remove the Musée d'Art Moderne altogether. And yet! In Paris, Berlin and London, in recent years larger art collections have been moved. Seraji does not mention a new location for the museum. It could be, for example, the Cinquantenaire, or on a new location in the canal zone awaiting new stimuli (impetuous ministers are now pricking up their ears!). Wouldn't Brussels then become a completely different city? Will the dispersal of culture, which Seraji so admires in Brussels and applies especially to private and small-scale initiatives, then not be officially endorsed and enhanced? Is the Mont des Arts not more inhabitable as a way-station in a network than as a top heavy epicentre?

But, on the other hand, is the collection of modern art not too lightweight to be given weight in this way? What is heavy? Measured against the Louvre or the Metropolitan the universalist pretentions of the Mont des Arts are insignificant, as Cathérine David correctly pointed out. Although she assisted Seraji in her proposal and obviously shares her preference for urban interference and a decentralised cultural model, she does not reduce the cultural load of the Mont des Arts in her contribution, rather the opposite. Her proposals for an integration of the museums with the Palais des Beaux-Arts are pragmatic and attractive. Her pragmatism is undoubtedly a result of the absence of any plans on the part of the authorities – ignoring the tentative Fondation Roi Baudouin – but also by the programmatic anaemia the Mont des Arts suffers from. At a location where there is a considerable number of empty properties, it is always better to fan the smouldering opportunities than to extinguish them. The oxygen has to come from outside. Because the Mont des Arts does not in itself possess centrality, it has to connect to the vibrant culture elsewhere in Brussels – David mentions the *KunstenFESTIVALdesArts*. She gambles that a more visible and less conformist supply of culture can shake this location out of its lethargy. The empty properties in the Galerie Ravenstein could be better filled with art, music and media (an experiment that incidentally Brussels 2000 has in its programme) than slide further into a metro tunnel which stigmatises the passer-by as a mere commuter. Her call for more active programming, including readings and debates in the Musée d'Art Ancien, indicates that she does not regard the museum visitor as a spoilsport and considers the barriers between the professional and amateur arts visitor to be permeable.

In short, what David wants is an postponement for Verschaffel's vatican. With a civil discourse in which art belongs to everyone and makes a contribution to public debate, she undermines the contrast he emphasises between tourist and specialist, between consumer and treasurer. An undermining of the contrasts in the literal sense we find in two plans which leave the ground level virtually untouched and exploit the underground: that of João Luís Carrilho da Graça, and that of Max. 1 & Crimson. The difference between the two plans is once again that between a local, detailed plan – the choice of lines – and an extensive plan – the choice of a field. The first plan, moreover, leans in a programmatic sense towards Seraji and injects the Mont des Arts with new urban programmes, including an exceptional shopping arcade. With the Galerie Saint Hubert and the Galerie Ravenstein, Brussels has a small but splendid genealogy of glass-covered arcades, to which Carrilho da Graça's ambitious proposal to excavate the Cantersteen relates admirably. Just as formerly in the Saint Hubert and the Ravenstein, modern day possibilities for the use of glass are exploited to the full: the glass roof of

the underground arcade is a floor at street level. This speculative operation with infrastructural implications reminds us of the resolute metropolitan future vision of the last
century – the type of images which the Brussels' strip cartoonists Schuiten and Peeters
revel in – or, more specifically for Brussels, the post-war period when developers conceived the Westbury and Martini Towers and the Manhattan plan. Reminders that present day, narrow-minded Brussels has declared to be taboo. The traffic flows crossing
each other at different levels remind us more of Victor Gruen's fatal Manhattan plan,
which caused the demise of the Quartier Nord, but the comparison is convincingly in
favour of the Cantersteen. The scope of the operation is more limited: both the higher
and lower levels connect to existing traffic routes and the development does not
destroy the existing situation but takes place within it. It is conceivable, perhaps in a
period of better prospects for the city and thus of generous funding, that such an
investment could signal the revival of the Mont des Arts. As for local linear interventions in the mikado of the Mont des Arts, one could ask oneself: Why here? Why precisely this line? Is the line of the north-south underground railway tunnel, where incidentally there are vacant spaces, not more meaningful in the urban plan? A comparison
with the Galerie Saint Hubert shows, however, that such an arcade in fact wants to be
an autonomous figure in the urban plan, between the historically relevant arteries. The
Cantersteen, now a redundant end of a boulevard, its hard building lines giving it
modest quality, can, once excavated, become a sublime urban fragment. The excavation
would, moreover, form the missing link between the underground levels on the eastern side and the ones inside the railway tunnel, which are separated from each other
now, rendering maximum utilisation possible.

One can be more brief about Carrilho da Graça's second proposal: the wooden float
above the Jardin de l'Albertine. The float is a square that is no longer a through way,
which makes its destiny uncertain. As a roof, however, sheltering a sort of vestibule for
the cultural institutions, the wooden float is more acceptable. The idea of a common
distribution centre for the neighbours on the Mont des Arts, a space that stimulates
new types of uses and more intense relationships between the institutions, brings us
to Max. 1 & Crimson. They do not design this space, they discover it. Where the Portu-
guese are bold, the Dutch are unassuming, almost passive. Their approach is more
topographic than architectural: as speleologists they sound out the walls of their cave
to dig out a hole or passageway where they can, until they have reached all the cavi-
ties. They are simply sounding out, looking for small breakthroughs, expanding what
the Fondation Roi Baudouin has already started. Moreover they show themselves to be
grateful and inventive with even the most unsightly discoveries in the area: the endless

series of transverse lamp shades in the passages to the metro, the eye-shaped garden at the bottom of the Jardin de l'Albertine, the statue of the horseman of the soldier king – but we run ahead of ourselves.

First we must return to Hilton Judin and Isabelle Graw, who both in their own ways search for a common ground, yes even a national identity for the passers-by fleeing from the Mont des Arts. In the view of Design + Urbanism, the historical project of the city, in which our political, social, economic and geographical origin is visible, could be this common denominator. Isabelle Graw wants the agent provocateur Schlingensief to ask the Belgians the questions with which he harassed the Austrians. But Max. 1 & Crimson beat him to it. Their appeal to the subconscious of the Belgians is so un-ashamed and so poignant that it hurts. We are Belgians only with respect to our royal family, which we do not want to see and cannot do without. Our common history is etched in their vicissitudes. Our relationship to the southern hemisphere is revealed in the cruelty of Leopold II's rubber plantations and Baudouin taking offence at Lumumba. The dilemmas of the war are reflected in the ambiguous opposites of the struggling Albert I and the capitulating Leopold III and in the suffering of the unworldly Astrid: our insignificant personal tragedies are abated.

That architects allow evocative, emotional images to catch space unawares, such as advertising overprints do with whole vehicles or even buildings, contains a theoretical architectural stance. A cult version of John Jerde is what Max. 1 & Crimson once said they were aiming at. It means that the strategy of the master scenic designer of shop-ping malls is used, but not for an obligatory feel-good message. Incidentally, contex-tual reasons can be put forward for making the excessive use of images at this location acceptable. Underground the Mont des Arts is still a Montagne de la Cour where some-times a crown can be found on a door. Underground orientation is via pictograms, for example in a car park – which are in fact their cultural agora. Finally revenge is desired for the public images which are the most dispiriting offered by the Mont des Arts: the manic peals of bells on the Palais de la Dynastie and Paul Delvaux's immense rows of glazed virgins in the Palais des Congrès where the panorama of the Lower Town should be. Such images on such a renowned location say nothing at all. Their escapism is shocking. They deserve to be parried, as cited by Max. 1 & Crimson, with some "sad and beautiful monuments."

VOYAGE AÉRIEN

(Dessin d'Amédée Lynen.)

L'AVIATEUR. — *Dites donc, Monsieur, où sommes-nous ici?*
LE MONTAGNARD. — *Vous êtes à Bruxelles, Monsieur le Voyageur, sur le Mont des Arts.*

COLOPHON

PUBLICATION VACANT CITY

Edited by
Bruno de Meulder, Karina Van Herck

Picture editing
Maureen Heyns, Veronique Patteeuw, Jurgen Persijn

Translation
Wendy Galloway, Dave Hardy, Douglas Heingartner, Andrew Maclagan, Peter Mason,
Arthur Payman, Andrew Taylor, Paul Schwartzman, Hans van Bemmelen

Copy editing
Helen Peers

Photographic assignments
Marie-Françoise Plissart, Angelo Vermeulen

Graphic Design
Jurgen Persijn for IYO

Production
Caroline Gautier

Printing and lithography
Drukkerij Die Keure

© 2000 NAi Publishers, Rotterdam / Bruxelles/Brussel 2000, Brussels / OSA K.U.Leuven, Leuven

The publication was made possible, in part, by Ministerie van de Vlaamse Gemeenschap

Available in North, South and Central America through D.A.P./Distributed Art Publishers Inc,
155 Sixth Avenue 2nd Floor, New York, NY 10013-1507, Tel. 212 6271999, Fax 212 6279484.

Available in the United Kingdom and Ireland through Art Data, 12 Bell Industrial Estate,
50 Cunnington Street, London W4 5HB, Tel. 181 7471061, Fax 181 7422319.

Printed and bound in the Netherlands
ISBN 90-5662-167-X

PROJECT VACANT CITY/MONT DES ARTS

Curator
Bruno De Meulder

Project co-ordination
Veronique Patteeuw

Co-ordination Bruxelles/Brussel 2000
Guido Minne

Co-ordination Koning Boudewijnstichting/Fondation Roi Baudouin
Marie-Laure Roggemans

Project assistant
Christine Sommeillier

Research
Tom Avermaete, Karl Beelen, Tom Bonnevalle, Peter Casier, Bieke Cattoor,
Veronique Charlier, Tine Daems, Dieter De Clercq, Bruno De Meulder, Nancy Meijsmans,
Veronique Patteeuw, Michael Ryckewaert, Karina Van Herck, Els Van Meerbeek,
Ilke Verhoeven, Students Cultural Studies 1999-2000 Seminar 'Cultural Identity and
Contemporary Urbanity' (Culturele identiteit en hedendaagse stedelijkheid) K.U.Leuven,
Architecture Students 1998-2000 K.U.Leuven

Design project
Jurgen Persijn for IYO

The project is a coproduction of
Bruxelles/Brussel 2000, OSA (Onderzoeksgroep Stedelijkheid en Architectuur)
K.U.Leuven, Koning Boudewijnstichting/Fondation Roi Baudouin, BBL.

The project was made possible in part by
Stimuleringsfonds voor Architectuur; EU-Japan Fest Japan Committee;
Ministerie van de Vlaamse Gemeenschap, Publicatiefonds; Ministerie van de
Vlaamse Gemeenschap, Administratie Cultuur, afdeling Beeldende Kunst en Musea;
AFAA; Audiovisuele Dienst K.U.Leuven; Departement Architectuur Stedenbouw en
Ruimtelijke Ordening (ASRO) K.U.Leuven.

PHOTOGRAPHIC ASSIGNMENTS

Marie-Françoise Plissart: pp. 257-264
Angelo Vermeulen: pp. 17-35, 200, 202-213, 220, 234-236, 246, 247

ADDITIONAL CAPTION INFORMATION

(pp. 12-13) Panorama of the Mont des Arts, 1975; (p. 45, bottom) *Cahier d'Urbanisme 6*, 1930s; (pp. 56-57) *Journal de Bruxelles Illustré*, 1911; (pp. 66-67) *Le Patriote Illustré*, 1909; (pp. 68-69) The Square du Mont des Arts by Vacherot, circa 1930; (p. 71) *Face à Main*, 1949; (p. 72) Palais des Beaux-Arts, building site, 1925; (p. 37) *Bulletin de la Classe des Beaux-Arts*, 1939; (pp. 78-79) Panorama of the north-south rail link, building site, Sergysels, 1941; (p. 80) Advertising brochure for the Office National pour l'Achèvement de la Jonction Nord-Midi, 1938; (p. 81) Revue about the north-south rail link, 1913; (pp. 82-83) Brochure about the inauguration of the north-south rail link, 1952; (p. 85) Advertisement for the Sabena Air Terminus, 1960; (p. 89, bottom) *Architecture 1/2*, 1969; (p. 92) Carrefour de l'Europe, 1968; (p. 93) Aerial view of Brussels' city centre, Isselée, 1970; (pp. 94-95) Carrefour de l'Europe, circa 1968; (pp. 96-97) Carrefour de l'Europe, 1968; (pp. 98-99) *Auto Touring*, 1962; (p. 105) Musée d'Art Moderne, well of light, 1984; (p. 106) Musée d'Art Moderne, exhibition hall, 1984; (p. 134, 4) *L'Émulation*, 1909; (p. 135, 3&4) *L'Émulation*, 1909; (p. 138, 7) *L'Émulation 9/10*, 1926; (p. 191) The demolition of the Rue Coudenberg, 1956 ; (p. 142, 12) *La Cité 10*, 1931; (p. 143, 13&14) *La Cité 10*, 1931; (pp. 146-147) *Cahiers de Belgique 6*, 1928; (p. 148,3) *L'Émulation 7/8*, 1928; (p. 149, 4) *L'Émulation*, 1909; (p. 150, 5) *Rythme 4*, 1964; (p. 158, 17) *Habitat et habitations 9/10*, 1954; (p. 216) Commuters, 1950s; (pp. 226-227) Commuters on their way to the Gare Centrale, 1968; (pp. 242-243) Panorama of the Mont des Arts, Haine, 1962; (p. 291) The fundamental cycle of documentation, Otlet, 1944; (endpaper) Aerial view of the Mont des Arts and its surroundings.

CREDITS

Our grateful thanks to the photographers, organizations, and individuals for providing material and kindly permitting its reproduction. References are to pages.

Architectuurarchief van de Provincie Antwerpen: 163(2), 168(7&8), 170(11), 171(12&13); Archives Abeels, Gustave: 118(2); Archives d'Architecture Moderne: 139(9), 140(10), 141(11), 154(11), 155(12&13), 162(1), 166(4), 167(5), 172(14), 173(15&16); Archives d'Architecture Moderne, Dossier n°1 (Brussels,1973): 178(3); Archives Bastin, Roger: 101, 102, 103, 104, 175(1); Archives Beel, Stéphane: 184(8), 185(9); Archives Belgian Shell: 156(14&15); Archives De Geyter, Xaveer: 90, 186-188; Archives Royales: 121(5), 133(1), 138-139(8); Archyves Dumont: 157(16), 159(18), 160(19); Archives Générales du Royaume, Cartes et Plans Manuscrits: 114(2), 115(3), Papiers de la Fondation Albert Ier: 167(6); Archives du Palais des Beaux-Arts: 193; Archives de la Ville de Bruxelles, Travaux Publics: 65, Cartes Postales: 68-69, 94-95, 137(6), Fonds Iconographique: 59, 60, 63, 64, 93, Fonds Lebouille: 56-57, 71, 81, 85, 98-99, Grands Plans: 43, 44 , Plans Portefeuilles: 47, 116(5), 118(1), 120(4), 124(8), 123(8&9), 126(11), 125(11), 128(13), 127(13&14), 122(7), 129(16); Bibliothèque Royale: 38-39, Cabinet des Estampes: 115(4), 136(5); Collection Dexia: 45(top of the page); Fondation Roi Baudouin: 296; Haine: 242-243; Institut Géographique National: endpaper, 51; I.R.P.A.: 105, 106; Klinger, Johann: 357; Ministère des Travaux Publics: 49, 169(9), 191, 218; Mundaneum (Mons): 291; Musée de la Ville de Bruxelles: 113(1), 130(17), 131(18), 170(10); Musée Horta: 72, 152(7), 153(8,9&10); O.S.A. KULeuven: 55, 194, 196, 197, 198, 199, 217, 224; Palais des Congrès: 222, 239; Pauwels: 86; Quartier des Arts: 180(2), 182(4&5), 183(6&7); Collection Samin: 66-67, 78-79, 82-83, 119(3), 164-165(3), 160; S.N.C.B.: 12-13, 216, 227; Service Fédéral d'Information: 92, 96-97, 226-227; Service des Relations Publiques du Ministère des Travaux Publics, Le Musée d'Art Moderne à Bruxelles (Brussels, 1973): 176-177(2); Sint-Lukasarchief: 145(1), 151(6); Thijs, Tom: 193 (bottom); Collection Verpoest L.: 80; Werleman, Hans: 187 (model by Vincent de Rijck); Wetzel, Nina: 356, 358, 359.

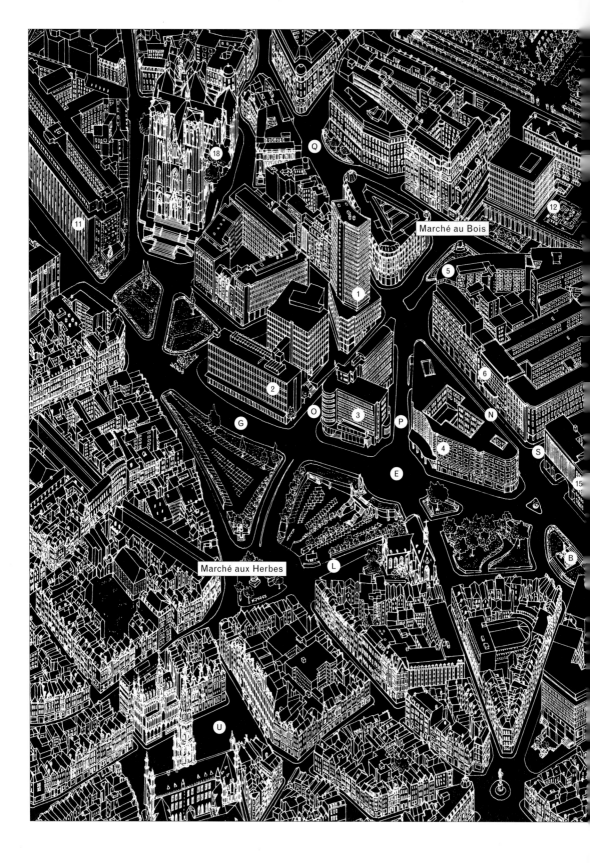

Marché au Bois

Marché aux Herbes

Place Royale

Place de la Justice

1. Westbury Tower
2. Telex building
3. Sabena Air Terminus
4. Gare Centrale
5. Shell building
6. Galerie Ravenstein
7. Palais des Beaux-Arts (PBA)
8. Old England
   Musée des Instruments
9. Palais Royale
10. St. Jacques-sur-Coudenberg
11. Banque Nationale
12. Fortis
13. Bibliothèque Royale Albert 1er
14. Musées Royaux des Beaux-Arts
15. Palais de la Dynastie
16. Archives Générales du Royaume
17. Palais des Congrès
18. Cathédrale Saint Michel

A. Jardin de l'Albertine
B. Place de l'Albertine
C. Place du Musée
D. Place des Palais
E. Carrefour de l'Europe
F. Boulevard de l'Empereur
G. Boulevard de l'Impératrice
H. Montagne de la Cour
I. Coudenberg
J. Rue Ravenstein
K. Rue Royale
L. Chaussée de la Madeleine
M. Rue de Ruysbroeck
N. Cantersteen
O. Rue du Cardinal Mercier
P. Rue de Loxum
Q. Rue des Colonies
R. Rue Mont des Arts
S. Rue des Sols
T. Parc de Bruxelles
U. Grand'Place

© Atelier Perspective

Ville européenne de la culture de l'an
Europese cultuurstad van het jaar 2000